Malcolm K. Hooke — Meta H. Miller

THE WOMAN'S COLLEGE, UNIVERSITY OF NORTH CAROLINA

FRENCH

REVIEW

GRAMMAR

Henry Holt and Company

PREFACE

The object of this grammar is twofold: first, to provide a thorough review of the material generally covered in the first year of college French or in an equivalent course in high school; second, to afford the student the opportunity to acquire sufficient additional knowledge of French grammar to prepare him for work in French composition.

In order to obtain adequate space in which to present a fairly comprehensive picture of French grammar, we have relegated to the appendix certain lists of forms, and have eliminated a small number of elementary rules.

As this book is intended for use as a review grammar and not as a composition book, it does not contain connected discourse in either English or French. The omission of connected prose in English is the result of our conviction that the satisfactory translation of such material is beyond the ability of the average Freshman or Sophomore. This omission is in itself sufficient to render of little value the inclusion of connected discourse in French, the main purpose of which is to aid the student in the translation of similar exercises in English. Moreover, the use of connected passages in French adds little to the student's training in reading, since his principal experience in that phase of learning is gained from the study of some literary work.

We wish to call attention to the following features of this grammar: (1) the inclusion of several chapters on the uses of certain common prepositions, verbs and nouns; (2) the treatment of *falloir* and *devoir*, of the modal auxiliaries, and of the uses of *ce* and *il;* (3) the simplification of the rules governing the use of the imperfect indicative; (4) the comparison of the uses of the pluperfect indicative, the past anterior and the *passé surcomposé;* (5) the presentation of the indefinite pronouns and of the subjunctive mode.

The treatment of the subjunctive is quite different from that found in the usual review grammar. Instead of placing it near the end of the book — a procedure which gives the student only incidental contact with this mode from the end of one year to the end of the next — we present in the first thirteen chapters a review of ten clear-cut uses of the subjunctive. As a result of this psychological approach, the student is "conditioned" to a number of obligatory uses of the subjunctive before he is called upon to struggle with uses for which the rules are more complicated and less categorical.

In order to make the discussion more complete and more readily available to the student, we have repeated one or two important rules of grammar. Repetition of a different type will be found in the sentences for translation, where an effort has been made to give the student a constant review of the idioms and constructions found in preceding lessons.

In general, we have avoided the use of English sentences the translation of which would bring up difficulties not discussed in the grammar portion of the lessons. In a few instances in which such problems might arise, the information necessary to their solution has been included in footnotes or in the body of the exercises.

Treatment of points of syntax more difficult than, but related to, those covered in the grammar's twenty-two chapters, will be found in the supplementary grammatical notes. It is hoped that this section of the book will be helpful to the student and that it will tend to stimulate his interest.

In order that the style of the French and English sentences be that of lively current speech, we have included a number of expressions and constructions peculiar to the familiar language. In the English sentences, for example, frequent use has been made of the contractions characteristic of unaffected speech. Moreover, we have not hesitated to use *so* [1] as a synonym of *therefore*, and *each other* [2] in place of *one another*.

Among the texts consulted during the preparation of this grammar, we found the following particularly helpful: *Comment on parle en français*, by Philippe Martinon (Larousse, 1927); and *Syntaxe du Français moderne*, by Le Bidois and Le Bidois (Stechert, 1938).

We wish to acknowledge our indebtedness to our colleagues, Lieutenant (j.g.) Katherine Taylor and M. René Hardré: to the former, for her work in preparing mimeographed copies of the manuscript for experimental use in classes at Woman's College; to the latter, for his kindness in offering many invaluable suggestions and in reviewing the manuscript. We have also had the benefit of helpful criticism from Professor H. Linn Edsall of Yale University, Professor Jean-Albert Bédé of Columbia University, and Lieutenant Cecil G. Taylor U. S. N. R. of the U. S. Naval Academy. We wish, however, to emphasize the fact that we alone are responsible for any errors which may be present in this text.

M. K. H.
M. H. M.

---

[1] Albert H. Marckwardt, *Scribner Handbook of English*, p. 242, 1940.
[2] Webster's Dictionary, 2nd edition, *each other*.

CONTENTS

I. PRESENT TENSE
FUTURE TENSE

The subjunctive after *jusqu'à ce que* and *avant que;*
the indefinite pronoun *quelqu'un*

1 The Present Tense (*le présent*).

A. In French, the present tense is generally used as in English. As the examples given below indicate, one French form translates the three English forms, the simple present, the progressive present, and the present with *do*.

Vous travaillez. *You work. You are working.*
Travaillez-vous ? *Do you work? Are you working?*
Nous allons souvent au cinéma. *We often go to the movies.*
Nous partons demain. *We leave tomorrow. We are leaving tomorrow.*
Je sais, je crois, il dit, etc., qu'il part demain. *I know, I think, he says, etc., that he is leaving tomorrow.*   § 100 ¹

---

¹ The numbers on the right of the page refer to sections of the Supplementary Grammatical Notes.

The present indicative, however, cannot be used to replace the future in subordinate noun clauses introduced by verbs more emphatic than those mentioned in the last example in § 1, A.

> Il affirme qu'il partira (*or:* va partir) demain. *He affirms that he will leave tomorrow.*
> J'espère (J'espère bien) qu'il viendra demain. *I hope (I do hope) he comes (will come) tomorrow.*

B. The present tense is used in the "if" clause of a conditional sentence when the result clause contains the present or future.

> Si je travaille bien, j'ai de bonnes notes. *If I work hard, I get good grades.*
> Si elles partent à huit heures, elles arriveront à Paris à midi. *If they leave at eight o'clock, they will reach Paris at noon.*

C. The present tense is used to express action or state begun in the past and continuing in the present. This construction is also used when the action which began in the past falls just short of reaching the present. In both cases the preposition *for* is translated by **depuis.**

> Depuis combien de temps joue-t-elle du piano? *How long has she been playing the piano?*
> Elle joue du piano depuis une heure. *She has been playing the piano for an hour.*
> Depuis quand m'attendez-vous? *How long have you been waiting for me?*
> Oh! peut-être depuis dix minutes. *Oh, for ten minutes, perhaps.*
> Depuis quand [1] sont-ils à Paris? *How long have they been in Paris?*
> Ils sont à Paris depuis le 15 mai. *They have been in Paris since May 15.*

---

[1] Theoretically, **depuis combien de temps** is correctly used when the answer expected is one of duration of time, **depuis quand** when the answer indicates a fixed point in time. This distinction, however, is not always made.

Suis-je en retard ? *Am I late?*
Oui, mon ami. Je vous attends depuis vingt minutes. *Yes,
my friend. I have been waiting for you for twenty minutes.*

With a negative other than **ne . . . plus,** the tense used is
regularly the same as in English.

Je ne l'ai pas vu depuis six mois. *I haven't seen him for six
months.*
Il n'habite plus ici depuis trois ans. *He hasn't lived here for
three years.* § 101

Instead of the construction with **depuis,** the more emphatic
il y a, voici, voilà . . . que are frequently used.

Il y a (Voici *or* Voilà) dix jours qu'ils sont à Paris. *They have
been in Paris for ten days.*
Il y a (*or* Voilà) huit jours que je ne l'ai vu.[1] *I have not seen
him for a week.*
Voilà deux mois qu'il n'habite plus ici. *He hasn't lived here
for two months.*
Combien de temps y a-t-il qu'il habite ici ? *How long has he
been living here?* § 102

2 The Future Tense *(le futur).*

A. The future tense is regularly used as in English.[2]

Il arrivera la semaine prochaine. *He will arrive next week.*

B. After conjunctions of time, with the exception of those
which govern the subjunctive, the future is used when the
action in the subordinate clause has yet to take place. The
future perfect is regularly used when the action of the subordinate clause has ended before that of the main clause
begins.

---

[1] In literary style, **pas** is omitted in a compound tense after **il y a** (**voici,
voilà**) **. . . que.**

[2] Future time, when near the present, is generally expressed in familiar
French by the present or by **aller** and the infinitive.

Je pars demain. *I am leaving tomorrow.*
Je vais partir demain. *I am going to leave tomorrow.*

3

Tant qu'il sera ici, vous n'aurez rien à craindre. *As long as he is here, you will have nothing to fear.*

Je vous dirai cela, quand nous serons chez nous. *I shall tell you that when we are at home.*

Quand je le verrai, je lui parlerai de vous. *When I see him, I shall talk to him about you.*

Aussitôt que vous aurez fini votre travail, vous sortirez. *As soon as you have finished your work, you will go out.* § 103

C. The future, sometimes, and the future perfect, more commonly, are used respectively to express present and past probability.

Qui a fait cette gaffe? Ce sera (probablement) votre frère. *Who made that "break"? It was probably your brother.*

Il aura encore fait des siennes. *He has probably been up to his old tricks.*

3 Subjunctive with Temporal Conjunctions.

jusqu'à ce que, que, avant que

The temporal conjunctions **jusqu'à ce que** and **avant que** are followed by the subjunctive mode. After **attendre, jusqu'à ce que** is regularly shortened to **que**. When the subordinate clause does not contain **personne** or **rien,** a redundant **ne** is sometimes used after **avant que.**

Vous resterez à la maison jusqu'à ce que je vous dise de sortir. *You will remain in the house until I tell you to go out.* § 104

J'attendrai qu'elle soit de retour. *I shall wait until she is back.*

Je lui parlerai avant qu'il (ne) sorte. *I shall speak to him before he goes out.*

Je lui dirai cela avant qu'il ait vu personne. *I shall tell him that before he has seen anyone.*

4 Indefinite Pronouns.

quelqu'un

The indefinite pronouns *someone, somebody,* are translated by **quelqu'un, quelqu'une,** and *some,* by **quelques-uns,**

4

quelques-unes. **Quelqu'une** is regularly used only with a complement. **Quelques-unes** generally follows this rule, but may be used as subject without a complement, if it refers to a specific antecedent.

Quelqu'un est arrivé. *Someone has come.*
Quelques-uns (d'entre eux) sont arrivés. *Some (of them) have arrived.*
Nous avons vu quelqu'un. *We have seen someone.*   § 105
Il paraît qu'il a raconté cela à quelqu'un. *It seems that he told somebody about that.*
Voilà quelqu'un que nous connaissons bien. *There's someone whom we know well.*
Quelqu'une de ces dames désire-t-elle me poser des questions ? *Does one of these ladies wish to ask me some questions?*
Avec qui va-t-il se marier ? Avec quelqu'un [1] que vous ne connaissez pas. *Whom is he going to marry? Someone whom you do not know.*
J'en ai vu quelques-uns, *or*, quelques-unes. (**En** must be used when **quelques-uns,** the object, has no other complement.) *I saw some of them.*
Il en resterait quelques-uns, quelques-unes. *Some of them would be left (would remain).*
Connaissez-vous ces jeunes filles ? Oui, quelques-unes sont déjà venues me voir. *Do you know these girls? Yes, some have already come to see me.*

EXERCISES

I. VERBS [2] TO REVIEW:

   aller, partir, sortir, dire

II. IDIOMATIC EXPRESSIONS:

   jouer du piano, du violon, etc., *to play the piano, the violin, etc.*   § 106
   jouer au tennis, aux cartes, etc., *to play tennis, cards, etc.*

---

[1] The masculine singular is used here because no complement is present.
[2] Irregular verbs are listed in alphabetical order in § 247.

5

être, *or*, arriver, en retard, en avance, à l'heure, *to be, or, to arrive, late* (i.e., *behind time*), *ahead of time, on time*

faire des siennes, *to be up to one's old tricks*

faire de brillantes études, *to make a brilliant record*

faire une gaffe, *to make a "break," a blunder*

monter, descendre, l'escalier en courant, *to go (come) running up, to go (come) running down, the stairs*

être de retour, *to be back*

la semaine prochaine, *next week*

III. SENTENCES FOR TRANSLATION:

1. Are you going to the movies tomorrow? No, I am leaving tomorrow for New York. 2. Do you get good grades when you work hard? 3. How long has she been back? She has been here for a week. 4. How long have you been waiting for me? For two hours. You are always late. 5. We haven't played cards for two years.

6. When he comes (*arriver*), tell him that I should like to see him next week. 7. When she goes out, she always puts on gloves. 8. He has probably forgotten what he told you. 9. If you leave now, you will arrive at the lycée ahead of time. 10. Some of our former students (*anciens élèves*) are making brilliant records at the university.

11. Do you know many of our former students? I know a few. 12. She always runs up the stairs when she comes home (*rentrer*) late for (*le*) dinner. 13. She is going to marry someone that you know well. 14. Where are our trunks? The janitor has just taken them upstairs. 15. If he comes back tomorrow, I shall go to see him.

16. Is Mary's brother playing the piano? 17. Her husband has probably been up to his old tricks again. Careful, old man. There she is. Don't make any breaks. 18. Don't you want to play tennis before it gets dark? 19. She will stay here until you tell her to leave. 20. I hope he comes home as soon as he has finished his work.

21. I see them every day when they leave the house. 22. If they wish to have a good time, they will have to learn to play cards. 23. Will you (*Voulez-vous*) wait until I come back to (*pour*) show

it to me? 24. He will spend the summer in Spain and in Italy.
25. He is never on time.

IV. DRILL: Translate the words in parentheses: *write*

1. Combien de temps y a-t-il (*that she has been playing the piano*)?
Voilà une heure et demie (*that she has been playing the piano*).
2. Depuis quand (*have you been here*)? Je suis ici (*since the first of
June*). 3. Va-t-il toujours à l'école? (*I haven't seen him*) depuis
trois mois. 4. Je verrai (*some of your friends*). 5. Vous les
verrez quand (*they arrive*), n'est-ce pas?

6. (*If they come tomorrow*), nous les verrons. 7. J'espère (*that
she arrives*) avant que (*you leave*). 8. (*Somebody*) m'a dit que (*you
are always making breaks*). 9. (*She falls and breaks*) la jambe. *se casser*
10. A quelle heure (*does she get up*)?

11. Vous resterez très tranquille jusqu'à ce que (*he has sat down*)
à son bureau. 12. Attendez (*until he tells you*) de partir. 13. Je
vous téléphonerai aussitôt que (*she arrives*). 14. Elle n'arrive
toujours pas; elle (*probably has forgotten*) son rendez-vous.
15. Depuis combien de temps (*have you been playing cards*)?

V. VERB EXERCISE:

A. Translate the English words: *oral*

1. *Is he going to* jouer du piano? 2. *Leave* la salle! 3. *She used
to go out* tous les jours. 4. *They left* à six heures. 5. *Did she go
out* hier? 6. *We shall go* à l'église. 7. *Let's leave* tout de suite.
8. *Have they gone* au cinéma? 9. *Before she goes* en ville, je serai
de retour. 10. *Tell me* la vérité.

B. Give the present and past participles of **aller, partir,**
and **dire.**

C. Translate:

1. When we have left... 2. I had said. 3. Would they go?
4. She was saying... 5. He would go. 6. We said. (past def.)
7. Go! (2d pers. sing.) 8. She is leaving. 9. They are going
there. 10. Has she left? 11. They would have gone there.
12. Until we leave... 13. I shall say. 14. When you go out
(future)...

7

II.

PAST INDEFINITE
PAST DEFINITE

The auxiliaries *avoir* and *être;* the subjunctive
of purpose; the indefinite pronoun *on*

5 The Past Indefinite and the Past Definite *(le passé
indéfini* or *le passé composé* and *le passé défini* or *le passé
simple).*

A. The past indefinite translates the English present perfect in both the spoken and literary language.

Il a souvent dit cela. *He has often said that.*
Il n'est pas encore arrivé. *He hasn't come yet.*
Je ne l'ai pas vu aujourd'hui. *I haven't seen him today.*
Molière a exercé une influence profonde sur la comédie
moderne. *Molière has had a profound influence on the
modern comedy.*

It also regularly translates the English simple past in spoken
French and in letter writing. It is used in literary French

8

as the equivalent of the English past when the effect of the action in question may be considered as extending to the present time.

Je l'ai vu hier. *I saw him yesterday.*
La guerre a éclaté en septembre 1939. *The war began* (literally: *broke out) in September, 1939.*
Balzac a d'abord écrit des romans historiques. *At first, Balzac wrote historical novels.*
C'est surtout de la farce que Molière s'est inspiré. *It was especially from the farce that Molière drew his inspiration.*

§§ 107, 108

B. The past definite translates the English simple past in formal narration or discourse. <u>One of its principal functions is to narrate a succession of events or actions</u>. It is, therefore, the tense regularly used in purely biographical and historical sketches.

A son retour à Paris, Mauperin entra au lycée Condorcet, où il fit de brillantes études. *On his return to Paris, Mauperin entered the lycée Condorcet, where he was a brilliant student.*
Jean-Jacques Rousseau naquit à Genève en 1712. *Jean-Jacques Rousseau was born in Geneva in 1712.*

The past indefinite, except in the southern part of France and in Normandy, has almost completely replaced the past definite in spoken French and in letter writing. In writing the exercises in this grammar, do not use the past definite unless instructed to do so.

C. The past indefinite is formed by adding to the present tense of **avoir** or **être** the past participle of the verb in question. <u>All transitive</u> verbs must be conjugated with **avoir;** <u>all reflexive verbs,</u> with **être.** The past participle of verbs conjugated with **avoir** and of reflexive verbs agrees with the preceding direct object. § 109

Je les ai vus hier. *I saw them yesterday.*
Quelle maison avez-vous achetée ? *Which house did you buy?*
Il a couru vers la maison. *He ran toward the house.*

9

Elle s'est bien amusée. *She had a good time.*

Elle s'est lavé les mains (*se* here is indirect object, therefore no agreement of past participle). *She washed her hands.*

Verbs conjugated with "être."

D. Certain intransitive verbs, the most common of which are listed below,[1] are conjugated with **être.** The past participle of such verbs agrees in gender and number with the subject. The agreement with **vous** is determined by the number and gender of the noun for which it stands. When the verbs *descendre, entrer, rentrer, monter, passer* and *sortir* are used transitively, they must be conjugated with **avoir.**

§ 111

Vous êtes parti(e)(s) sans moi. *You left without me.*

Qu'est-elle devenue? *What has become of her?*

Ils sont nés en 1920. *They were born in 1920.* (Note the tense used in the French example.)

Le concierge a descendu la malle. *The janitor took down the trunk.*

Il a monté l'escalier en courant. (This is considered a transitive use.) *He went running up the stairs.*

6 Subjunctive after Conjunctions of Purpose.

The subjunctive must be used after conjunctions denoting purpose, i.e., *unattained* result. In clauses of *attained* result, however, the indicative is retained.

---

[1] aller *to go*
arriver *to arrive*
demeurer *to remain* (When **demeurer** means *to reside*, it is conjugated with **avoir.**)
descendre *to go down*
devenir *to become*
entrer *to enter*
monter *to go up*
mourir *to die*
naître *to be born* § 110

partir *to leave*
passer *to pass* (*by*) (may be conjugated with **avoir** if the action, rather than the state, is stressed.)
rester *to stay, remain*
rentrer *to return*
revenir *to come back*
sortir *to go out*
tomber *to fall*
venir *to come*

10

Il fera de son mieux pour que son petit garçon comprenne ce qu'on lui a dit. *He will do his best in order that his little son may understand what has been said to him.* § 112

Faites en sorte que $\Big\}$ tout le monde suive votre exemple. *Act*
Agissez de sorte que
so that everyone will follow your example.

RESULT:

Il a travaillé dur si bien qu'il (de sorte qu'il) a réussi à tous ses examens. *He worked hard; so he passed all his examinations.*

7 Indefinite *on.*

The indefinite *people, one, they, you* is rendered by **on** in French.

On dit qu'elle va divorcer. *They say she is going to get a divorce.*
On ne peut pas contenter tout le monde. *You can't please everyone.*

For the sake of euphony, especially in the written language, **l'** is used before **on** after **où, si, and et,** less commonly after **que.** § 113
L' should not be used if **on** is followed by a word beginning with **l. L'on** at the beginning of a sentence is sometimes found but is generally considered an affectation.

Il m'a demandé où l'on devait mettre ses affaires. *He asked me where their (his, her) things should be put* (literally: *where one should put one's things*).
Si l'on ne réussit pas, il faut recommencer. *If you don't succeed, you must begin again.*
Ce que l'on comprend mieux, c'est son désir de partir. *What one understands better, is his desire to leave.*
Si on le lui offrait [*Not* Si l'on le lui . . .], il le refuserait. *If you offered it to him, he would refuse.*

With **on** the reflexive form used is **se,** the possessive **son,** etc., the nonreflexive direct and indirect object forms are **nous,** or **vous,** and the possessives, **notre** and **votre.**

On se persuade facilement que ses enfants ont toujours raison. *People are easily persuaded that their children are always right.*

Si l'on attrape une abeille et qu'elle vous pique... *If you catch a bee and it stings you ...*

On aime toujours les gens qui vous (nous) flattent. *You (we) always like people who flatter you (us).*

On n'aime pas les gens qui nous prennent notre argent. *We don't like people who take our money.* § 114

EXERCISES

I. VERBS TO REVIEW:

faire, écrire, avoir, être

II. IDIOMATIC EXPRESSIONS:

la semaine dernière, *last week*
d'abord, *at first*
faire de son mieux pour (plus infinitive), pour que (plus clause), *to do one's best to*
avoir du retard, *to be late* (of a train)
s'amuser, *to have a good time*
avoir faim, *to be hungry*

§ 115

avoir soif, *to be thirsty*
avoir raison, *to be right*
avoir tort, *to be wrong* (in doing something), *to be in the wrong*
se tromper, *to be mistaken, to make a mistake*
se tromper de leçon, *to study the wrong lesson*
se tromper de chemin, *to take the wrong road*
donner faim, soif, à quelqu'un, *to make someone hungry, thirsty*
serrer la main à quelqu'un, *to shake hands with someone*

III. SENTENCES FOR TRANSLATION: *use to contradict*

1. Your brother hasn't come yet? Oh yes! (*Mais si*) he is always ahead of time. 2. Did you see John yesterday? Yes, he came running down the stairs to (*venir*) shake hands with me. 3. She got up, washed her face and hands (hands and face), and sat down

12

to write John a letter. 4. In what year (*En quelle année*) were you born? I was born in 1920. 5. What has become of his son? He has made a brilliant record at the lycée Condorcet.

6. Victor Hugo prolonged (*past def.*) Romanticism by (*de*) a quarter of a century. 7. He did his best last week to arrive on time. 8. Your walk made you hungry, didn't it? You are right! I am hungry and thirsty. 9. You are tired, too, aren't you? You're mistaken. I'm not tired at all. 10. I'm going to work hard so that my parents will be satisfied with me.

11. I am told (*On me dit*) that parents are never satisfied. 12. What movies (*films, m.*) did you see last week? They say that *Gribouille* is an excellent picture. 13. Did you have a good time yesterday? Yes, I went to the movies (*cinéma, m.*) to see a show (*film*) which had not been recommended to me. 14. You never have a good time when you go to the movies with your children. 15. Let's do our best to persuade him to stay at home.

16. Are you going to bring up the trunk? No, Madam, the concierge is going to bring it up (*C'est le concierge qui . . .*). 17. She has traveled widely (*un peu partout*) so that she is well acquainted with the world's greatest cities (greatest cities of the world). 18. At what time did you get in last night? We got in very early . . . this morning. 19. I am not surprised. Your train was probably late again, wasn't it? 20. You are right. In the first place, that train is always late. In the second place, people are wrong to meddle with what (*ce qui*) does not concern them.

IV. DRILL: Translate the words in parentheses:

1. En quelle année (*was she born*)? 2. (*What has become of*) votre sœur? (*We haven't seen her*) depuis six mois. 3. Où sont les fleurs (*which you have bought*)? 4. (*When you see him*), dites-lui que (*we have gone to the movies*). 5. (*She will do her best to*) réussir à l'examen.

6. (*If she is mistaken*), elle vous fera des excuses. 7. (*You would be wrong*) de l'accuser. 8. (*She took the wrong street*) de sorte qu'elle (*got home very late*). 9. (*She washed her hands*) plusieurs fois pour que sa maman ne la gronde pas. 10. Il fait de son mieux pour que (*we have a good time*).

11. (*I haven't written him*) depuis trois semaines. 12. (*When I am hungry*), je vous le dirai. 13. (*If he is thirsty*), il vous le dira.

14. Le voilà qui (*is running down the stairs.*) 15. (*At first he took down the trunk*); ensuite (*he came back*) chercher les valises.

V. Verb Exercise:

A. Translate:

1. I used to make. 2. You (*Tu*) are writing. 3. Having written . . . 4. Are they ill? 5. Is he in the wrong? 6. We wrote (*past def.*). 7. They will do. 8. You have had. 9. They were writing. 10. We have been. 11. Do your work. 12. You (*Tu*) would be . . . 13. We would have. 14. Are you hungry? 15. Be good! (*2nd pers. sing.*) 16. They had (*past def.*). 17. While writing . . . 18. I shall have been . . . 19. Don't make any "breaks"! 20. Let's be gay!

B. Translate the English words:

1. Elle *would be* bête, si elle *did* cela. 2. Si vous *do* votre travail tout de suite, je *shall be* content. 3. Elle *would have written* la lettre. 4. Quand *you have done* vos devoirs, vous pourrez sortir. 5. Il veut manger jusqu à ce qu'il *is no longer hungry*. 6. On m'a dit qu'elle *was always right*.

14

III.

THE ARTICLES: USE AND OMISSION

8 Use of the Article.

The definite article is regularly used before:

A. Nouns used in a general sense.

> Le pain n'est pas cher en ce moment. *Bread is not expensive now.*
> La vie est trop courte. *Life is too short.*
> Les hommes sont des animaux. *Men are animals.* — why des?
> L'été est sa saison préférée. *Summer is his (or her) favorite season.*

B. Names of continents and countries.[1]

> L'Asie, l'Europe, l'Amérique, la France, l'Angleterre, l'Espagne, les États-Unis, etc. *Asia, Europe, America, France, England, Spain, the United States, etc.*

---

[1] With a few exceptions, the article is not used with names of cities or towns. *In, at,* or *to* are translated by the preposition à.

Il va *or* habite [1] au Portugal, aux États-Unis, au Canada, etc.
He goes to, or *lives in, Portugal, the United States, Canada, etc.*
§§ 116, 117, 118
Il revient du Portugal, du Canada, etc. *He comes back from Portugal, Canada, etc.*

When the name of the continent or country is <u>feminine</u> and <u>unmodified</u>, *to* and *in* are translated by **en,** *from,* by **de,** and the <u>article is omitted</u>. § 119

Nous allons, *or* habitons, en Amérique, en France, en Angleterre, etc. *We are going to,* or *living in, America, France, England, etc.*
Il revient de France, d'Angleterre, etc. *He returns from France, England, etc.*

If the name of the continent or country is <u>modified</u>, **en** is replaced by **dans** and the <u>definite article reappears</u>.

Nous allons, *or* habitons, dans l'Amérique du Nord. *We go to,* or *live in, North America.* § 120

C. Titles, or adjectives, followed by a proper noun, except in direct address.

Le docteur Ledoux, le président Lebrun, le général Gamelin. *Dr. Ledoux, President Lebrun, General Gamelin.*
Je suis le docteur Martin. *I am Dr. Martin.* § 121

Paris, Marseille, Lyon sont des villes de France. *Paris, Marseilles, Lyons are French cities.*
Elle va, *or* demeure, à Paris, à Marseille, etc. *She goes to,* or *lives in, Paris, Marseilles, etc.*
Il vient de Londres. *He comes from London.*

Common exceptions are **La Nouvelle-Orléans, La Havane, Le Havre, La Haye** (*The Hague*), **Le Caire** (*Cairo*).

A la Nouvelle-Orléans, au Havre, de la Havane, de la Haye, du Caire.

If the name of the city or town is modified, the definite article reappears.

Le vieux Paris, le Paris de Victor Hugo, le Paris d'avant-guerre. *Old Paris, the Paris of Victor Hugo, Paris before the war.*

[1] **Habiter** is frequently used transitively.

Il habite le Portugal, les États-Unis, Paris, etc. *He lives in Portugal, the United States, Paris, etc.*

Le petit Pierre, le grand Meaulnes, etc. *Little Peter, Big
Meaulnes, etc.*
But: Bonjour, docteur Ledoux. *How do you do, Dr. Ledoux.*

The titles **monsieur, madame, mademoiselle,** and **maître**
are not preceded by the article. They are, however, followed
by the article when they precede another title. § 122

Bonjour, monsieur. Monsieur Duval est là? *Good morning,
sir. Is Mr. Duval in?*
Madame la comtesse est sortie? *Did the countess go out?*
Non, monsieur le comte. *No, sir.*

D. Names of languages, except after the preposition **en.**

L'italien est une belle langue. *Italian is a beautiful language.*
Nous étudions le français. *We study French.*
Comment dit-on cela en français? *How is that said in French?*
Il parle couramment le français. *He speaks French fluently.*

The definite article is frequently omitted, however, after
parler, especially when the verb is not modified by an
adverb.

Parlez-vous français? *Do you speak French?* § 123

E. Expressions of weight and measure.

Deux francs la livre. *Two francs a pound.*
Il a payé ce vin vingt francs la bouteille. *He paid twenty
francs a bottle for this wine.*
Dix francs le mètre. *Ten francs a meter.*

F. Days of the week.

Le dimanche on va à l'église. *On Sundays people go to church.*
Le jeudi on a toujours congé. *We always have a holiday on
Thursday.*
Il est arrivé le mardi 22 octobre. *He arrived on Tuesday,
October 22.* § 124

However, if *Monday, Tuesday,* etc., are equivalent to *this,
next,* or *last Monday, Tuesday,* etc., no article is used.

Il partira lundi (prochain). *He will leave Monday.*
Il est arrivé mardi (dernier). *He arrived Tuesday.*
C'est aujourd'hui lundi. *Today is Monday.*

17

9 Omission of the Article.

The article is regularly omitted:

A. Before nouns in apposition. This omission is especially frequent in official and impersonal style.

> Paris, capitale de la France ... *Paris, the capital of France* ...
> Louis XIV, roi de France. *Louis XIV, king of France.*
> M. Durand, directeur de l'usine X, domicilié au 244 de la rue de Vaugirard, a été arrêté hier par des agents de la Sûreté. *Mr. Durand, manager of the factory of X, who resides at 244 Vaugirard Street, was arrested by government detectives yesterday.*

The article regularly reappears in a more familiar style, where the personal identification is stressed.

> Nous avons invité Mme Dacheux, une amie de notre fille. *We invited Mrs. Dacheux, a friend of our daughter's.*
> Vous y verrez M. Meyer, le directeur de la banque, M. Collinot, le directeur du casino, et son ami M. Olive. *You will see there Mr. Meyer, the president of the bank, Mr. Collinot, the manager of the casino, and his friend Mr. Olive.*

When the noun in apposition is modified by an adjective, the *indefinite* article may be omitted; the *definite* article must be used.

> X., (un) petit village sur la Seine,[1] ... *X., a little village on the Seine,* ...
> M. Reynaud, l'homme d'État bien connu ... *Mr. Reynaud, the well-known statesman* ...

The definite article must be used if the noun in apposition is a proper name preceded by a title, other than **M., Mme, Mlle, Me**.

> Je lui ai été présenté par mon camarade, le capitaine Ledoux. *I was introduced to him by my comrade, Captain Ledoux.*

---

[1] The indefinite article is now frequently used to identify a noun in apposition modified by an adjective and a clause.

> Le conférencier, un jeune économiste anglais qui venait d'arriver aux États-Unis, ... *The lecturer, a young English economist who had just arrived in the United States,* ...

In general, when one wishes to *classify*, the article is omitted; when one wishes to *identify* or *individualize*, the article is used. The indefinite article, therefore, is much more frequently omitted than the definite article.

> Pasteur, savant chimiste français, né à Dôle en 1822 ...
> *Pasteur, a learned French chemist, born at Dôle in 1822 ...*
> Wagner, le célèbre compositeur allemand, a exercé une influence profonde sur la musique. *Wagner, the famous German composer, exerted a profound influence on music.*

B. Before predicate nouns which indicate profession, nationality, religion, etc., unless they are modified by an adjective, or introduced by **ce**.

> Elle est Française. *She is a Frenchwoman.*
> Mon père est médecin. *My father is a doctor.*
> Nous sommes catholiques. *We are Catholics.*
> On l'a élu président du cercle français. *He was elected president of the French Club.*
> Julie est une cuisinière excellente. *Julia is an excellent cook.*
> Il est médecin? C'est un médecin? *Is he a doctor?*
> Oui, c'est [*Not* il est] un médecin célèbre. *Yes, he is a famous doctor.*

If the predicate noun and its adjective are so closely connected as to form a unit, the article is regularly omitted.

> Il est bon catholique. *He is a good Catholic.*
> Il est beau joueur. *He is a good loser.*

C. After the preposition **en**.

> Il pense toujours en professeur. *He always thinks like a professor.*
> En été, en automne, en hiver, en mai, en ville, en voiture, etc. *In summer, in fall, in winter, in May, in town, in a vehicle, etc.*
> §§ 125, 126

Exceptions: Certain stereotyped expressions:

> En l'air, en l'honneur de, en l'absence de, etc. *In the air, in honor of, in the absence of, etc.*

EXERCISES

I. Verbs to Review:

venir, voir, prendre

II. Idiomatic Expressions:

avoir congé, *to have a holiday*

en été, en hiver, en automne, au printemps, *in summer, in winter, in autumn, in spring*

en l'air, *in the air*

en l'honneur de, *in honor of*

en l'absence de, *in the absence of*

par terre, *on the ground*

par hasard, *by chance*

apprendre le français, *to learn, to study French*

apprendre (enseigner) quelque chose à quelqu'un, *to teach someone something* (**apprendre** cannot be used to mean *teach* unless it has both a direct and an indirect object.)

à l'église, *to, in church*

Quand est-ce Noël? [1] *When is Christmas?*

Pâques tombe toujours un dimanche. *Easter always comes on (a) Sunday.*

Noël tombe le 25 décembre. *Christmas comes on the 25th of December.*

C'est demain Noël. *Tomorrow is Christmas.*

C'est aujourd'hui lundi. *Today is Monday.*

C'est aujourd'hui le 16 novembre. *Today is November 16.*

deux fois par mois, par an, par jour, *twice a month, a year, a day* § 127

Qu'est-ce que vous voulez comme boisson, comme dessert, etc.? *What do you wish to drink, for dessert, etc.?*

III. Sentences for Translation:

1. Cats are intelligent animals. 2. The United States is doing its best to aid England. 3. Mr. Hughes, an English lecturer, is making a tour of the United States. 4. In France, living is very expensive now; bread costs fifteen francs a kilo, red wine, ten

---

[1] Some French people prefer the more formal expression: **Quand est la Noël?** (i.e., **la fête de Noël**).

francs a liter. 5. Dr. Ledoux has been living in New Orleans since 1918.

6. On what day of the week does Easter come? 7. On Tuesday we shall have a holiday in honor of the founder of the university. 8. After leaving (use the past infinitive) England, we shall go to France, Italy, and North Africa. 9. Has he come back from Spain? He has never been in Spain. 10. He is a good Catholic; he always goes to church on Sunday.

11. What is your favorite season? I don't know. In winter I think it (ce) is summer, and in summer I think it is winter. 12. In the absence of our professor, a music student taught us some French songs. 13. Good morning, Dr. Ledoux. I have come to see if by chance I might make an appointment for ten o'clock. 14. Mary's son is studying French. He takes a private lesson three times a week. 15. Our teacher speaks French very slowly so that we may be able to understand her.

16. How do you say this in French? I don't know. I have never studied (use *étudier*) French. I am learning Italian. 17. Next Tuesday when we have a quiz, we shall see whether you have learned your lessons well. 18. To-day is Thursday. We always have a holiday on Thursday. 19. Little Henry has been very ill. We had to send for Dr. Legrand. 20. Washington, the capital of the United States, is the most beautiful city in North America.

21. The students at (de) the University of Paris know and admire Galsworthy, the famous English novelist. 22. His wife is a Frenchwoman. He met her during the war and he married her in 1920. 23. He never puts his books away; so he never knows where they are. 24. Put my books away so that I will know where they are. 25. Spring begins in March.

IV. Drill: Translate the words in parentheses:

1. Depuis combien de temps (*has Dr. Ledoux lived in Spain*)? 2. (*In Mexico*) il pleut souvent (*in summer*). 3. Est-il revenu (*from England*)? Non, il est toujours (*in London*). 4. Depuis combien de temps (*have you been studying French*)? 5. Connaissez-vous Mlle Duval, (*the president of the French Club*)? 6. En ce moment (*coffee*) est très cher. Il coûte 25 francs (*a pound*). 7. M. Dupuis, (*a grocer in* [de] *the*) rue Legendre a

21

disparu il y a quinze jours. 8. Tu lui écris toujours (*in French*)? 9. (*Next Monday*) nous allons donner une réception (*in honor of*) Mme Cottin. (*She is a Frenchwoman*), n'est-ce pas? 10. Pourquoi donnez-vous toujours vos réceptions (*on Monday*)?

11. Si on est (*a good Catholic*) on va souvent (*to church*). 12. (*Dr. Duval*) est sorti. Il faudra que (*little Helen*) revienne demain. 13. Le professeur fait de son mieux pour que vous (*learn*) vos verbes français. 14. Allez-vous souvent au cinéma? Oui, j'y vais (*three times a week*). 15. Apprenez-vous (*French*)? Non, je préfère (*Italian*).

V. VERB EXERCISE:

A. Give the following forms in all the simple tenses:

1. *prendre*, first person singular and plural. 2. *venir*, third person singular and first person plural. 3. *voir*, third person singular and plural.

B. Translate;
1. Coming... 2. I have taken. 3. They would have come. 4. She had seen. 5. You came (*past def.*). 6. Until he takes... 7. Taking... 8. In order that she may see... 9. They used to come. 10. Will they see?

6. Jusqu'à ce qu'il prenne
7. Prenant
8. Pour qu'elle voie
9. Ils venaient.
10. Verront-ils?

22

IV.

THE USE OF CERTAIN PREPOSITIONS

10 *Pendant, de, pour.*

When a period of time which is the object of the preposition
for expresses the total duration of the action of the verb, *for* is
translated by **pendant.** This preposition is often omitted.
Its use emphasizes the idea of duration.

> Il est resté à l'hôpital pendant quinze jours. Il est resté
> quinze jours à l'hôpital. *He stayed in the hospital for two
> weeks.* (Note the different word order in the two French
> sentences.)
> Je resterai quelques années à Paris. Je resterai à Paris
> pendant quelques années. *I shall stay in Paris for a few
> years.*

In negative sentences, **pendant** is sometimes replaced by **de.**

> Il n'avait pas mangé de la journée. *He hadn't eaten all day
> long.*
> On ne me reverra pas de quelques années. *They won't see
> me again for a few years.*

When the verb marks the starting point of the period of time governed by the English *for*, *for* is translated by **pour.**

> Nous sommes ici pour deux mois (i.e., pour y rester deux mois). *We are here for two months.*
> Il est revenu à Paris pour quinze jours (i.e., pour y rester quinze jours). *He came back to Paris for two weeks.*

11 *Pour, envers, avec.*

To after adjectives indicating feeling toward or treatment of is regularly translated by **pour.**

> Il est très bon pour vous. *He is very good to you.*
> Elle est aimable pour tout le monde. *She is kind to everyone.*

In literary style, this *to* is frequently translated by **envers,** in colloquial style, by **avec.**

12 *Dans, sur.*

On the street is translated by **dans la rue,** *on the avenue,* by **dans** or **sur** [1] **l'avenue,** *on the boulevard,* by **sur** [2] **le boulevard.** When the name of the street is given, however, the preposition is generally omitted.   § 128

> Dans cette rue, il y a plusieurs maisons d'édition. *On this street there are several publishing houses.*
> Il habitait rue de Courcelles, boulevard Saint-Michel, etc. *He lived on Courcelles Street, Saint-Michel Boulevard, etc.*
> *Cf.:* Elle habite 75, rue de Vaugirard (au 75 de la rue de Vaugirard). *She lives at 75 Vaugirard Street.*
> Il allait tous les jours rue Jouffroy. *Every day he went to Jouffroy Street.*

Sur la rue would mean *looking out on the street.*

> Il a un appartement (qui donne) sur la rue.

---

[1] When it is a question of a very broad avenue **sur** is especially indicated: sur l'avenue des Champs-Élysées.

[2] The use of **sur** with **boulevard** is the result of the fact that the latter word formerly meant *rampart,* or the street which later replaced the rampart.

24

13 *Avant* versus *devant.*

Before, when it indicates priority, is translated by **avant**; when it is a synonym of *in front of,* it is translated by **devant**.

> Elle est arrivée avant moi. *She arrived before me.*
> Combien y en a-t-il avant vous? *How many are there ahead of you?*
> Il vous a fait passer avant moi. *He had you go ahead of me.*
> Elle mettait le garde-feu devant la cheminée. *She was putting the screen in front of the fireplace.*
> Elle est passée devant vous. *She passed in front of you.*

14 *A, en, dans.*

The English prepositions *to* and *in* are frequently translated by à when the object is a place more or less public in character.

> à l'école, *to, in, school*
> à l'église, *to, in, church* (**dans** l'église, if one wishes to stress position inside the church)
> à la bibliothèque, *to, in, the library*
> à l'hôpital, *to, in, the hospital*
> au salon (dans le salon), *in the living room*
> à la salle à manger (dans la salle à manger), *in the dining room*
> à la cuisine (dans la cuisine), *in the kitchen*

In the bedroom, however, is always **dans la chambre**.
À la ville is regularly contrasted with **à la campagne**.

> demeurer à la ville, à la campagne, *to live in town, in the country*
> Le paysan va à la ville (pour) vendre son blé. *The peasant goes to the city to sell his grain.*

When a person is already in the country:

> J'aime me promener **dans la campagne**. *I like to take a walk in the country.*

En ville means *down town,* or *out,* in the sense of away from home, *to town* for the suburbanite, also *in town,* as opposed to *to, at, the seashore, to, in, the mountains, the country,* etc.

> Nous allons en ville cet après-midi. *We are going to town,* or *down town, this afternoon.*

J'ai dîné en ville hier. *I dined out yesterday.*

Cette année nous n'allons pas au bord de la mer, nous restons en ville. *This year we are not going to the seashore, we are staying in town.*

When it is a question of a person's coming from another town, *to town, in town*, is translated by **à** plus the name of the town, or occasionally by **dans cette ville.**

La prochaine fois que vous serez à Paris ... *The next time that you are in town (i.e., in Paris) ...*

When the emphasis is placed on position inside the limits of the town, **dans** is used before the name of the town.

Au cours de ses promenades dans Paris, il a appris bien des choses. *In the course of his walks in Paris, he learned lots of things.*

Il n'y a pas d'usines dans Paris, mais il y en a beaucoup dans la banlieue. *There aren't any factories in Paris, but there are many in the outskirts.*

15 Prepositions used with *prendre.*

As the French verb **prendre** conveys little or no idea of motion, it is followed by a preposition of location, where *to take* would require a preposition expressing the idea of separation.

Il a pris le cahier sur la table. *He took the notebook from the table.*

Allez prendre mes gants dans le tiroir. *Go get my gloves from the drawer.*

EXERCISES

I. VERBS TO REVIEW:

mettre, se promener,[1] **jeter,**[1] **recevoir**

II. IDIOMATIC EXPRESSIONS:

faire des emplettes, *to do (some) shopping*
se mettre à, plus infinitive, *to begin to*

---

[1] Cf. orthographical changing verbs. § 246 **D** and **F**

se mettre à table, *to sit down at the table*
mettre la table, *or*, le couvert, *to set the table*
mettre, *to put on (of clothes)*
(aller) jeter un coup d'œil, *to take a look*   (Use **aller** if *to go* ✓
   is implied.)
mettre deux heures pour (à) faire quelque chose, il lui faut
   deux heures pour faire quelque chose, *it takes him two hours*
   to do something.
mettre de l'argent de côté, *to put some money aside*
se mettre en colère, *to get angry*, être en colère, *to be angry*
être reçu à l'examen, *to pass the examination*
penser à, *to think of, i.e., to turn one's thoughts to, toward*
penser de, *to think of (to have a good or bad opinion of)*
Je pense à lui, *I am thinking of him.*
J'y pense, *I am thinking of it.*
Que pensez-vous de lui? *What do you think of him?*
Qu'en pensez-vous? *What do you think of it?*
          (what opinion)   en = de + pronoun
                                      y = à

III. Sentences for Translation:

1. He isn't kind to anyone when he is angry. Does he get angry
often? No, not (*pas*) very often.   2. I came back to Paris for
two weeks, and I stayed there two years. ③ You won't see him *nég*
again for a long, long time.   4. Where does Mrs. Dulot live? She
lives on Guynemer Street, near the Luxembourg Garden.   5. How
long does it take you to walk there? I never walk there, I always
drive (*y aller en auto*). *Combien de temps mettez-vous pour y aller à pieds*
Je n'y vais jamais à pieds, j'y vais toujours en auto.
6. I never take more than five minutes to set the table.   7. Let's
take a look at the house which looks out on Monceau Park (*le
parc Monceau*).   8. How long did you work in the library?   I
worked there for three hours.   9. How long has he been in the
hospital? He has been there for ten days.   10. When did you see
him? A few days before Christmas. He was waiting for a bus
in front of the Louvre.

11. After taking him to the station, I am going (*je vais aller*) down
town to do some shopping.   12. If she passes her examinations,
she will go to the seashore.   13. Do your parents live in the city
or in the country?   14. Before sitting down at the table, go get
some spoons out of the drawer of the sideboard.   15. When she
dines out, she always puts on her jewels.

16. I think (*Je crois*) that he has begun to put some money aside in order that his son may be able to go to college next year. 17. What do you think of his idea? I don't know; I've never thought about it. 18. Is your hotel situated in Paris or in the suburbs? 19. Did you go to France last summer? Yes. How long did it take you to cross the ocean? 20. It took us five days. If you go (*y*) by plane, it takes less than (*de*) two days.

21. What are you thinking of? I am thinking of what your friend said last night. 22. You don't think much of his arguments, do you? (much = *grand'chose*) 23. I should like to look at your manuscript again before you send it to the publisher. 24. One day when (*que*) I was walking along Tronchet Street, I saw a poor fellow throw himself under (the wheels of) a bus. 25. What street does he live on? He lives at 88 LaFayette Street (*rue LaFayette*).[1] Are there many boardinghouses on that street? I don't know (*Je n'en sais rien*).

IV. DRILL: Translate the words in parentheses:

1. (*In summer we do our shopping*) dans la matinée. Ne parlez pas de ça maintenant. Venez (*sit down at the table*). 2. Qu'est-ce qu'il y a (*in front of that house*)? 3. Y a-t-il une maison à louer (*on the boulevard*)? 4. Non, mais il y en a beaucoup (*on Delambre Street*). 5. Il est parti (*before your arrival*). Savez-vous s'il (*has passed his examination*)?

6. A l'insu de sa mère, (*the child stayed in the park for two hours*). 7. Il est allé à Paris (*for several months*). 8. Moi, je croyais que nous ne le reverrions pas (*for several years*). 9. Les Quakers sont bons (*to everyone*). 10. (*In the country*) on se lève de bonne heure, (*in the city*) on fait souvent la grasse matinée.

11. Au lieu d'aller (*to church*) j'aurais dû travailler (*in the library*). 12. Où allez-vous passer l'été? (*At the beach or in town?*) 13. Votre frère est-il (*in the hospital*)? (*Yes, he has been there for two weeks*). 14. Après avoir pris ses livres (*off the table*), elle est sortie précipitamment. 15. (*She always gets angry*) quand elle

---

[1] **De** is used in street names which refer to places but not in those which refer to persons.

La rue de Rennes (place).
La rue Guynemer (person).

(takes more than five minutes to set the table). 16. *(Take a look at)* ce veston; je pourrais toujours *(put it on)*, n'est-ce pas?

V. VERB EXERCISE:

A. Translate the English words:

1. Je vais la gronder jusqu'à ce qu'elle *gets angry.* 2. Nous *throw* la balle. 3. *Will he receive* la lettre? 4. Si elle *put on* cette robe, elle *would receive* beaucoup de compliments. 5. *Mail* la lettre ce matin pour qu'il *may receive it* cet après-midi. 6. *I am receiving* mes amies aujourd'hui. 7. Il *throws* son chapeau en l'air. 8. Le dimanche les Parisiens *walk* sur les grands boulevards. 9. Elle *was putting on* ses gants quand elle *received* la nouvelle. 10. Avant cinq heures, elle *will have set the table.* 11. Si on le lui permettait, *he would go out* tous les soirs.

B. Translate:

1. Take a look *(2nd pers. sing.)* at my exercise. 2. Are you walking (taking a walk)? 3. Don't receive him. 4. While throwing . . . 5. She began to cry. 6. Let's not get angry. 7. I put *(past def.).* 8. They had walked (taken a walk). 9. We shall throw. 10. We threw *(past def.).* 11. Put the book on the table.

V.

PARTITIVE ARTICLE
PARTITIVE PRONOUN

The subjunctive of concession; the indefinites:
*quelque, un peu de, peu de, quelque chose,
autre chose, rien, personne*

16 The Partitive Article.

A. When a noun is used to express part of a class, it is regularly preceded by the partitive article.

> Il a du pain et de la viande. *He has (some) bread and meat.*
> Donnez-moi de l'argent. *Give me some money.*
> Nous avons des [1] amis à Paris. *We have friends in Paris.*

B. The noun in the partitive sense is preceded by **de** alone:

1. In a general negation.

> Elle n'a pas d'amis à Paris. *She hasn't any friends in Paris.*
> Il n'y a pas de viande sur la table. *There isn't any meat on the table.*

---

[1] The contraction **des** is regularly the plural of the indefinite article and is so designated by most French grammarians.

Il n'a pas de pain ni de beurre. *He hasn't any bread, or any butter.*

Il ne mange jamais de viande. *He never eats meat.*

Il n'avait d'yeux que pour elle. *He had eyes only for her (He had no eyes except for her).* §§ 129, 130, 131

Je n'aurai de paix avec moi-même qu'après lui avoir dit la vérité. *I shall be at peace with myself only when I have told him the truth (I shall have no peace with myself until . . .).*

[When the noun in the partitive sense is limited by the **que** of **ne . . . que,** it is excluded from the negation; hence the full form of the partitive article is used.

Je n'ai mangé que de la viande. *I ate only meat (I ate nothing but meat).*

Il n'a que du pain. *He has only bread (He has nothing but bread).*]

2. After expressions of quantity.

beaucoup de viande, *a lot of meat*
assez de beurre, *enough butter*
trop de soin, *too much care*
un kilo[1] de pain, *two pounds of bread*
une boîte de cigares, *a box of cigars*
un verre de vin, *a glass of wine*

Exceptions:

bien des livres, *many books*
encore du vin, *more wine*
la plupart des gens, *most people*

If a noun is used in a specific sense, the definite article is required.

Beaucoup des gens que nous connaissons sont des étrangers. *Many of the people whom we know are foreigners.*

3. Before a noun preceded by an adjective.

Il a de bons livres. *He has good books.*
Ils ont de beaux enfants. *They have beautiful children.*

---

[1] *Kilo* is the abbreviation of *kilogramme.* A kilogram is approximately equivalent to 2.2 American pounds.

Many Frenchmen who disregard this rule when the noun is singular, practically always observe it when the noun is plural. In many instances, the use of the full form of the partitive article in violation of the rule is characteristic of familiar or childish speech.

With abstract nouns, however, and in many frequently used expressions when the noun and adjective seem to form a unit, the full form of the partitive reappears.

> du vrai bonheur, *true happiness*
> de la grande éloquence, *great eloquence*
> des jeunes gens, *young people, young men* (who have not yet started on their career)
> des petits pains, *rolls*
> des petits pois, *green peas* § 132

Omission of the partitive.

C. The partitive is omitted:

1. After **avec** (in adverbial phrases of manner of a type equivalent to a single adverb), **sans, ni . . . ni.**

> Il l'a reçu avec plaisir (volontiers). *He received it with pleasure.*
> On ne peut rien faire sans talent. *You can't do anything without talent.*
> Il n'a ni pain ni beurre. *He has neither bread nor butter.*

When the phrase with **avec** expresses accompaniment, instrument, or means, the full form of the partitive is used.

> Il prend toujours son café avec du lait. *He always takes his coffee with milk.*
> On a fait cela avec des épingles. *That was done with pins.*
> Avec du talent, on fait bien des choses. *With talent one does many things.*
> Avec du courage, on surmonte beaucoup de difficultés. *With courage one surmounts many difficulties.* § 133

2. When the noun in the partitive sense is already the object of the preposition **de.**

> Il a besoin d'argent [*Not* de de l'argent]. *He needs money.*
> La salle était pleine de monde. *The hall was full of people.*

32

un chapeau de paille, *a straw hat*
des bas de soie, *silk stockings*

17 The Partitive Pronoun *en*.

The partitive as a pronoun is expressed by **en**, in referring both to persons and to things.

> Avez-vous du beurre? Oui, j'en ai. *Do you have some butter? Yes, I do (I have some).*
> Avez-vous des amis à Paris? Oui, j'en ai. *Do you have friends in Paris? Yes, I do.*

En must be used to translate the idea *of it, of them,* when the object of the verb is an expression of quantity or number.

> Avez-vous du vin? Oui, j'en ai une bouteille. *Have you some wine? Yes, I have a bottle.*
> Avez-vous des amis à Paris? Oui, j'en ai deux (beaucoup). *Have you friends in Paris? Yes, I have two (many).*

18 The Subjunctive in Clauses of Concession.

The subjunctive must be used in clauses of concession introduced by conjunctions such as **quoique, bien que,** or **encore que.**

> Bien qu'il (Quoiqu'il) fasse beau, nous ne sortirons pas. *Although the weather is fine, we shall not go out.*

19 Indefinites.

quelque, un peu de, peu de

The student should distinguish **quelque**, *some, a few,* from **un peu de,** *a little* and from **peu de,** *few, little* (not much).

> quelques amis, *some (a few) friends*
> un peu d'argent, *a little money*
> peu d'amis, *few friends*
> peu d'argent, *little money*

33

Quelque used adverbially to modify the numeral adjective is invariable.

> Il habite à quelque deux cents mètres d'ici. *He lives some two hundred yards from here.*

quelque chose

Although **chose** is feminine in most instances, the indefinite pronouns **quelque chose** and **autre chose** are masculine.

> J'ai quelque chose pour vous. Je vais vous le montrer. *I have something for you. I'll show it to you.*
>
> Voici encore autre chose. Faites-le-moi voir. *Here's something else (still another thing). Show it to me (Let me see it).*

rien, personne

When a verb is present, *nothing* is translated by **ne . . . rien,** *no one* by **ne . . . personne.** When **rien** is the direct object of a verb in a compound tense, it stands between the auxiliary and the past participle. **Personne,** on the other hand, is never placed in this position. If no verb is present, these words are used without **ne.** When **rien** and **personne** are used as subjects, they precede the verb.   § 134

> Il n'entend rien. *He hears nothing.*
> Il n'a rien entendu. *He heard nothing.*
> Je ne vois personne. *I see no one.*
> Je n'ai vu personne. *I saw no one.*
> Rien ne m'intéresse. *Nothing interests me.*
> Personne n'est venu. *No one came.*
> Il n'a parlé à personne. *He spoke to no one.*
> Il n'a renoncé à rien. *He gave up nothing.*
> Il n'a besoin de rien. *He needs nothing.*
> Il n'a besoin de personne. *He needs no one.*
> — Qui est venu ? — Personne. *Who came? No one.*
> — Qu'est-ce qu'il vous a dit ? — Rien. *What did he tell you? Nothing.*

Note that **pas** is *not* used in the same clause with **rien, personne,** or **jamais.**

When **quelque chose, rien, personne** are followed by an adjective, **de** is regularly required.

Je vous montrerai quelque chose be beau. *I shall show you something beautiful.*

Je n'ai rien vu d'intéressant. *I saw nothing interesting.*

Il n'y a personne de raisonnable parmi vous. *There is not a reasonable person among you.* § 135

EXERCISES

I. Verbs to Review:

connaître, vouloir, pouvoir, pleuvoir

II. Idiomatic Expressions:

Il fait beau (temps).
Le temps est beau. } *The weather is beautiful.*

Il fait mauvais (temps).
Le temps est mauvais. } *The weather is bad.*

Il fait de la pluie. *It is raining.*

Il fait du brouillard. *It is foggy.*

Il fait du vent. *It is windy.*

Il pleut à verse. *It is pouring (rain).*

Le temps (le ciel) se couvre. *The weather is getting cloudy.*

Le ciel est couvert. *It is cloudy.*

Le temps s'éclaircit (se lève). *It's clearing up.*

On dirait qu'il va pleuvoir. *It looks as if it's going to rain.*

Le soleil va se montrer. *The sun is going to come out.*

avoir besoin de, *to need*

se passer de, *to do without*   Do not have 14-25

III. Sentences for Translation:

1. Does she have any friends at college? Yes, she has a great many. 2. Although it is pouring rain, he says that he doesn't need an [1] umbrella. 3. He is right. I think the sun is going to come out at any minute. 4. I still have many of the books that he gave me last year. 5. Do you have many English books? No, I have only French books.

6. There are few young people who study with pleasure. 7. I know a few who study all the time. 8. Do you have some good

---

[1] Do not translate *an.*

35

pictures of your roommate? No, I don't have any. No one has any photos of that creature. 9. Will you have (*Voulez-vous*) a little salt? No, thanks. I never take either salt or pepper. Will you have a glass of wine? With pleasure (*Bien volontiers*), mademoiselle, I always take wine with (*à*) my meals. 10. He heard from Monica only through her friends. *recevoir des nouvelles de*

11. With perseverance most of the students will be able to pass their examinations. 12. I think that they will need intelligence too, don't you? 13. A few students told me they had found nothing interesting in his lecture. 14. There is no one intelligent in that class (*cette classe-là*). 15. It seems (*Il paraît*) that Rip van Winkle slept for twenty years. Really? That's what I call true happiness.

16. Is it raining? No, it's foggy; but I think it's going to clear up. 17. It is clouding up. It looks as though it were going to rain. It's very windy, too. 18. If the weather is good tomorrow, we are going to play tennis. If it's bad, we'll play bridge. 19. Although I have seen no one leave (*sortir de*) the house, I am certain that the murderer is no longer there (*y* before the verb). 20. For some time we have been doing our best to save our silk stockings.

21. When it is foggy, the plane is generally late. 22. In the country it is hard to have a good time when the weather is bad. 23. What's new (*Qu'est-ce qu'il y a de nouveau*) in the paper? Nothing. 24. Who is willing to lend me some money? No one. 25. Well, I'm going to ask father to give me some. You (*On*) can't do without money.

IV. DRILL: Translate the words in parentheses:

1. Sur la table il y a (*a lot of bread, a little butter, a few rolls and some vegetables*); mais il n'y a pas (*any coffee*). 2. Je ne vais prendre que (*some vegetables*). Comment? Vous n'allez manger (*either meat or bread*)? 3. (*Most*) hommes d'affaires fument (*too many*) cigares. 4. (*Many of the*) élèves qui ont échoué à l'examen avaient eu (*good grades*) avant d'entrer au collège. 5. Voilà (*some young people*) qui ont trouvé (*some real happiness*).

6. Prenez-vous votre café (*with sugar*)? Non, je le prends toujours (*without sugar*). 7. Si vous faites cela (*with care*), il vous faudra (*much patience*). C'est vrai, mais (*with patience*) j'en viendrai à

bout. **8.** Quoiqu'on (*can do without*) bien des choses, on a toujours besoin (*of money*). **9.** Il y a (*few*) Français dans cette partie des États-Unis. (*Do you know any?*) **10.** Je n'en connais pas. (*How many do you know?*) (*I know*) trois ou quatre.

11. Si vous avez (*something*) pour moi, (*give it to me*). (*I have nothing*) pour vous. (*No one*) n'a rien pour moi? (*No one.*) **12.** Parmi tous ces jeunes gens il n'y avait personne (*likable*). **13.** Si (*the weather is fine*) cet après-midi, j'aurai (*something interesting*) à vous proposer. **14.** Avant qu'il (*rains*), (*the weather gets cloudy and the wind blows*). Quelques minutes plus tard, (*it is pouring rain*). **15.** Ne dirait-on pas (*that it is going to rain*)? Au contraire, je crois (*that the sun is going to come out*). **16.** Bien que (*it is foggy*) maintenant, je crois que (*the weather is going to clear up*).

V. VERB EXERCISE:

A. Match the English sentences with the correct French translation.

1. *Do you know Mrs. Durand?*
2. *I should like to go home.*
3. *He could not leave yesterday.*
4. *It will rain soon.*
5. *Could you go?*
6. *I should have liked to go to that concert.*
7. *We don't want to leave.*
8. *If it rains, we shall be unable to go out.*
9. *Be kind enough to continue.*
10. *If she knew you, she would speak to you.*
11. *Will you have some coffee?*
12. *May I do that?*
13. *Although it is raining, they don't want to stay at home.*
14. *They cannot sing.*
15. *Have they been able to find their son?*

1. J'aurai voulu aller à ce concert.
2. S'il pleut, nous ne pourrons pas sortir.
3. Veuillez continuer.
4. Si elle vous connaissait, elle vous parlerait.
5. Puis-je faire cela?
6. Voulez-vous du café?
7. Connaissez-vous Mme Durand?
8. Il pleuvra bientôt.
9. Ont-ils pu trouver leur fils?
10. Je voudrais aller chez moi.
11. Ils ne peuvent pas chanter.
12. Nous ne voulons pas partir.
13. Il n'a pas pu partir hier.
14. Quoiqu'il pleuve, ils ne veulent pas rester à la maison.
15. Pourriez-vous y aller?

B. Translate:

1. She used to know them. 2. Will you (*tu*) go out? 3. It would rain. 4. Before he is able to do it... 5. Until he wants to learn... 6. We wished (*past def.*). 7. I should like to know her. 8. I have known her since January. 9. Would you be able to do that? 10. It is raining.

VI.

PERSONAL PRONOUNS

The subjunctive after expressions of emotion

20 Forms of the Personal Pronouns.

	CONJUNCTIVE PRONOUNS			DISJUNCTIVE PRONOUNS
SUBJECT	INDIRECT OBJ.	DIR. OBJ.	REFLEX.	
je	me	me	me	moi
tu	te	te	te	toi
il	lui	le	se	lui ⎱ soi
elle	lui	la	se	elle ⎰
nous	nous	nous	nous	nous
vous	vous	vous	vous	vous
ils	leur	les	se	eux ⎱ soi
elles	leur	les	se	elles ⎰

§§ 136, 137

21 Position of Conjunctive Pronouns.

A. Conjunctive pronoun objects, including the pronominal adverbs **y** and **en,** precede the verb, unless the verb is in the

39

affirmative imperative. In the latter case, the pronoun objects are placed after the verb. With the exception of **y** and **en,** *the verb may have two conjunctive pronoun objects only when the direct object is one of the three pronouns* **le, la,** *or* **les.** **Y** comes last in any series of pronouns except when **en** is present, in which case **en** comes last.

1. The following table indicates the order when the objects precede the verb:

INDIRECT OBJECT	DIRECT OBJECT	INDIRECT OBJECT
me	le	lui
te	la	leur
se	les	
nous		
vous		

Note that the indirect object precedes the direct object unless both objects are in the third person and not reflexive.

> Il me l'envoie. *He sends it to me.*
> Il se l'est donné (à lui-même). *He gave it to himself.*
> Ne le lui envoyez pas. *Don't send it to him.*
> On ne les leur a pas envoyés. *They didn't send them to them.*
> Vous l'a-t-il envoyé? *Did he send it to you?*

2. When the affirmative imperative has two pronoun objects, the accepted order is: direct object, indirect object. When **y** and **en** follow the imperative, their position with regard to other pronoun objects is that mentioned in § 21A. **Me** and **te,** unless followed by **y** or **en,** are replaced by **moi** and **toi.**   § 138

> Envoyez-le-lui. *Send it to him.*
> Envoyez-les-moi. *Send them to me.*
> Envoyez-lui-en. *Send him some.*
> Envoyez-m'en. *Send me some.*
> Va-t'en! *Go away!*
> Allez-y! *Go to it! Go ahead!*
> Servons-nous-en. *Let's use it.*
> Méfiez-vous-en. *Beware of it.*

40

22 Use of Disjunctive Pronouns.

Disjunctive pronouns are used in the following cases:

A. To translate the indirect object, when the direct object is in the first or second person, or a reflexive. *ou is not le, la, les.*

> Il m'a envoyé à vous. *He sent me to you.*
> Elle s'adresse à lui. *She applies to him.*
> Présentez-moi à elle. *Introduce me to her.*
> Ne vous présentez pas à eux. *Don't introduce yourselves to them.*

B. To translate the indirect objects of certain verbs expressing *literal* motion and of a small number of verbs which do not permit a preceding object referring to persons.

> Il est venu à moi. *He came to me.*
> *But*: L'idée m'est venue. *The idea came to me.*
> Pensez à moi. *Think of me.*
> Renoncez à lui. *Give him up.*
> Il ne tenait pas à elle. *He didn't care for her.*
> Ne faites pas attention à lui. *Don't pay any attention to him.*

C. After prepositions.

> Vous parlez toujours de lui. *You always talk about him.*
> sans moi, avec elle, près de lui, pour elles, *without me, with her, near him, for them*
> l'un [1] de nous, deux d'entre eux, beaucoup d'entre nous, *one of us, two of them, many of us*

When a third person subject is general or indefinite, **soi** is used as the corresponding disjunctive.

> Chacun pour soi. *Everyone for himself.*
> On pense à soi. *One thinks of one's self.*
> Il faut travailler pour soi. *You must work for yourself.*

D. After **être** when the subject is **ce.**

> C'est moi, vous, elle, nous. *It is I, you, she, we.*
> Ce sont eux. *It is they.*

---

[1] After numerals greater than *one* and after adverbs of quantity, **d'entre** is used instead of **de** before a personal pronoun.

E. When used without a verb, or for emphasis or contrast.

> Qui frappe à la porte? Lui. *Who is knocking at the door? He.*
> Lui est parti, elle est restée. He *left*, she *stayed.*
> Je l'ai fait moi-même. *I did it myself.*
> Donnez-les-lui, à elle. *Give them to* her.
> Moi, je ne le crois pas. I *don't think so.*

F. When the subject is separated from the verb by any word other than **ne, y, en,** or a personal pronoun. § 139

> Moi, qui l'ai vu, je vous le jure. *I, who saw it, I swear it to you.*
> Lui aussi me l'a dit. *He too told me it.*

Disjunctives of the third person may stand alone as subject, whereas those of the first and second person are regularly accompanied by the conjunctive form. § 140

G. When the subject or object is compound.

> Lui et moi (nous) irons au cinéma. *He and I shall go to the movies.*
> Je les ai rencontrés, lui et elle. *I met him and her.*

H. After **ne . . . que.**

> Il n'a vu que moi. *He saw only me.*

I. After **que** in comparisons.

> Elle est aussi grande que moi. *She is as tall as I.*
> Elle est plus grande que moi. *She is taller than I.*

23 The Pronominal Adverb *en.*

When an English preposition equivalent to **de** governs an object which refers to a thing, the phrase is regularly translated by the pronominal adverb **en.**[1]

> Je n'en ai jamais entendu parler. *I've never heard of it.*
> Vous en parlez toujours. *You always talk about it.*
> Venez-vous de Paris? *Do you come from Paris?*
> Oui, j'en viens. *Yes, I come from there.* § 141

---

[1] For the partitive use of **en,** cf. § 17.

24 The Use of Y.

Y is equivalent to the prepositions **à, dans, sur** plus a disjunctive pronoun referring to a thing or to a place. It frequently translates the English *there* when the place has already been mentioned. §§ 142, 143

Votre père est-il au (dans le) jardin? *Is your father in the garden?*
Oui, il y est. *Yes, he is.*
Etes-vous allé à Lyon? *Did you go to Lyons?*
Non, je n'y suis pas allé. *No, I didn't go.*
N'y pensez pas! *Don't think of it!*
Etes-vous à Paris? *Are you in Paris?*
Non, je n'y suis pas. *No, I'm not.*
Votre maison donne sur la rue? *Does your house face the street?*
Oui, elle y donne. *Yes, it does.* §§ 144, 145

25 The Subjunctive after Expressions of Emotion.

The subjunctive is used after expressions of emotion. After verbs of fearing, when no negation is present, and after the conjunctions **de crainte que** and **de peur que,** a redundant **ne** generally precedes the subjunctive. § 147

C'est dommage qu'il pleuve. *It's too bad it's raining.*
Je regrette qu'il ne puisse pas y aller. *I am sorry that he can't go.*
Je suis content qu'il vous l'ait dit. *I am glad that he told you.*
J'ai peur qu'il ne vienne. *I'm afraid he is coming.*
Avez-vous peur qu'il ne vienne? *Are you afraid that he will come?*
Il est parti précipitamment de peur que le patron ne le voie. *He left in a hurry for fear that the boss would see him.*
Il n'a pas voulu me le dire, de peur que son père ne le punisse. *He wouldn't tell me for fear that his father would punish him.*
But:
Je n'ai pas peur qu'il vienne. *I am not afraid that he will come.*
N'avez-vous pas peur qu'il vienne? *Aren't you afraid that he will come?*
J'ai peur qu'il ne vienne pas. *I'm afraid that he will not come.*

EXERCISES

I. VERBS TO REVIEW:

envoyer, croire, s'asseoir, s'en aller

II. IDIOMATIC EXPRESSIONS:

tenir à quelqu'un, *to esteem, value someone*
tenir à, *plus infinitive, to be anxious to*
faire attention, *to pay attention*
Il y va de sa vie. *His life is at stake.*
Je n'y vois pas. *I can't see (there).*
Vous n'y êtes pas. *You don't understand.*
Vous n'y pensez pas! *You don't mean it! The very idea!*
Y pensez-vous! *Not at all! By no means.*
en vouloir à quelqu'un, *to be annoyed with someone, to have a grudge against*
en être pour sa peine, *to have one's trouble for nothing*
venir à bout de quelqu'un, *to get the best of someone*
venir à bout de quelque chose, *to accomplish something, to carry something out successfully*

III. SENTENCES FOR TRANSLATION:

1. She gave them to me. I sent it to him. Give it back to me. He sent it to us. Don't give it to her. Give him some. Don't give me any. 2. He introduced you to us. Apply to him. Go away (familiar and polite forms). Don't go away (familiar and polite forms). 3. I am thinking of him. Pay attention to her. Don't give it up. I saw only her. Tell me about it. 4. Don't give them to her, give them to him. *They* are sleeping, while (*tandis que*) *I* am working. 5. Don't sit down near her; sit down by me.

6. Who said that? I am the one who said it. Well, you and I are going to come to blows. 7. Introduce us to him. Don't pay attention to her! She is more intelligent than he. 8. He talked about it for an hour. I have never thought about it. 9. Where do you want to go? To the movies. It's too bad that you insist on (*pour*) going there. 10. I am afraid that he is anxious to leave at once.

11. He, too, is afraid that you will not pass your examinations. 12. Aren't you afraid that he will say that? No, I'm afraid that

he won't say it. 13. I am going to wait for him here for fear that he will go out without seeing me. 14. Pay attention to what he says. Your life is at stake. 15. Did he work hard? Yes, but I am afraid he has had his trouble for nothing.

16. He's a man that it's easy to get the best of. 17. I am annoyed with him for (de) not paying any attention to me. 18. Can you see? No, it's too dark. Turn on the light, then (donc, immediately after the verb). 19. But you don't understand! He says that he saw you and her this morning. 20. Well, you can tell him that I don't care to (tenir à) see him.

21. We play bridge twice a week. 22. I prefer to have a holiday in winter because I don't like the heat of summer (les grandes chaleurs). 23. Today's the day that (C'est aujourd'hui que) they are going to give a dinner in honor of the dean. 24. How long does it take to learn to speak a foreign language? 25. Although the weather is bad, most of the guests insist (plural verb) on going out.

IV. DRILL: Translate and insert in the proper position the words in parentheses: Do not have 1-12

1. Envoyez (it to us). N'envoyez pas (it to them). Il a donné (it to you). Nous avons donné (them to him). J'ai donné (him some). 2. Je me suis adressé (to her). Je ne pense pas (of him). Que pensez-vous (of them)? Qui a présenté (you to us)? J'ai présenté (her to him). 3. (He and I) nous nous sommes mis à table (opposite them). 4. (I) travaille tout le temps; (he) ne fait jamais rien. 5. (He's the one), je crois, qui (has a grudge against you). 6. Elle va (to introduce herself to him). se présenter à lui J'espère qu'elle (doesn't ask him) ne lui posera pas trop de questions. 7. Bien qu'elle (is) moins intelligente (than he), elle a (better grades). 8. (You and she) vous cotez trop dur. Personne ne (passes your examinations). 9. Taisez-vous et (pay attention to me). 10. Les avez-vous vus tous les deux? Non, je (saw only her). des timbres en a beaucoup 11. Avez-vous (any stamps)? Oui, je (have a lot of them). 12. (He invited you and me) à dîner. Eh bien, moi (I'm not going). 13. Si vous (don't pay attention to) ce qu'elle dit, elle va (have a grudge against you). 14. (The very idea!) Vous savez bien que (his life is not at stake). 15. De peur qu'il (will have his trouble for nothing),

45

(he is anxious to) renoncer à ce projet.   16. C'est là une entreprise *(which he will never be able to carry out successfully)*.

V. VERB EXERCISE:

A. Translate the English verbs and conjugate them in the tense and mode given:

1. C'est dommage que *I am going away.*   2. Il regrette que *I believe that.*   3. Elle est contente que *I have sent it* (f.) *to you.*   4. Quand *shall I send it to her?*   5. Ils ont peur que *I shall sit down.*

B. Give the imperative of **envoyer,** and the affirmative and negative imperative of **s'asseoir.**

C. Give the present and past participles of **envoyer** and **croire.**

D. Identify the following forms:

1. Nous nous assîmes.   2. Tu croyais.   3. Ils croiraient.   4. Elle s'assiéra.   5. Vous en allez-vous?   6. Je l'ai cru.   7. Allez-vous-en!   8. Nous enverrions.   9. Il s'assit.   10. Elle s'est assise.

VII.
SIMPLE & COMPOUND PAST TENSES

Indirect discourse after a past tense; subjunctive and infinitive after verbs of volition; agreement of verb and subject

---

26 The Imperfect Tense (l'imparfait).

A. The imperfect tense, as its name implies, expresses action or state which *at a certain point* in past time had not come to an end; one of its principal functions, therefore, is to describe the mental or physical *setting* of a past action. In this fundamental use of the imperfect is included the imperfect with **depuis, il y avait . . . que,** where English uses the pluperfect.

> Quand je suis entré, il chantait à tue-tête. *When I entered, he was singing at the top of his voice.*
> Pendant qu'elle lisait, lui écrivait. *While* she *was reading*, he *was writing.*

Quand je l'ai connue, elle était très jeune. *When I met her, she was very young.*

Deux minutes plus tard il frappait à la porte. *Two minutes later he was knocking at the door.*

J'avais peur de lui dire la vérité. *I was afraid to tell him* (or *her*) *the truth.*

Il était à Paris depuis quinze jours, *or* Il y avait quinze jours qu'il était à Paris, quand nous y sommes arrivés. *He had been in Paris for two weeks when we arrived there.* §§ 148, 149

Le ciel était bleu, il faisait du soleil, il n'y avait pas un nuage au ciel. *The sky was blue, the sun was shining, there wasn't a cloud in the sky.*

B. By an extension of this rule the imperfect is used to denote a past habitual [1] or repeated action or state.

Quand il était à Paris, il allait au cinéma tous les jours. *When he was in Paris, he went to the movies every day.*

J'étudiais beaucoup l'année dernière. *I used to study a lot last year.*

Il s'asseyait, se levait, marchait. *He kept sitting down, getting up, walking about.*

Cette femme-là était toujours en colère. *That woman was always angry.*

C. In conditional sentences, the imperfect is used in the " *if* "-clause when the conditional is used in the result clause. If the tenses are compound, this rule applies to the auxiliaries.

Si elle venait demain, je ne la verrais pas.

$$\left. \begin{array}{l} \textit{If she} \left\{ \begin{array}{l} \textit{came} \\ \textit{were to come} \\ \textit{did come} \\ \textit{should come} \end{array} \right\} \\ \textit{Were she to come} \end{array} \right\} \textit{tomorrow, I would not see her.}$$

Si elle était venue la semaine dernière, je ne l'aurais pas vue. *If she had come last week, I would not have seen her.*

---

[1] In English, past habitual action is often expressed by *would*.
She would often go to sleep in my class. Elle s'endormait souvent dans ma classe.

48

27 The Past Indefinite (le passé indéfini or le passé composé).

A. The past indefinite is used to narrate a single action which was completed in past time.

Il était malade, quand je l'ai vu. *He was ill when I saw him.*

Il est arrivé à midi. *He arrived at noon.*

§ 150

1. Passing from one state to another is considered a single act and is therefore expressed by the past indefinite.

L'obus a éclaté si près de l'enfant, qu'il a eu peur. *The shell burst so near to the child, that he was (i.e., became) frightened.*
J'ai été content de recevoir votre lettre. *I was glad to get your letter.*
Quand j'ai reçu cette nouvelle, j'ai cru que j'allais m'évanouir. *When I received that news, I thought I was going to faint.*

Compare the use of the imperfect in the following sentences in which the state which *already* existed continued to exist:

Quand je l'ai vu, il avait (déjà) peur. *When I saw him, he was (already) afraid.*
J'étais (déjà) malade quand j'ai reçu votre lettre. *I was (already) ill when I received your letter.*
Quand vous m'avez demandé où elle était, je croyais qu'elle était partie. *When you asked me where she was I thought that she had gone.*

B. The past indefinite is also used to narrate repeated or habitual action, provided that some expression, such as **plusieurs fois,**[1] **très souvent, tous les jours,** etc., makes this repetition or habit clear.

---

[1] As the imperfect tense expresses primarily action pictured as unfinished, or habitual, at a certain time in the past, it cannot be used to express repeated action when the total number of repetitions is given. Compare the following examples:

Quand j'étais à Paris, je suis allé plusieurs fois (dix fois, cent fois, etc.) au théâtre. *When I was in Paris, I went to the theater several times (ten times, a hundred times, etc.).*
Quand j'étais à Paris, j'allais au théâtre plusieurs fois par semaine. *When I was in Paris, I went (used to go) to the theater several times a week.*

Quand j'étais à Paris, je suis allé plusieurs fois voir la tour Eiffel. *When I was in Paris, I went to see the Eiffel tower several times.*
Quand j'étais à la campagne, je me suis levé tous les jours à six heures. *When I was in the country, I got up at six o'clock every day.*

C. If the duration of a completed action is given, the verb must be in the past indefinite (in literary style, the past definite).

Il a été ici pendant quelque temps. *He was here for some time.*
Pendant trois ans, il a écrit (il écrivit) deux articles par semaine. *For three years he wrote two articles a week.*

28 The Pluperfect *(le plus-que-parfait)* and the Past Anterior *(le passé antérieur).*

A. The pluperfect, which is formed by adding the imperfect of the auxiliary to the past participle, is used very much as in English.

Quand nous sommes arrivés, ils n'avaient pas fini de déjeuner. *When we arrived, they hadn't finished lunch.*
Il m'avait déjà mis au courant de ce qui s'était passé. *He had already informed me about what had happened.*

B. The past anterior, which is formed by adding the preterit of the auxiliary to the past participle, is now essentially a literary tense. Its use is largely confined to clauses introduced by conjunctions of time which do not require the subjunctive (**quand, lorsque, aussitôt que, après que,** etc.). The action of the subordinate clause generally precedes immediately that of the main clause, the verb of which is in the preterit.

Quand elle eut raconté son histoire, elle éclata en sanglots. *When she had told her story, she burst into sobs.* § 151

29 The Conditional *(le conditionnel)* and the Past Conditional *(le conditionnel passé).*

A. The conditional and the past conditional (conditional of the auxiliary plus the past participle) are used in general as in English.

> Si j'étais à votre place, je n'irais pas en ville aujourd'hui. *If I were you* (lit., *in your place*), *I wouldn't go to town today.*
> Si j'avais été à votre place, je ne serais pas allé en ville. *If I had been in your place, I wouldn't have gone to town.*
>
> §§ 152, 153

B. The conditional is used to express doubt or hearsay information about the present.

> Serait-il à Paris? *Could he be in Paris?*
> D'après les journaux le roi d'Italie serait malade. *According to the papers the king of Italy is (said to be) (supposed to be) ill.*

C. The past conditional is used to express doubt and hearsay information about the past.

> Se serait-elle prêtée à cette comédie? *Could she have lent herself to that farce?*
> Le roi d'Italie aurait été malade. *The king of Italy is (or was) said to have been ill.*
> Il s'agit d'un roman qu'il aurait écrit. *It's a question of a novel which he is (or was) supposed to have written.*

30 Indirect Discourse after a Past Tense.

Regularly in indirect discourse, after a past tense, the imperfect, the conditional, and the pluperfect respectively replace the present, the future, and the past indefinite of direct discourse.

> Il a dit: « Je n'aime pas cela. » *He said, "I don't like that."*
> Il a dit qu'il n'aimait pas cela. *He said that he didn't like that.*
> Il a dit: « Je vous reverrai demain. » *He said, "I shall see you again tomorrow."*

Il a dit qu'il me reverrait demain. *He said that he would see me again tomorrow.*

Il a dit: « Je n'ai pas eu le temps de finir mon devoir. » *He said, "I didn't have time to finish my exercise."*

Il a dit qu'il n'avait pas eu le temps de finir son devoir. *He said that he hadn't had (didn't have) time to finish his exercise.*

31 Subjunctive and Infinitive after Verbs of Volition.

Verbs of *wishing*,[1] *willing*, and *preferring* require the infinitive if there is no change of subject. If there is a change of subject, they *must* be followed by a clause with the subjunctive.

Que voulez-vous faire? *What do you want to do?*

Il ne veut pas aller au cinéma. *He doesn't want to go to the movies.*

Que voulez-vous que je fasse? *What do you want me to do?*

J'aimerais mieux ne pas y aller. *I'd rather not go.*

Il ne veut pas que nous allions au cinéma. *He doesn't want us to go to the movies.*

J'aimerais mieux que vous partiez tout de suite. *I'd rather have you leave at once.*

32 Agreement of Verb and Subject.

A. When the subject is a collective noun, followed by a plural complement, a plural verb is regularly used.

Une foule d'étudiants sont entrés dans la salle. *A crowd of students came into the hall.*

1. If the emphasis is on the collective noun rather than on its complement, a singular verb is used.

La foule de spectateurs était si épaisse que nous n'avons pas pu voir le défilé. *The crowd of spectators was so dense that we were not able to see the parade.*

---

[1] The milder conditional of **vouloir** frequently replaces the more emphatic present, especially in the first person. **Je veux que tu fasses cela** may be practically equivalent to a command; whereas, **Je voudrais (bien) que vous fassiez cela** means simply, *I'd like to have you do that.*

2. When the subject is a collective of number followed by a plural complement, expressed or implied, a plural verb is almost always used.

> Un grand nombre (de voyageurs) sont arrivés. *A great number (of travelers) have come.* § 154

B. When the subject is a so-called adverb [1] of quantity, followed by a plural complement, expressed or implied, a plural verb is used. If the complement is singular, a singular verb is used.

> La plupart (des soldats) sont partis. *Most (of the soldiers) have left.* § 155
>
> Peu de monde y restait.
> *Better:* Il y restait peu de monde. *Few people were left.* § 156

C. With compound subjects used with **ni . . . ni,** connected by **et,** or used without a conjunction, the verb is regularly in the plural. § 154

> Ni Jean ni son père ne sont arrivés. *Neither John nor his father has arrived.*
>
> Jean et son père sont arrivés hier. *John and his father arrived yesterday.*
>
> L'eau, le vin, le lait sont des boissons très utiles. *Water, wine, and milk are very useful drinks.*

EXERCISES

I. VERBS TO REVIEW:

craindre, lire, vouloir

II. IDIOMATIC EXPRESSIONS:

> à tue-tête, *at the top of one's voice*
> à côté de, *beside*
> à haute voix, *aloud*
> avoir peur, *to be afraid*
> faire chaud, *to be warm (of weather)*

---

[1] The "adverbs" of quantity frequently play, as here, the rôle of nouns.

53

faire froid, *to be cold, to get cold* (*of weather*)
faire du soleil, *to be sunny*
être en colère, *to be angry*
près de, *near*
tous les jours, *every day*

Do not have 1-13

III. SENTENCES FOR TRANSLATION:

1. When the child saw the doctor, she was afraid (i.e., she became frightened). Were you told that? Yes. Well, it isn't true. 2. If he should be angry, he would yell at the top of his voice. 3. They want to leave tomorrow, and they want you to go with them. 4. The children had been needing shoes for a long time. I know it. But one can't always give one's children everything they need (*tout ce qu'il leur faut*). 5. If you are not afraid of me, I shall sit down beside you.

6. She used to write a letter to her mother every day. 7. The doctor said that he would come back to see us tomorrow. 8. When we went to town, the sun was shining; when we came back home, it was cold and cloudy. 9. If the child had not been afraid of the doctor, she would have sat down near him. 10. The student said that the professor and his wife were getting angry.

11. The professor read aloud for two hours. Many parents read to (*faire la lecture à*) their children every evening. 12. She was reading when I came into the living room. 13. I saw him several times when I was in Paris. 14. For two years he came to see me twice a week. 15. According to the captain the general is supposed to be angry.

16. He wants me to write two letters this evening. 17. When we were in Rome, it was very warm. 18. She would often read two or three books a week. 19. She said that he would get angry if you were afraid. 20. If he had written me a letter, I would have read it.

21. You wouldn't be jealous, by any chance? 22. Don't get angry, doctor; we shall need you later. 23. If you came at noon, I would go to meet you (*aller chercher*). 24. She will stay in the United States until her parents come back (present) from France. 25. If he needed any books, I would lend him some. Most of my books, however, are in very bad condition.

IV. Drill: Translate the words in parentheses:

1. Elle (*had been writing*) depuis une demi-heure quand (*I came in*).
2. Elle a dit qu'elle (*would like*) aller en ville avec moi. 3. Quand elle (*was*) petite, elle (*was afraid*) de tout. 4. Pendant deux ans il (*read*) un livre tous les quinze jours. 5. Si (*I wrote*) la lettre ce soir, (*would you read it*)?

6. (*Would you like me to read it?*) 7. Il a dit qu'il (*didn't want to read*) ce que (*I had written*). 8. Comme (*it was sunny*), (*I didn't need*) mon imperméable. 9. Il y avait trois semaines qu'il (*had been*) ici, quand son père (*died*). 10. Nous (*are reading*) maintenant les lettres que vous nous (*wrote*).

11. Bien que (*Lt. Ledoux wishes*) partir tout de suite, ce n'est pas possible. La plupart des officiers (*want him to stay here*). 12. Il n'a pas (*any information*) à ce sujet; donnez (*him some*). 13. (*Do they want*) aller au cinéma? 14. Nous (*want*) faire un pique-nique avant qu'il (*gets cold*). 15. Je regrette qu'il (*gets angry*) si souvent. Oui, (*one doesn't like*) les gens qui (*scold one*) tout le temps.

V. Verb Exercise:

A. Give the plural of the verbs in the following sentences:

1. Il craint la nuit. 2. Elle lit le journal. 3. Je veux partir.
4. Tu lisais un livre. 5. Elle voudra s'en aller. 6. Il lut la lettre.
7. Lis cette phrase. 8. Il est content que je veuille le faire.
9. Lirais-tu? 10. Ne l'a-t-il pas craint?

B. Give the singular of the plural verbs in the following sentences:

1. Elles voulaient partir. 2. Nous craignîmes les avocats.
3. Nous lirions toute la page, si vous vouliez bien nous donner dix francs. 4. Ils m'en veulent. 5. Nous voulons qu'ils lisent la nouvelle. 6. Voudriez-vous me le donner? 7. Ne craignez rien! 8. Elles auraient voulu y aller. 9. S'il ne pleuvait pas, nous ne craindrions rien. 10. Que voulez-vous que nous lisions?

VIII.

FALLOIR
DEVOIR

The subjunctive of necessity, advisability, possibility; the indefinite *tout*

33 Distinctive Uses of *falloir* and *devoir*.

As may be seen from the following examples, there are certain cases in which these verbs are used with entirely different meanings.

falloir

Qu'est-ce qu'il vous faut? *What do you need?*
Combien de temps (vous) faut-il pour aller à l'école à pied? *How long does it take (you) to walk to school?*
Combien d'argent faut-il? *How much money does it take?*

devoir

Je lui dois cinquante francs. *I owe him fifty francs.*
Je lui dois d'être toujours en vie. *I owe it to him that I am still*

alive. (Note that **devoir** meaning *to owe* requires **de** before the dependent infinitive.)

Il doit chanter ce soir. *He is to sing tonight.*   § 157

Il devait chanter hier soir. *He was to sing last night.* (Note that the English *to be to* plus the infinitive *must* be translated by **devoir** and not by **être**.)

C'est à lui que je dois d'être toujours en vie.

34 Synonymous Uses of *falloir* and *devoir*.

In theory, **falloir** expresses necessity or obligation from without, **devoir,** necessity or obligation from within. In practice, however, the two verbs are in large measure used interchangeably to express not only these ideas but also the idea of probability.[1]

A. Moral obligation (equivalent to the English *ought* or *should*).

> Vous devriez étudier davantage. *You should study more.*
> Si vous aimiez tant votre femme, vous n'auriez pas dû la quitter. (Although the idea of moral obligation exists to a certain extent throughout the whole verb **devoir,** it is especially strong in the conditional and past conditional tenses.) *If you loved your wife so much, you ought not to have left her.*   §§ 159, 160, 161, 162

Note: English *should* is not always equivalent to *ought*.

> *How should I read this verse?* Comment faut-il lire ce vers?

B. Necessity. While **falloir** and **devoir** are both used to express necessity, the former verb is the more frequent in conversational French. Note that the future and past tenses of **devoir** and **falloir** to be used in each case are the same as those used in the corresponding simple statements.   § 163

---

[1] Since **falloir** is less frequently used than **devoir** to express moral obligation and probability, examples of these uses have been placed in the Supplementary Grammatical Notes.   § 158

Il faut que j'aille chez le dentiste.
Rather than: Il me faut aller . . .[1] ⎫ *I must go to the dentist's.*
Je dois aller chez le dentiste. ⎭

Il ne faut pas [2] qu'il sorte. ⎫ *He must not go out.*
Il ne doit pas sortir. ⎭

Il fera deux discours par mois. *He will make two speeches a month.*

Il devra faire deux discours par mois. ⎫ *He will have to make*
Il faudra qu'il fasse deux discours par ⎬ *two speeches a*
mois. ⎭ *month.*

Il a passé un examen. *He took an examination.*

Il a dû passer un examen. ⎫ *He had to take an examination.*
Il a fallu qu'il passe un examen. ⎭

Quand je voulais le trouver, je montais toujours chez sa sœur. *When I wanted to find him, I always went up to his sister's.*

Quand je voulais le trouver, je devais ⎫
toujours monter chez sa sœur. ⎪ *When I wanted to find*
Quand je voulais le trouver, il ⎬ *him, I always had to*
fallait toujours que je monte ⎪ *go up to his sister's.*
chez sa sœur. ⎭

---

[1] The obsolescent construction with the indirect pronoun object and the infinitive is now generally replaced by a clause with the subjunctive or, if it is perfectly clear to whom the necessity applies, by the infinitive without a preceding pronoun.

> Nous sommes déjà en retard; il faut partir tout de suite. *We are already late; we must leave at once.*

The infinitive construction should be used instead of a clause with *on* (everybody) as subject.

> Il faut manger. (*Not:* Il faut qu'on mange.) *One must eat.*
> Il ne faut pas perdre son temps. (*Not:* Il ne faut pas qu'on perde son. temps.) *One must not waste one's time.* §§ 164, 165

[2] The position of the negative in both of these examples should be noted. **Il ne faut pas** and **il ne doit pas** regularly indicate a prohibition and are not equivalent to *it is not necessary.* The negative of *to be necessary* may be expressed in various ways.

> Il n'est pas nécessaire qu'il sorte. ⎫ *It isn't necessary for him to go out.*
> Il n'est pas obligé (*or* forcé) de sortir. ⎭

Il ne faut pas is, however, occasionally used with the meaning *it is not necessary.* § 158

C. Probability. **Devoir** is used to express both present and past probability.[1] The tense of **devoir** to be used in each case is the same as that used in the simple statement.

Il est au salon. *He is in the parlor.*
Il doit être au salon. *He must be in the parlor.*
Il avait l'air idiot; tout le monde a éclaté de rire. *He looked very foolish; everyone burst out laughing.*
Il devait avoir l'air idiot, car tout le monde a éclaté de rire. *He must have looked very foolish, for everyone burst out laughing.*
Il était deux heures quand elle est rentrée. *It was two o'clock when she came home.*
Il devait être deux heures quand elle est rentrée. *It must have been two o'clock when she came home.*
Il avait soixante-cinq ans quand il est mort. *He was sixty-five years old when he died.*
Il devait avoir soixante-cinq ans quand il est mort. *He must have been sixty-five years old when he died.*
Il croyait qu'elle avait rencontré un jeune homme. *He thought she had met a young man.*
Il croyait qu'elle avait dû rencontrer un jeune homme. *He thought that she must have met a young man.*

35 The Subjunctive of Necessity, Advisability, Possibility.

Clauses depending upon expressions of necessity, advisability, possibility, must have their verbs in the subjunctive.

Il faut que nous partions de bonne heure. *We must leave early.*
Il n'est pas nécessaire que vous veniez ce soir. *It is not necessary for you to come this evening.*
Il est important qu'elle apprenne cela. *It is important for her to learn that.*
Il convient que vous alliez le voir dès demain. *It is advisable for you to go to see him tomorrow.*

---

[1] Future probability is expressed in other ways.

Il sera ici demain probablement. ⎱
Il est probable qu'il sera ici demain. ⎰ *He will probably be here tomorrow.*

Il se peut que la bonne soit en retard. *It may be that the maid is late, the maid may be late.*

Il est possible que j'aie abusé de votre bonté. *It is possible that I have taken advantage of your kindness.*

36 The Indefinite *tout*.

tout = "all," "every," "any," "each"

A. The adjective **tout** may be used to translate *all, any, every,* or *each.* Note that it is regularly not followed by the preposition **de**. **Tout** is regularly repeated before each noun it modifies.　　　　　　　　　　　　　　　　　§ 166

> tous les hommes, *all men*
> toutes les femmes, *all women*
> toutes les femmes et tous les hommes, *all women and men*
> tout le monde, *everybody* (cf. le monde entier, *the whole world*)
> Toute peine mérite salaire. *Every trouble deserves a recompense (The laborer is worthy of his hire).*
> Toute femme qui s'est mariée jeune comprendra. *Every (Any) woman who married young will understand.*
> J'ai dormi toute la nuit. *I slept all night.*
> Il a joué toute la journée. *He played all day long.*

tout = "quite," "all," "very"

B. Tout when it translates the adverbs *quite, all, very,* is invariable, unless it modifies a feminine adjective beginning with a consonant or an aspirate *h.*

> Elle en était tout émue. *She was quite affected (moved) by it.*
> Elle était toute seule. *She was all alone.*
> Elle était toute honteuse de lui parler. *She was quite bashful about talking to him.*
> Ils étaient tout petits. *They were very little.*　　　　　　§ 167

tout = "anything," "everything"

C. Tout is used as an indefinite pronoun or noun in the sense of *anything, everything,* or *the whole.*

> Il est capable de tout. *He is capable of anything.*
> Tout est beau. *Everything is beautiful.*

Il a renoncé à tout. *He gave up everything.*

Je vous donne le tout pour six francs. *I give you the whole lot for six francs.*

Elle a tout préparé. *She prepared everything.*

Je vais tout vous dire. *I am going to tell you everything.*

Tout ce qu'il a dit est vrai. *Everything he said is true.*

Tout ce qui reluit (*or* brille) n'est pas or. *All that glitters is not gold.*

tous, toutes

D. The pronouns **tous** and **toutes** may be used as subject, indirect object, or in apposition with subject, indirect object, direct object. When used as subject, they precede the verb. More often they are used in apposition with the subject and are placed after the verb. This position is especially necessary in the case of a negative sentence.

Tous sont venus. ⎫
Ils sont tous venus. ⎬ *They all came.*

Toutes ont répondu. ⎫
Elles ont toutes répondu. ⎬ *They all answered.*

Elles n'ont pas toutes accepté. *They didn't all accept.*

Nous leur avons répondu à toutes (*preferred to:* Nous avons répondu à toutes.) *We answered them all (We answered all of them).*

Il nous parlait à tous. *He was speaking to all of us.*

Je le (leur) ai dit à tous. *I said it to them all.*

Il s'est présenté à tous. *He introduced himself to all.*

Nous les voyons tous. (*Not:* Nous voyons tous.) *We see them all.*

E. **Tous** and **toutes** are also used as the objects of prepositions other than **à,** and in apposition with such objects.

envers et contre tous, *against everybody, against all opposition,* etc.

Il travaille pour nous tous. *He works for us all.*

Elle s'est brouillée avec vous tous. *She has quarreled with all of you.*

Il a besoin de nous tous. *He needs us all.*

Il s'est fâché contre vous tous. *He became angry with all of you.*

EXERCISES

I. VERBS TO REVIEW:

falloir, devoir

II. IDIOMATIC EXPRESSIONS:

être tard, *to be late* (an impersonal expression)
tout de suite, *immediately*
avoir l'air, *to appear, to look*
de bonne heure, *early*
venir (aller) à pied (à bicyclette), *to walk (to ride a bicycle)*
venir (aller) en auto (en avion), *to come (go) in a car (in an airplane)*
à l'école, *to school, at school*
passer un examen, *to take an examination*
réussir (échouer) à un examen, *to pass (fail) an examination*
chez Marie, *at Mary's, to Mary's house*
faire un discours, *to make a speech*
éclater de rire, *to burst out laughing*
avoir soixante-cinq ans, *to be sixty-five years old*
n'avoir qu'à, *plus infinitive, to have only to . . .*

III. SENTENCES FOR TRANSLATION:

1. We must all leave at once, since it will take us at least two hours to go there (*y aller*). 2. If she wanted all that information, she ought to have asked for it. 3. It is possible that she will look ridiculous in (*avec*) that hat. 4. How much money do they owe the grocer? Four hundred francs. Is that (*C'est*) all they owe him? Yes, that's all. 5. One must not cross the street without looking to the left and the right.

6. His book is to appear next month. That is why (*C'est pourquoi*) he is so excited. 7. You will have to get up early if you wish to arrive at the station before the train leaves. 8. He needs ten dollars to go to New York. 9. It isn't necessary to read the newspapers to know what (*ce qui*) is going on; one has only to listen to the radio. 10. The maid must be late; it is very late and she still (*encore*) has not arrived.

11. If she wishes to take the examination, she will have to work hard. 12. You must have read that book very recently in order

to recall so many details. 13. They were to leave at two o'clock; it's four o'clock, and they are still here. 14. It may be that this remedy will cure him. 15. Do you walk to school? No, I ride (I go there in a car).

16. He will probably fail his French examination. 17. While he was making a speech, she burst out laughing. 18. He had to take two examinations yesterday. He worked the whole day. 19. It is absolutely necessary that I pass the examination. 20. Although he is sixty-five years old, he still rides to Mary's house on a bicycle.

21. We were to go to France last summer, but we postponed our trip on account of the war. 22. If he had given them to you, he would not have lost them. 23. Why do you have to go to the dentist's today? 24. You should have told me why you needed so much money. 25. It's too bad that you must leave so early.

IV. DRILL: Translate the words in parentheses:

1. (*It was not necessary*) de me dire cela. (*We all*) le savons.
2. (*They had to*) aller à l'école hier. 3. Comme (*it was very hot*), (*I had to*) rester chez moi. 4. Si vous étiez en retard, (*would you make*) un discours? 5. (*He must do*) son travail, s'il veut (*pass the examination*).

6. Combien d'argent (*would I need*) pour aller (*to*) New York? 7. Il est possible que (*you will need*) cent dollars. 8. Où (*must I put*) cela? Mettez (*everything*) dans la salle à manger. 9. (*It must have been*) deux heures, quand elle (*left*). 10. (*Weren't you to*) faire un discours hier soir?

11. Si je fais cela, mademoiselle, vous (*will owe me*) dix dollars. Oui, je le sais. J'en suis (*quite ashamed*). 12. Elle (*ought to*) faire de son mieux pour ne pas (*fail the examination*). 13. (*It is necessary that*) tout le monde (*do his duty*). (*That is all that*) je sais vous dire. 14. Quand (*you finish*) vos devoirs, (*you will have to go out*) un peu. Vous ne devez pas travailler (*the whole night*). 15. Si la guerre éclate, (*we shall have to*) rester (*in the United States*).

V. VERB EXERCISE:

A. Translate:

1. Je dois aller lundi à New-York. 2. Il faut qu'elle s'en aille. 3. Il a dû y aller. 4. Il faudra qu'il lise deux pages. 5. Devrait-il

y aller? 6. Je devais écrire cela hier soir. 7. Il ne faut pas donner son argent aux enfants. 8. Combien vous faut-il d'argent? 9. Elle aurait dû y aller. 10. Nous lui devons cinq francs.

B. Give the third person singular, and the first person plural, of the verb **devoir,** in all the simple tenses.

IX. ADJECTIVES: POSITION & AGREEMENT

The subjunctive after *sans que* and *à moins que;*
the indefinites *chaque* and *chacun*

37 Position of Adjectives.[1]

A. In modern French, the normal position of adjectives is
after the noun. Except in the case of poetic or figurative
language, the student may consider this rule particularly
binding for adjectives of color, nationality, shape, and those
formed from past participles.

> un manteau gris, *a gray coat*
> l'armée française, *the French army*
> une balle ronde, *a round ball*
> une femme aimée, *a beloved woman*

A certain number of very common adjectives are still generally placed before the noun, as in old French. These ad-

---

[1] Cf. § 239 for list of irregular adjectives.

jectives regularly express an inherent rather than an accidental quality.

bon	mauvais
gros, grand	petit
beau, joli	vilain
jeune	vieux
long	court
gentil	vilain, méchant

In the same way, many adjectives which ordinarily follow the noun retain the older position when they express an inherent quality, i.e., one which is regularly possessed by all the nouns of a class. This position before the noun is especially common in poetic and figurative uses.

un chapeau blanc, *a white hat*
les blanches épaules d'une femme, *a woman's white shoulders*
un homme maigre, *a thin man*
un maigre repas, *a meager meal* (cf.: un repas maigre, *a meatless meal*)
un esprit faible, *a weak mind*
un faible enfant, *a helpless child* (who has the weakness inherent to all children)
un homme fort, *a strong man*
une forte colère, *a great wrath*
un chien savant, *a trained dog* (i.e., one good at tricks)
un orateur savant, *a learned orator*
un savant professeur, *a learned professor*

Changed position = changed meaning

B. Certain adjectives change their meaning with the change of position.

une église ancienne, *an old church*
un ancien élève, *a former pupil*
un homme grand, *a tall man*
un grand [1] homme, *a great man*

---

[1] When this adjective is used with the word **femme,** or when there is another adjective expressing a physical characteristic, **grand** means *tall* even when it precedes. **Une grande femme,** *a tall woman.* **Un grand homme maigre,** *a tall, thin man.* For *a great woman,* one would say: **une femme célèbre** or **illustre.**

des gens braves, *brave people*   § 168
de braves gens, *good, kindly people*
un livre cher, *an expensive book*
un cher ami, *a dear friend*
un homme pauvre, *a poor (indigent) man*
un pauvre homme, *a poor (pitiable) man*
la semaine dernière, *last week (the week just past)*
la dernière semaine du mois, *the last week of the month*
la semaine prochaine, *next week (the week after this:* a definite
    time)
la prochaine fois que vous le verrez ... *(the) next time you
    see him ...*
des solutions différentes, *different solutions*
les différents pays (les divers pays) de l'Europe, *the various
    countries of Europe*
des opinions diverses, *different opinions*
un fait certain, *a certain (sure) fact*
un certain individu, *a certain individual*
une robe nouvelle, *a new dress* (of a new style or model)
une nouvelle [1] robe, *a new dress* (not necessarily a new style)
un roman nouveau, *a recently published novel*   § 169
un nouveau roman, *another novel*

plural modifiers

C. When a noun is modified by several adjectives which
regularly precede, they may all be placed before the noun,
provided one of them forms a unit with the noun.

    un gentil petit jeune homme, *a nice little young chap*

If two adjectives which ordinarily precede the noun do *not*
form a unit with the noun, they may be joined by **et** and
placed before, or after, the noun.

    un grand et beau garçon, ⎫
or: un garçon grand et beau, ⎬ *a tall, handsome boy*

If these adjectives ordinarily follow the noun, they are co-
ordinated and placed after the noun.

    une jeune fille saine et forte, *a strong, healthy girl*

---

[1] In sentences such as: *I'm going to buy a new dress. How do you like my
new dress?* use: *une nouvelle robe* or *ma nouvelle robe.*

67

If a noun is modified by an adjective which may precede and by an adjective which regularly follows, each adjective usually retains its normal position. If the adjectives are of such a nature that they may be co-ordinated, i.e., if they express the same type of characteristic, they may be joined by the conjunction **et** and placed after the noun.

une grande femme maigre,
or: une femme grande et maigre, } *a tall, thin woman*

une petite table blanche,
not: une table petite et blanche, } *a little white table*

une admirable étude scientifique, } *an admirable scientific*
not: une étude admirable et scientifique, } *study*

The conjunction **et** is not used to join two adjectives placed after the noun when one of the adjectives forms a unit with the noun in question.

une erreur judiciaire regrettable, *a regrettable judicial error*
des alliances internationales inconcevables, *inconceivable international alliances*
une étude scientifique admirable, *an admirable scientific study*

38 Agreement of Adjectives.

When a predicate adjective or one which follows its noun modifies two or more nouns of different genders, it is generally placed in the masculine plural. When the adjective is not a predicate adjective it is usually preferable to have a masculine noun precede immediately the masculine plural adjective, as in the second example. § 170

Mon oncle et ma tante sont très intelligents. *My uncle and aunt are very intelligent.*
Il nous faut des revues et des livres nouveaux. *We need new magazines and books.*
Les femmes et les vieillards étaient bien fatigués. *The women and the old men were quite tired.*

If the adjective precedes its noun, it is repeated.

> un petit garçon et une petite fille, *a little boy and girl*
> de bons parents et de bons amis, *good relatives and friends*
>
> §§ 171, 172

When the adjective is used in an adverbial sense, it is invariable.

> des cheveux coupés court, *hair cut short*
> coûter cher, *to be expensive*
> aller tout droit, *to go straight ahead*

39 The Subjunctive after *sans que, à moins que.*

The subjunctive must be used after the conjunctions **sans que** and **à moins que.**
A redundant **ne** is frequently used after **à moins que.**

> Il est parti sans que je l'aie vu. *He left without my seeing him.*
> A moins qu'il (ne) fasse beau, je ne partirai pas. *Unless the weather is fine, I shall not leave.*

40 The Indefinites *chaque, chacun.*

The adjective *each* and the pronoun *each one* are translated by **chaque** and **chacun** respectively.

> A chaque jour suffit sa peine. *Sufficient unto the day is the evil thereof.* (Lit.: *To each day suffices its toil.*)
> Il venait chaque jour (tous les jours) [1] à la même heure. *He came each day at the same time.*
> Il faut que chaque membre paie sa cotisation. *Each member must pay his dues.*
> A chaque instant on entend le signal de l'alerte. *At every moment one hears the alarm signal.*
> Chacun pour soi. *Every fellow for himself.*
> Chacun son goût. *Each one to his own taste.*
> Chacun de nous le chantera. *Each of us will sing it.*

---

[1] **Tous les soirs** and **tous les matins** are more frequent in conversation than **chaque soir** and **chaque matin.** In expressions such as *every other day, every three days, every ten minutes*, etc., *every* should not be translated by **chaque** but by **tout.**

> tous les deux jours, *every two days* (*every other day*)
> tous les trois jours, *every three days*
> toutes les dix minutes, *every ten minutes*

EXERCISES

I. Verbs to Review:

paraître, manger,[1] mener [1]

II. Idiomatic Expressions:

faire la connaissance de, *to meet, to make the acquaintance of*
faire paraître, *to publish, to bring out*
qui vient de paraître, *which has just appeared, been published*
se peigner, *to comb one's hair*
à la mode, *fashionable*
mener à bien, *to carry out successfully*
avoir de belles relations, *to have influential acquaintances*
d'occasion, *secondhand*
faire maigre, *to do without meat, to eat fish and vegetables*
faire gras, *to eat meat*

III. Sentences for Translation:

1. The soldiers of the French army used to wear horizon blue uniforms.[2] 2. Have you met that pretty little girl? She is a former pupil of mine (one of my former pupils). 3. Last week I bought an old square table which I shall put into the kitchen. 4. On Fridays all good Catholics do without meat. On other days of the week, however, they are accustomed to eat meat. 5. When the English troops entered the village, they found there only helpless old men and starving children. All the strong and active people had already left.[3]

6. Have you any secondhand books? No, but you will find many of them on the quay. Here we sell only recently published books. 7. That book which has just come out is the work of a learned professor. 8. I do not like her new dress. It is not becoming to her

---

[1] Cf. § 246 **B** and **D**.

[2] Begin sentence with **autrefois**.

[3] The adjective modifying **gens** is feminine if it immediately precedes and has a special form for the feminine. In other cases it is masculine. When more than one adjective precedes, these adjectives must be of the same gender.

> Tous les gens, tous les braves gens, les petites gens, toutes les vieilles gens, les vieilles gens soupçonneux, les vieilles gens sont querelleurs.
> *All the people, all the good people, humble folk, all (the) old people, suspicious old people, old people are quarrelsome.*

and it is out of style. 9. At the antiquarian's most of the thorough scientific treatises are very expensive books. 10. It will take more than one great man to make plans for the reorganization of the economy of the various countries of Europe at the end of this war.

11. Next month an English publisher will bring out a certain book which will please everyone. 12. Unless each one of us does his best, we shall not carry out this enterprise successfully. 13. My cousin is going to marry a young man who has influential acquaintances. 14. Unless you wash your hands and comb your hair, you must not come into the parlor to greet the guests. 15. This good woman never pays any attention to style; she has never had her hair cut. Her daughter, however, wears her hair cut very short.

16. Did you take the wrong road? Yes, I ought to have gone straight ahead at X. instead of turning to the left. 17. The next time you see that poor woman, be kind to her, for she has lost her whole family. 18. Each student must write a review of a book. 19. Mrs. Brown has two beautiful children, hasn't she? Yes, John is a tall, handsome boy, and Helen a blond, rosy-cheeked girl. 20. He left without my being able (having been able) to talk to him about that matter.

21. My brother and sister were quite moved on learning that their friend had had to undergo an operation. 22. If you knew how to cook, you would not need to eat a meager meal. 23. Before the war comes to an end, it is possible that we shall all be wearing dresses [that are] out of style. 24. Good books and magazines are always expensive. 25. I left without having been able (use infinitive) to see him.

IV. Drill: Translate the words in parentheses:

1. Quand est-ce qu'Hachette (*will publish another novel*) de Julian Green? Je ne sais pas. Le dernier (*has just appeared*), n'est-ce pas? 2. Si vous (*meet* [1]) Mme Brown, je vous prie de (*introduce*

---

[1] *Become acquainted with.* Note that the verb *to meet* may have two other meanings.

Je l'ai rencontré ce matin. *I met him this morning* (by chance).

Nous allons nous retrouver devant le théâtre (by appointment). *We are going to meet* (*again*) *in front of the theater.*

Il va venir me trouver ici. *He's going to meet me here* (by appointment).

me to her). 3. Si l'on faisait (a "meatless" meal), on (would eat) d'ordinaire du poisson. 4. (The last week of May) est le moment où (American students) passent leurs examens. 5. Que pensez-vous de ce roman? (Each one of us) en a (a different opinion).

6. Son mari est (a tall, handsome boy) qui s'habille (fashionably). 7. Il y a (many old churches) dans la petite ville où habitent (these good people). 8. (Most learned men) ne sont pas de (great men). 9. Chez les bouquinistes on trouvait (many secondhand books). 10. Elle portait toujours (a little white dress [that was] out of style).

11. A moins que (you go straight ahead), (you will take the wrong road) et elle ne vous trouvera pas au rendez-vous indiqué. 12. Elle est partie (without my having met her). 13. (A little boy and girl) que je connais viendront me voir (next week). 14. Tous ces problèmes ont (different solutions) qui (will appear) bien étranges à (our dear friends). 15. Dans ce milieu, les dames et les messieurs étaient (charming). En outre, (they all had influential acquaint-ances).

V. VERB EXERCISE:

A. Replace the dashes by the present indicative, the imperfect indicative, and the past definite of the verb which precedes each of the following sentences:

1. (manger)   Ne — —-t-il pas beaucoup?
2. (mener)   Je — — l'enfant à l'église.
3. (manger)   Ils — — les pommes.
4. (paraître) Elle — — souffrante.

B. Translate the English verbs and conjugate them in the tense used in the French sentences:

1. Il se peut que je *shall lead* la danse. 2. Il est important que je *eat* du poisson. 3. Faut-il que je *seem* souffrant?

C. Translate:

1. It seems. 2. They would eat. 3. We ate (past def.). 4. I used to lead. 5. You (Tu) would seem. 6. It has just appeared. 7. Let's eat it. 8. Will she not have taken the child to school? 9. Don't eat it. 10. We were leading. 11. They led (past def.). 12. They were eating. 13. We shall take. 14. Eat them now.

72

X.   COMPARISON: ADJECTIVES & ADVERBS

The position of adverbs; possessive adjectives
and pronouns [1]

41   Comparison of Adjectives.

plus (moins) + adjective

A. In comparisons of inequality, the comparative is formed
by placing **plus** or **moins** before the adjective.   The superlative is obtained by placing the definite article before the
comparative.   The comparative, therefore, when preceded
by the definite article, is identical in form with the superlative.

> Elle est plus (moins) intelligente que sa sœur.   *She is more
> (less) intelligent than her sister.*
> Pourquoi avez-vous choisi la phrase la plus (la moins) difficile

---

[1] Cf. § 240 for lists of possessive adjectives and pronouns.

de toutes? *Why did you choose the most (the least) difficult sentence of all?*

Lequel des deux frères est le plus sympathique? *Which of the two brothers is the more likable?*

Lequel des trois frères est le plus sympathique? *Which of the three brothers is the most likable?*

aussi (si) que

B. In comparisons of equality *as ... as* is translated by **aussi ... que.** After a negative, **aussi** may be replaced by **si.**

> Elle est aussi grande que moi. *She is as tall as I.*
> Elle n'est pas aussi (si) grande que moi. *She is not as tall as I.*
> § 173

In the second member of a comparison of inequality, a redundant **ne** is regularly used before the verb.

> Elle est plus forte en français que vous ne (le) pensez. *She is better in French than you think.* §§ 174, 175

C. In comparisons of inequality, the word which expresses the measure of difference is preceded by **de.**

> La salle à manger est plus large (moins large) que le salon de deux mètres. *The dining room is two meters wider (narrower) than the living room.*
> Elle est plus âgée[1] que son mari de trois ans (*or:* Elle est de trois ans plus âgée que son mari). *She is three years older than her husband.*

D. If the possessive adjective is used with the superlative of an adjective which precedes the noun, the article is omitted.

> mon plus cher ami, *my dearest friend*
> le plus cher ami de mon père, *my father's dearest friend*
> § 176

E. *In* after a superlative is expressed by **de.**

> la plus grande maison de la ville, *the largest house in the town*
> le meilleur élève de la classe, *the best pupil in the class*

---

[1] One may also say: Elle a trois ans de plus que son mari.

F. The following adjectives are compared irregularly:

bon	meilleur	le meilleur
mauvais	{ plus mauvais { pire	le plus mauvais le pire
petit	{ plus petit { moindre, *less(er)*	le plus petit le moindre, *the least*

mauvais

1. When **mauvais** modifies a concrete noun, it is usually compared regularly.

> Ce vin-ci est plus mauvais que celui-là (i.e., d'une qualité inférieure). *This wine is worse than that (i.e., of inferior quality).*
>
> C'est le plus mauvais joueur de l'équipe. *He is the worst player on the team.*

2. When **mauvais** modifies an abstract noun, or when it is used in the sense of *harmful*, it is generally compared irregularly.

> L'avarice est son pire défaut. *Avarice is his worst fault.*
>
> Le cognac est pire (i.e., plus nuisible) que le vin. *Cognac is worse (i.e., more harmful) than wine.*

pire, le pire

3. **Pire** and **le pire** are also used in contrast with **meilleur,** and in comparisons with **mauvais** and **le mal.**[1]

> Elle n'est ni meilleure ni pire que sa sœur. *She is neither better nor worse than her sister.*
>
> Celui-ci est mauvais (le meilleur), mais celui-là est pire (le pire de tous). *This one is bad (the best), but that one is worse (the worst of all).*

While there are many cases in which either **plus mauvais** or **pire** may be used, the former is more frequently used in everyday French and the latter in the literary language.

§ 177

---

[1] **Le pire** is frequently used as a "neuter" noun with the meaning of *the worst, the worst thing to do,* etc.

42 Position of Adverbs.

In general, the adverb follows immediately the verb it modifies. In compound tenses this rule applies to the auxiliary.[1]

> Vous comprenez bien. *You understand well.*
> Il parle mieux le français que l'italien. *He speaks French better than (he does) Italian.*
> Vous allez souvent au théâtre, n'est-ce pas? *You often go to the theater, don't you?*
> Vous avez bien compris. *You understood well.*
> Il était déjà rentré. *He had already come home.*
> Elle m'a souvent parlé de vous. *She has often spoken to me of you.*

A. The adverbs **ici, là, hier, aujourd'hui, demain, tard** and, generally, **tôt,** do not come between the auxiliary and the past participle of a compound tense.

> Il est arrivé hier. *He arrived yesterday.*
> Je l'aurai fini demain. *I'll have finished it tomorrow.*

B. Long adverbs frequently stand at the beginning or at the end of a sentence. Adverbs of time are also often placed at the beginning of a sentence.

> Malheureusement, il a plu aujourd'hui. ⎱ *Unfortunately it*
> *or:* Il a plu aujourd'hui, malheureusement. ⎰ *rained today.*
> Apparemment votre père ne va pas venir.[2] *Apparently your father isn't going to come.*
> Aujourd'hui nous n'avons rien à faire. *Today we have nothing to do.*
> Déjà il commençait à reprendre ses forces. *He was already beginning to recover his strength.*

---

[1] Adverbs are frequently shifted from their normal position when it is desired to render the style more emphatic, more varied, or more pleasing to the ear.

[2] In familiar French, certain adverbs ending in –**ment** may be joined to a following clause by the conjunction **que.**

> Certainement (Apparemment) qu'il ne va pas venir. *Certainly (Apparently) he's not going to come.*
> Heureusement qu'il n'en a rien dit. *Fortunately he said nothing about it.*

C. Y and **en** *must*, except in the imperative affirmative, and **aussi, non plus** *may*, precede the verb. Cf. Chapter VI for examples.

D. Short adverbs modifying an infinitive regularly precede.[1]

Il croyait bien faire. *He thought he was doing right.*
Ce n'est pas trop demander. *That's not asking too much.*
Pour mieux comprendre ce que dirait le conférencier, je m'étais assis au premier rang. *In order better to understand what the lecturer would say, I had taken a seat in the front row.*

43 Comparison of Adverbs.

Adverbs are compared in the same way as adjectives except that the definite article used is always the masculine singular form **le.**

Il parle moins bien que sa sœur. *He doesn't speak as well as his sister.*
Vous conduisez plus vite que moi. *You drive faster than I.*
C'est elle qui a couru le plus vite. *She was the one who ran the fastest.*
Elle ne chante pas aussi (si) bien que vous. *She doesn't sing as well as you.*

bien, mal, beaucoup, peu

The following adverbs are compared irregularly:

bien	mieux	le mieux	
mal	{ plus mal	le plus mal	
	pis	le pis	
beaucoup	plus	le plus	
peu	moins	le moins	§ 179

---

[1] This is also the regular position of the indefinite pronouns **tout** and **rien,** except when the infinitive is compound.   § 178

Je vais tout vous dire. *I'm going to tell you everything.*
Elle est rentrée sans rien dire. *She came in without saying anything.*
Il craint d'avoir tout perdu. *He's afraid that he lost everything.*
Elle partit sans avoir rien vu. *She left without seeing anything.*

44 Possessive Adjectives.[1]

A. The possessive adjective must be repeated before each noun which it modifies, *unless the same person or thing is designated.*

> mon père et ma mère, *my father and mother*   § 180
> son ami et sa sœur, *his friend and his sister*
> sa fidélité et son habileté, *his fidelity and (his) cleverness* (Note that the masculine form is used before a feminine noun beginning with a vowel sound.)
> mon collègue et ami, *my friend and colleague* (Note order.)

B. To emphasize ownership or to avoid ambiguity, the disjunctive pronoun is placed after the noun modified by the possessive.

> mon livre à moi, **my** *book*
> son livre à elle, **her** *book*

C. Before parts of the body the possessive adjective is generally replaced by the definite article.

> Elle a les yeux bleus. *She has blue eyes.*   § 181
> Elle lève la main. *She raises her hand.*
> Nous avons mal à la tête. *We have a headache.*

1. If there is action from the outside on a part of the body, the indirect object pronoun is added.

> Elle se lave les mains. *She washes her hands.*
> Il s'est fait mal aux pieds. *He hurt his feet.*
> Je lui ai fait mal au bras. *I hurt his arm.*

2. If the part of the body is the subject of **être,** the possessive adjective reappears.   § 182

> Ses yeux sont bleus. *Her eyes are blue.*

D. Before articles of clothing the possessive adjective is regularly used.

> Elle a ôté son chapeau. *She took off her hat.*
> Vous avez déchiré votre veston. *You have torn your coat.*
> Il les met dans sa poche. *He puts them in his pocket.*

---

[1] Cf. Appendix for a list of possessive adjectives and pronouns.

E. When clothing and a part of the body are both mentioned:

1. The definite article is regularly used if a typical or usual combination is *described.*

> Il est entré le manteau sur le bras, les gants à la main. *He entered with his coat on his arm, his gloves in his hand* (Cf. l'épée à la main, *sword in hand*).

2. The possessive adjective is regularly used if an *action* is *narrated.*

> Elle a fourré ses mains dans son manchon. *She thrust her hands into her muff.*

F. *To be* plus an English possessive, when equivalent to *to belong to*, is regularly translated by **être à** and the disjunctive pronoun. In other cases, the English possessive is rendered by the corresponding French form.

> A qui est ce stylo? Il est *(colloquially:* C'est) à moi. *(Emphatic:* à moi.) *Whose pen is this? It's mine.* § 183
> A qui sont ces livres? Ils *(not:* Ce) sont à moi. *Whose books are these? They are mine.*
> Je n'ai pas de gants. Voulez-vous que je vous prête les miens? *I haven't any gloves. Do you want me to lend you mine?*
> Ces chaussures-là sont à vous? Non, les miennes sont dans le placard. *Do these shoes belong to you? No, mine are in the closet.*

EXERCISES

I. Verbs to Review:

conduire, courir, ouvrir

II. Idiomatic Expressions:

> avoir mal à la tête, *to have a headache*
> avoir mal à la gorge, *to have a sore throat*
> avoir mal aux dents, *to have a toothache*
> se faire mal, *to hurt one's self*
> faire mal à quelqu'un, *to hurt someone*
> envoyer chercher, ⎫ *to send for*
> faire venir (lit., *to make come*), ⎭
> tant pis, *so much the worse*

tant mieux, *so much the better*

de mal en pis, *from bad to worse*

aller bien, *to be well;* aller mal, *to be ill*

être en bonne santé, *to be in good health*

avoir bonne mine, *to look well;* avoir mauvaise mine, *to look bad, ill*

en avoir plein le dos de quelque chose, de quelqu'un, *to be fed up with something, someone*

III. Sentences for Translation:

1. She is not so intelligent as her sister, but she is cleverer than you think. 2. The youngest pupil in the class is a year older than the teacher. 3. My best friend (*f.*) arrived yesterday from England. 4. Apparently her worst fault is (*c'est*) that she never puts money aside. 5. It is in the country where one likes tea the best that one finds the worst tea in the world.

6. The doctor we sent for prescribed a diet that was worse than the illness. 7. Although she looks well, it seems (*il paraît*) she has a sore throat. 8. Without doing anything extraordinary, my brother and sister succeeded in having a good time. 9. If she has hurt her hand, she cannot put on her gloves. 10. Unless she has blue eyes and black hair, she should never wear that color.

11. I understood very well that his business was going from bad to worse, but I did not realize that he was not in good health. 12. To avoid washing his hands, the child put his hands in his pockets. 13. His tutor and friend is using my book, since he has lost his. 14. Whose gloves are these? They are mine. You cannot wear them. Your hands are too small. 15. He was there, as always, behind the counter with his cap (*bonnet, m.*) over one ear.

16. I could hardly walk yesterday because she had hurt my foot while we were playing hockey. 17. Have you a headache? Yes, and I also have a high fever. I shall have to send for the doctor. 18. If he is right, all the better; but I am convinced that he is wrong. 19. Are you going to the dentist's this afternoon? No, I'm not going. And if you had the toothache? If I had the toothache, I would go. 20. I think that my wife looks very bad this evening. If she is not better tomorrow, I'm going to call in another doctor. 21. If you do that, Dr. Leblanc will get mad. Who cares? I'm fed up with Dr. Leblanc.

IV. DRILL: Translate the words in parentheses:

1. (*I hurt my foot yesterday*) pendant que (*I was playing tennis*).
2. Bonjour, madame, inutile de vous demander (*if you are well*).
Tiens, je ne savais pas que (*I looked so well*). 3. Bien que Marie
(*is two years younger than*) son frère, elle (*drives much better*) que
lui. 4. Vous savez? Je crois que (*I am much better today*). Je
viens de (*run up the stairs*). Vous êtes (*less intelligent than I
thought*). 5. Les femmes (*are neither better nor worse*) que les
hommes. 6. (*My aunt and uncle*) se sont levés de très bonne
heure et sont partis (*without my having seen them*).
7. (*The best tea in the world*) vient de la Chine. 8. (*Run wash
your hands*), mon enfant! Et puis va me chercher un comprimé
d'aspirine. (*Do you have a headache?*) Oui, malheureusement,
(*and my throat is sore, too*). 9. Ne reste pas là (*with your hands in
your pockets*)! Va dire à la bonne (*to call in the doctor*). 10. Qu'est-
ce que tu as à pleurer comme ça? (*Did you hurt yourself?*) Non,
mais (*I tore my trousers*). 11. Tous ceux qui peuvent résoudre ce
problème voudront bien (*raise their hands*). 12. Presque toutes
les héroïnes des romans du moyen âge ont (*blue eyes and blond hair*).

V. VERB EXERCISE:

A. Identify the following forms:

1. Ouvert
2. Conduisant
3. Nous ouvrîmes.
4. Tu courrais.
5. Il a couru.

6. Vous ouvrez.
7. Ils conduisaient.
8. Ouvres-tu?
9. Ne cours pas.
10. Elle courait.

B. Write the following sentences in the conditional, the past
definite, the pluperfect, and the imperfect indicative.

1. Elle court à la porte. 2. J'ouvre la fenêtre. 3. Nous conduisons
l'auto.

XI. NUMERALS: CARDINAL & ORDINAL

Fractions; and expressions of time [1]

45 Cardinals.

cent, mille

A. Contrary to English usage, the adjectives **cent** and **mille** are used <u>without</u> the indefinite article.

> cent hommes, *one hundred men*
> mille hommes, *one thousand men*

quatre-vingts, cent

B. Quatre-vingts and **cent** <u>agree</u> with the nouns they modify, provided that the nouns follow these numerals immediately.

> quatre-vingts hommes, *eighty men*
> deux cents hommes, *two hundred men*

---

[1] Cf. § 241 for list of numerals and pronunciation of numerals.

page deux cent, *page two hundred*
deux cent quatre-vingt-dix-neuf prisonniers, *two hundred
  ninety-nine prisoners*
en dix-neuf cent, *in 1900*

C. Except for **premier,** dates and titles are expressed by
the <u>cardinal</u>.

le premier mai, *May the first*
François premier, *Francis the First*
le douze juin, (*on*) *the twelfth of June*
Charles dix, *Charles* (*the*) *Tenth*
le jeudi vingt-sept octobre, *Thursday, October the twenty-seventh*
or: **on** *Thursday, October the twenty-seventh* (Note the position of
  the article and the fact that, contrary to English usage, no
  preposition is used in French.)   §§ 184, 185

les deux, tous les deux

D. *Both, all three, all four,* etc., when used as subject or
object, are expressed in French by **les deux, les trois, les
quatre,** or **tous les deux, tous les trois, tous les quatre.**
The former expressions are generally used of things, the
latter, of persons. When **tous les deux, tous les trois,**
etc., are used as direct objects, the verb must be preceded
by the pronoun **les.**

Les deux sont possibles. *Both* (*things*) *are possible.*
J'ai reçu les deux. *I received both.*
Tous les deux sont arrivés. ⎫
Better: Ils sont arrivés tous les deux. ⎬ *They both arrived.*
Je les ai invités tous les deux. *I invited them both.*
Je leur ai parlé à tous les deux. *I talked to them both.*   § 186

46 Ordinals.

A. Ordinals regularly precede the nouns they modify.

la première classe, *the first class*
le troisième jour, *the third day*
le troisième acte, *the third act*
la quatrième scène, *the fourth scene*

83

1. The chief exceptions to this rule are titles and headings.

> Acte premier, *Act One*
> Scène première, *Scene One*

second, deuxième

B. Either **second** or **deuxième** may be used, whether the series in question consists of two or more than two. In certain expressions, however, such as **en deuxième,** *in second class*, **au deuxième,** *on the third floor*, the use of **deuxième** without a noun is considered inelegant by some grammarians.

> le second acte, le deuxième acte, *the second act*
> Il voyage toujours en seconde (*or:* en deuxième classe). *He always travels second-class.*
> Il habite au second (étage) (*or:* au deuxième étage). *He lives on the third floor.* §§ 187, 188

C. When a noun is modified by both cardinal and ordinal, the cardinal regularly precedes. § 189

> les quatre premières leçons, *the first four lessons* (cf. ses quatre prochains romans, *his next four novels*)

47 Numerals used as Nouns.

The commoner numerals used as nouns are: **huitaine, dizaine, douzaine, quinzaine, vingtaine, trentaine, quarantaine, cinquantaine, soixantaine, centaine, millier, million, milliard.** These nouns are followed by the preposition **de.** The suffix –aine cannot be added to a compound numeral, such as **dix-sept, quatre-vingt-cinq,** etc., and is rarely used in forms other than those given at the beginning of this paragraph. § 190

> une cinquantaine de jours, *about fifty days*
> un million de francs, *a million francs*
> quatre milliards de dollars, *four billion dollars*

A. Numerals ending in –**aine** and **millier** are generally used to express approximate numbers. On occasion, however, they may express a definite number.

une huitaine, *about eight*

La cause a été remise à huitaine. *The case has been postponed for a week.*

une douzaine, *about twelve* (or: *exactly a dozen*)

Combien de dizaines en 290 ? *How many tens in 290?*

plusieurs centaines de francs, *several hundred francs*

un millier d'hommes, (*about*) *a thousand men*

des milliers d'hommes, *thousands of men*

B. Approximate numbers may also be expressed by the addition of **environ, à peu près, approximativement,** and, especially in expressions of price, **dans les.**

mille hommes environ (environ mille hommes), *about a thousand men*

cinquante mille personnes à peu près (à peu près cinquante mille personnes), *about fifty thousand persons*

six mètres à peu près (à peu près six mètres), *about six meters*

Je voudrais quelque chose dans les deux cents francs. *I should like something for about two hundred francs.*

48 Fractions.

Fractions are regularly expressed by both cardinal and ordinal.

les deux cinquièmes, *two-fifths* § 191

les cinq huitièmes, *five-eighths*

A. From *one-half* to *one-fourth* inclusive, fractions are expressed by the following words:

le demi, la moitié, le tiers, le quart

demi

1. In the precise sense, *half* is expressed by **demi.**

une demi-heure, *a half hour*

une demi-journée, *a half day*

une heure et demie, *an hour and a half*

trois mètres et demi (*never:* trois et demi mètres), *three and a half meters* § 192

Note that when **demi** precedes the noun, it is invariable and joined to it by a hyphen.

moitié

2. In the indefinite sense, *half* is expressed by **moitié.**

> une moitié d'orange (*or:* la moitié d'une orange), *half an
> orange*
> Donnez-moi une moitié d'orange. *Give me half an orange.*
> Il a mangé la moitié d'une orange. *He ate half an orange.*

tiers, quart

3. Like **moitié, tiers** and **quart** are preceded by the article,
preferably the definite article.[1]

> un tiers d'orange (*preferably:* le tiers d'une orange), *a
> third of an orange*
> un quart d'orange (*preferably:* le quart d'une orange), *a
> fourth of an orange*

49 The Number of the Verb ruled by a Numeral.

When a plural complement is present or implied, the number
of the verb whose subject is **une huitaine, une vingtaine,**
etc., **la moitié, le tiers, le quart,** etc., is regularly plural.

> Une vingtaine (de soldats) sont arrivés. *About twenty (soldiers)
> arrived.*
> La moitié (des soldats) sont partis. *Half (the soldiers) have left.*

When **la moitié, le tiers,** etc., are used with a singular
complement, expressed or implied, they regularly take a
singular verb.

> La moitié (de l'argent) vous suffira. *Half (of the money) will
> be enough for you.*

50 Expressions of Time.

> Il est deux heures. *It is two o'clock.*
> Il est deux heures et quart (*less frequently:* deux heures
> un quart). *It is a quarter past two.*

---

[1] The definite article cannot be used when it is a question of a precise
measure.

> un quart de livre de beurre (*not:* le quart d'une livre)

Il est deux heures moins le quart (*less frequently:* deux heures moins un quart). *It is quarter of two.*
Il est midi. *It is noon.*
Il est minuit. *It is midnight.*
Il est midi et demi. *It is half past twelve (in the afternoon).*
Il est minuit et demi. *It is half past twelve (at night).*
Il est deux heures moins vingt. *It is twenty minutes to two.*
Il est trois heures dix, trois heures quarante. *It is ten minutes past three, three forty.*

In official announcements such as railroad timetables, government posters, etc., time is reckoned on a twenty-four hour basis.

Le train arrivera à dix-sept heures. *The train will arrive at five o'clock in the afternoon.*
La représentation commencera à dix-neuf heures. *The play will begin at seven o'clock in the evening.*

EXERCISES

I. VERBS TO REVIEW:

commencer,[1] naître, mourir

II. IDIOMATIC EXPRESSIONS:

à cinq heures du matin, de l'après-midi, *at five o'clock in the morning, in the afternoon*
à huit heures précises, *at exactly eight o'clock*
Quelle heure est-il? *What time is it?*
tout à l'heure, *in a little while, a little while ago*
il y a quinze jours, *two weeks ago*
d'aujourd'hui en huit, *a week from today*
lundi, mardi, en huit, *a week from Monday, Tuesday*
dans une dizaine de jours, *in about ten days*
Quel âge avez-vous? *How old are you?*
(être) d'un certain âge, (*to be*) (*rather*) *elderly*
entre deux âges, *of middle age*

---

[1] Cf. § 246 A.

III. Sentences for Translation:

1. She arrived Wednesday the twenty-second of December at three o'clock in the afternoon. 2. What time is it? By (*à*) my watch, it is a quarter to ten. 3. In the parlor I saw an elderly gentleman who was talking with a middle-aged lady. Who are they? 4. Why, you know them both. I introduced them to you two weeks ago at Dr. Henriot's. 5. You are mistaken, my dear. I don't know them any more than I know Napoleon the First.

6. You're the one who is mistaken. At the Henriots' (*les Henriot*) you talked to both of them for at least five minutes. Don't you remember it? 7. During the war thousands of refugees would enter little towns which had only a few hundred inhabitants. 8. Three fourths of these poor people had neither money nor food. 9. I am surprised (*Cela m'étonne*) that they didn't all starve to death. 10. He told me a little while ago that he would see me again a week from today.

11. If the train is on time, it will pull into the station (*entrer en gare*) at exactly nine o'clock. It is generally late, however. 12. In Europe most people travel third-class, although the wooden benches which one finds in certain third-class coaches are not very comfortable. 13. Have you finished the fifth act? No, we stopped at (*en rester à*)[1] page 200. 14. Have we covered (*voir*) two thirds of this manual? No, we have covered only half of it, the first hundred pages. 15. What could we do (*Comment faire*)? There were eighty of us girls (We were eighty girls) and there were only thirty-two seats (*places assises*) in each trackless trolley.

16. Half an apple; a half hour; two hours and a half; two and one-half meters; a franc and a half (one franc fifty); half a pound of butter; a fourth of a kilogram, which is (*ce qui fait*) half a pound; about three meters. 17. If I went to that reception, I would have to buy a new dress. How much would you want to put into it? Oh, about two thousand francs. 18. Three hundred books; 285 post cards; 80 pages; 88 francs; 1000 volumes; a million dollars; Henry V; James I; on the first floor (ground floor); on the second floor[2]; in 1942. 19. It's a quarter to ten; it is 11:30; it is half past three; it is midnight; it is twenty minutes past four; it is ten minutes to five. 20. He said he would

---

[1] Insert *la*.

[2] Between the **rez-de-chaussée** and the *1 er étage* there is sometimes a floor called the **entresol** (*m.*). Cf. the English *mezzanine*.

arrive about (*vers*) [1] seven o'clock. What time is it? It's about [1] half past six.

21. If he doesn't fail the examination, he'll be back in about ten days. 22. I am exhausted. I'll have to take about a ten-day vacation. 23. Well, I'll do my best to do without you, until you are in good health again. 24. Have you seen John? Yes. When? (Add *ça*.) A little while ago. What did he say to you? 25. He told me that I would never be able (*pouvoir*) to play tennis if I held my racket as if it (*ce*) were a frying-pan.

IV. DRILL: Translate the words in parentheses:

1. (*Half the time*) il ne sait pas l'heure qu'il est. 2. (*He made a mistake*) sur l'heure de la réunion; par conséquent il y est arrivé (*a half-hour late*). 3. Quand la reverrez-vous? (*In about fifteen days*). 4. Quel âge avez-vous? (*I shall be twenty the first of June.*) 5. On l'a vu pour la dernière fois (*Monday the twenty-seventh of September*) en compagnie d'une (*elderly lady*).

6. La représentation (*will begin at exactly nine o'clock*) et se terminera (*at a quarter to twelve*). 7. Connaissez-vous Jacques et Paul Martin? Oui, (*I am very fond of* [*Use* **aimer bien**] *both of them*). Moi aussi. (*They have hundreds of friends.*) 8. Autrefois il arrivait en France chaque été (*thousands of tourists*). 9. Combien voulez-vous mettre à une nouvelle robe? (*About 3000 fr.*) 10. Quand allez-vous (*to the country*)? (*A week from Monday.*)

11. (*We have a holiday*) deux fois par mois. 12. Quand est-ce Noël? Noël c'est toujours (*the twenty-fifth of December*). 13. Elle est arrivée (*at three o'clock in the afternoon*). 14. J'ai demandé machinalement (*a second-class ticket*); je n'ai pas l'habitude de (*traveling first-class*). 15. (*When was he born?*) Je n'en sais rien; mais (*he died about 1450*).

V. VERB EXERCISE:

A. Translate the English words:

1. Saint Louis *was born* (*past def.*) en 1215 et *died* (*past def.*) en 1270. 2. Quand *was she born?* 3. *Hardly had he begun* à écrier

---

[1] The use of **vers** is generally confined to the translation of *about* before an expression of time or a date. It is regularly used only with a *verb* of *action* but never with the idea of duration or after another preposition.

son livre *when he died.* 4. Elles *will die* contentes. 5. *He was dying* quand *they began* à le ressusciter. 6. *I was beginning* à m'endormir. 7. *He said that he was born* au mois de juin. 8. *Let's begin* la leçon. 9. Si tu *began* à jouer du piano, elle *would die* de peur. 10. La guerre de cent ans *began (past def.)* en 1337. 11. *Let him die!* 12. *Begin it (2nd pers. sing.)* tout de suite. 13. Elles *will begin* lundi en huit. 14. Les réfugiés *will have died.* 15. *I am dying* de faim. 16. Restez avec moi jusqu'à ce qu'il *dies.*

B. Identify the following forms:

1. Il naissait.
2. Ils mourussent.
3. On avait commencé.
4. Nous mourrions.
5. Tu commenças.
6. Il commençât.
7. Mourez-vous?
8. Ne le commençons-nous pas?
9. né
10. mourant

XII.
VOULOIR & POUVOIR
SAVOIR & CONNAÎTRE

The subjunctive after *pourvu que;* the subjunctive in a main clause

51 *Vouloir.*

Some of the most important uses of **vouloir** are listed below.

> Je veux partir. *I wish (want) to leave.*
> Je ne veux pas partir. *I do not wish to leave. I won't leave.*[1]
> Je veux bien y aller. *I am willing to go (there).*
> Je voudrais y aller. *I should like to go there.*
> Je voulais y aller. *I wanted to go (there).*
> Je ne voulais pas y aller. *I did not want to go.* (No statement is made as to whether I actually went or not.)
> J'ai voulu y aller. *I wanted to go* (insisted on going, did go, started or made some effort to go).

---

[1] I won't leave, I will *not* leave, may also be translated by an emphatic *Je ne partirai pas.*

Je n'ai pas voulu y aller. *I would not go* (made no effort to go, refused to go).

J'aurais voulu y aller. *I should have liked to go.*

Voulez-vous me rendre un service? *Will you do me a favor?*

"will" ~~versus~~ and "would"

The student should distinguish between the different meanings of the English *will* and *would*.

Il ira au cinéma, s'il a le temps. *He will go to the movies if he has time.* (*Will* here expresses futurity.)

Voulez-vous encore un peu de sel? *Will you have a little more salt?* (*Will you have* is here equivalent to *Do you wish.*)

Il irait au cinéma, s'il avait le temps. *He would go to the movies if he had the time.*

Voudriez-vous m'aider à sortir ma malle? *Would you help me to take out my trunk?* (*Would* here equals *Are you willing to, do you wish to.*)

Il n'a pas voulu y aller. *He wouldn't go* (refused to go).

For *would* expressing past habitual action, cf. Chapter V, the use of the imperfect tense.

52 *Pouvoir.*

Constructions with **pouvoir** are quite similar to those with **vouloir.** If the student has difficulty in the translation of *can* and *could*, he may substitute the appropriate tense of *to be able to.*

Je peux venir. *I am able to come, I can come, I may come* (of permission or possibility).

Je ne peux pas venir. *I cannot come.*

Je peux ne pas venir. *I may not come* (possibility).

Il ne peut pas ne pas réussir. *He can't keep from succeeding.*

Je pourrai venir. *I shall be able to come, I can come.*

Je pourrais venir. *I could come, I might come.*

J'aurais pu venir. *I could have come, I might have come.*

Je pouvais venir. *I was able to come, I could come.* (Literary style: *I could have come.*)

Je ne pouvais pas venir. *I wasn't able to come, I couldn't come.* (This does not imply that any effort was made to come.)

J'ai pu venir. *I could come (and did come), I managed to come.*
Je n'ai pas pu venir. *I couldn't come (although I wanted to and perhaps tried).* § 193
J'ai pu oublier mon livre chez moi. *I may have left my book at home.*

53 *Savoir.*

The following examples will give the most important uses of **savoir.**

Il sait nager. *He can swim, knows how to swim.*
Il saura le faire. *He will be able, will know how, to do it.*
Il saurait le faire.[1] *He would be able to, know how to, do it.*
Il aurait su le faire. *He would have been able, would have known how, to do it.*
Il savait le faire. *He knew how to do it, he used to know how to do it, he was able to do it.*
Quand il était chez moi, il savait très bien le français. *When he was at my home, he knew French very well.*
Quand je l'ai vu, il savait (déjà) qu'il allait mourir. *When I saw him, he knew (already) that he was going to die.*
Quand le médecin l'a vue, il a su qu'elle allait mourir. *When the doctor saw her, he knew (became aware of the fact) that she was going to die.*
Il a su cela par un de vos amis. *He found that out from one of your friends.*
Il a su se faire aimer de tout le monde. *He was able to make everyone like him. He succeeded in making everyone like him.*
Il n'a pas su se faire aimer de tout le monde. *He was unable to, failed to, make everyone like him.*

54 *Savoir* versus *pouvoir.*

Savoir expresses aptitude (knowledge or skill gained from study or practice), whereas **pouvoir** may express both aptitude (innate ability, ability to put knowledge into practice) and physical ability.

[1] The conditional of **savoir** is sometimes equivalent to the present of **pouvoir.**

Je ne saurais vous le dire. *I can't tell you.*

Savez-vous nager? *Can you swim, do you know how to swim?*

Je ne sais pas résoudre ce problème. *I don't know how to solve this problem.*

Il sait nager, mais il ne peut pas nager parce qu'il s'est foulé le poignet. *He knows how to swim, but he can't swim because he sprained his wrist.*

Pouvez-vous nager? *Can you swim, are you able to swim?*

Je ne peux pas résoudre ce problème. *I can't solve this problem.*

Cet enfant aura beau étudier, il ne pourra jamais parler français. *No matter how much that child studies, he will never be able to speak French.*

Elle n'a pas pu traduire sa leçon. *She couldn't translate her lesson.*

your watch is 10 minutes fast!

55 *Savoir* versus *connaître.*

Savoir, *to know with the mind,* should be distinguished from **connaître,** *to be acquainted with.*

Elle sait sa leçon. *She knows her lesson.*

Elle sait que vous lui avez téléphoné. *She knows that you telephoned her.*

Elle connaît très bien Paris. *She knows Paris very well.*

Nous ne connaissons pas votre ami. *We do not know your friend.* § 194

C'est à Paris que je l'ai connu. *It was in Paris that I met him (I knew him).* (Note this meaning of the past indefinite.)

56 The Subjunctive after *pourvu que.*

The subjunctive must be used in clauses introduced by **pourvu que.**

Pourvu qu'il ne pleuve pas! *If only it doesn't rain!*

Il ira vous prendre au théâtre, pourvu qu'il finisse son travail à temps. *He will call for you at the theater, provided that he finishes his work in time.*

57 The Subjunctive in a Main Clause.

The subjunctive is used in a main clause to express a wish or command in the third person.

Qu'il meure! Ainsi soit-il! *Let him die! So be it!*
À Dieu ne plaise! *God forbid!*
Plaise à Dieu qu'il revienne! *May God grant that he return!*

EXERCISES

I. VERBS TO REVIEW:

résoudre, savoir, plaire

II. IDIOMATIC EXPRESSIONS:

vouloir bien, *to be willing, to be kind enough to*
vouloir dire, *to mean*
vouloir absolument, *to insist*
demander un service à quelqu'un, *to ask a favor*
rendre (un) service à quelqu'un, *to do a favor for someone*
n'en pouvoir plus, *to be exhausted*
Cela se peut (bien). *That may (very well) be.*
(un) je ne sais quoi,[1] *something (indefinable)*
faire savoir quelque chose à quelqu'un, *to let someone know
    something*
se connaître en (plus noun, or indefinite pronoun), *to be a good
    judge of, to be expert in*
se connaître à (plus infinitive, demonstrative pronoun, or noun
    modified by a demonstrative adjective) same meaning as
    se connaître en.
s'y connaître en (à) [familiar] = se connaître en (à)
Il s'y connaît en musique, à ces sortes de choses, etc. *He knows
    a lot about music, this kind of thing, etc.*

III. SENTENCES FOR TRANSLATION:

1. I wanted to go to see him yesterday to ask him a favor. 2. If
I had known that, I should have asked you to go with me. 3. I
couldn't have gone. I was too busy. I was too tired also. In
fact, I was exhausted. 4. I asked my sister several times to go
with me, but she wouldn't go. 5. Although I walked very fast,
I wasn't able to reach the station in time to tell my friends good-
bye.

---

[1] The article is regularly omitted when **quoi** is followed by **de** plus an
adjective.

6. Would you do me a favor? Gladly, old man, provided it's not a question of money. 7. What! You don't want to lend me a little more money? 8. I don't want to lend you any more money. If I should lend you three or four hundred francs, you might not pay them back to me. 9. That might very well be. Fine! You are not lacking in frankness (It is not frankness which is lacking to you) at any rate. And then, I would have a grudge against you and we would no longer be friends. 10. Well, my dear (*mon petit*) John, do you have (You have them) the four hundred francs?

11. Unfortunately, no. I wanted to "touch" him for a few hundred (a few hundreds of) francs, but I couldn't persuade him to give them to me. 12. So (*De sorte que*) he wouldn't listen to you, eh? Do you know what that means? No? Well, that means that you are not a good judge of men. 13. Allow me to inform you, if you absolutely insist that I tell you the truth, that your remarks have a certain something about them which is insulting. 14. As I know that he knows New York very well, I'm going to ask him to be kind enough (*bien vouloir*) to do me a great favor. 15. Although I have known how to swim for at least ten years, I shall never be able to swim as well as that young life-guard.

16. As soon as I saw her, I knew that she was going to hit us for a loan. 17. When your letter reached (*parvenir*) me, I already knew that he was very ill. How did you find it out? One of your colleagues (*C'est ... qui*) told (it to) me. 18. If only he doesn't recognize me! Have you known him long? Yes, I met him in London several years ago. 19. If you've known him for several years, how do you expect (Use *vouloir* and *que* clause) him not to recognize you? You are right. He can't keep from recognizing me. 20. I hope to the Lord he never comes back! Well, well, one would say that you don't find him very attractive (that he is not pleasing to you).

21. Have you solved all the problems? No, I've been working on them for two hours, but I can't solve them. I'm not very good (*être fort*) in mathematics, you know. 22. Will you help me solve them? I know you know a lot about mathematics. 23. You are mistaken. I don't know anything about mathematics. I prefer French. When you have some written work to do in French, let me know (it). 24. Where is your French grammar? You haven't lost it, I hope. I don't think so (*Je ne crois pas*). Well, look for it.

96

un peu partout

25. I've already looked for it practically everywhere, but I haven't found it. I may have left it in the Dean's office.
il se peut   *cabinet du doyen*

IV. Drill: Translate the words in parentheses:

1. J'ai voulu lui parler, mais (*I couldn't*) dire un mot.   2. (*I couldn't*) aller au-devant de lui; je n'étais pas habillé. 3. Si (*you will*) y aller avec moi, (*I am willing*) y aller.   4. Si (*I had known*) qu'il (*needed me*), (*I could have*) lui rendre le service qu'il (*wanted*). 5. (*I tried*) sortir malgré l'orage, mais (*I was forced*) de rentrer. 6. (*God forbid*) qu'elle (*find that out*). (*I should never be able*) le lui expliquer.   7. (*Do you know*) combien de ces personnes (*I know*)?   8. (*Do you know how to dance?*) Oui, mais (*I can't*) danser ce soir, j'ai mal au pied.   9. (*Could you*) mettre ces caisses dans le camion? Pas moi, (*I'm exhausted*).   10. (*Let him leave*) et (*let him never come back*). (*So be it.*) 11. (*I didn't know*) que le chauffeur était gris, mais quand l'auto a commencé à déraper, (*I knew*) que nous allions tomber dans la rivière.   12. Voulez-vous (*me to ask him this favor*)? Non, j'aime mieux (*ask him*) moi-même.   13. (*I know*) bien des élèves qui (*never know*) leurs leçons.   14. (*I absolutely insist*) que vous (*tell me what that means*). Je n'en sais rien. (*I'm not a good judge of that*).   15. Quelqu'un a sonné? Oui, c'est un sourd-muet. (*What did he want?*) (*He couldn't*) me faire comprendre (*what he wanted*).

V. Verb Exercise:

A. Put the verbs of the following sentences in the past definite, the imperfect indicative, and the future:

1. Je résous d'attendre jusqu'au soir.   2. Nous savons la vérité. 3. Cela me plaît.   4. On résout le problème.   5. Elle sait lire.

B. Translate:

1. While knowing...   2. After solving...   3. In order that he may know...   4. Would to God!   5. We would know.   6. I found out.   7. Did you solve?   8. I want you to know that. 9. They know it.   10. If you please.   11. That used to please her. 12. While solving...   13. Let's know it!   14. They will have solved it.   15. God forbid!

97

XIII.

THE NEGATIVES: POSITION & USAGE

The subjunctive after verbs of commanding and requesting

58 Position of Negatives.

A. Regularly the first part of the negative, **ne,** precedes the verb, while the second part follows.

> Je ne crois pas cela. *I don't believe that.*
> Elle ne parle jamais. *She never speaks.*

If the verb is in a compound tense, the second part of the negative is regularly placed between the auxiliary and the past participle. **Personne** and **aucun,** however, follow the participle.

> Il n'a rien dit. *He said nothing.*
> Je ne l'ai pas vu. *I did not see him.*

But:

> Je n'ai vu personne. *I saw no one.*
> Je n'en ai trouvé aucun. *I did not find a single one (of them).*

98

B. Personne, pas un, aucun, when subjects, precede
ne and the verb. **Jamais** may also precede.

> Personne n'est venu. *No one came.*
> Aucun d'eux n'a parlé. *Not one of them spoke.*
> Pas un ne réussit. *Not one succeeds.*
> Jamais il ne vous croira. *He will never believe you.*

C. Position of negatives with infinitive. The negatives
ne . . . pas, point, plus, jamais, rien, regularly precede
the infinitive which they limit. They regularly come together before a pronoun object of the infinitive. If the infinitive is compound, however, **jamais** and **rien** regularly
stand between the infinitive and the past participle. **Aucun**
and **personne** follow the simple infinitive or the past participle of a compound infinitive.   § 195

> Je lui ai dit de ne pas y aller. *I told him not to go there.*
> Il a fait mine de ne pas me voir. *He pretended not to see me.*
> Je regrette de ne pas l'avoir vu. *I regret not having seen him.*
> Je voudrais ne l'avoir jamais vu. *I should like never to have
> seen him.*
> Je regrette de ne vous avoir rien dit. *I'm sorry not to have told
> you anything.*
> Il est sûr de n'y avoir vu personne. *He is sure that he did not
> see anyone there.*

59 Combinations of Negatives.

A. No negatives can be combined in the same clause with
pas or **point.**[1]
Various combinations of **plus, rien, guère, personne,
jamais** are frequent.

> Il ne verra plus jamais personne. *He will never see anyone any
> more.*
> Il n'en a jamais rien dit à personne. *He never told anyone
> anything about it.*

---

[1] This rule does not refer to the repetition of the whole negative expression
ne . . . pas in sentences like the following:

> Il ne peut pas ne pas y consentir. *He can't keep from consenting to it.*

99

Personne ne le croira plus jamais. *No one will ever believe him any more.*

Jamais plus je ne lui en reparlerai. *I shall never speak to him about it again.*

Certain negatives may be used after **pas** or **point** in a dependent clause introduced by **que.**

Il ne veut pas que vous le disiez à personne. *He doesn't want you to tell it to anyone.*

Il ne faut pas qu'il le fasse jamais. *He must never do it.*

Je ne crois pas qu'il en ait parlé à aucun de ses amis. *I don't think he has spoken of it to any one of his friends.*

With **vouloir** and **falloir,** however, for greater emphasis the negation is often transferred to the subordinate clause.

Il veut que vous ne le disiez à personne (practically a command). *He doesn't want you to tell it to anyone.*

Il faut qu'il ne le fasse jamais (absolute necessity or prohibition). *He must never do il.*

60 Negation with *ne* alone.

In literary style, **pas** is frequently omitted with **cesser, oser,** and **pouvoir** (when these verbs are followed by an infinitive, expressed or implied) and with **savoir.** When **savoir** is followed by the interrogative pronoun **que** and the infinitive, in indirect interrogation, the **pas** is always omitted.

Il ne cesse d'écrire. *He writes unceasingly.*

Je n'oserais le lui demander. *I wouldn't dare to ask him.*

Nous ne pouvons nous décider. *We can't make up our minds.*

Je ne sais si je pourrai y aller. *I don't know whether I can go.*

Il ne sait que [1] faire (Less elegant: Il ne sait pas quoi faire). *He doesn't know what to do.*

Elle ne savait que devenir. *She did not know what was going to become of her.*   § 196

In literary style, **pas** may be omitted after **si** in a conditional sentence, after **il y a ... que, voilà ... que** (in

---

[1] Cf. the affirmative: Il sait ce qu'il faut faire. *He knows what he must do.* Il sait ce qu'il va faire. *He knows what he is going to do.*

compound tenses). This omission also occurs in certain set expressions.

> Si je n'avais confiance en vous, je ne vous aurais pas fait venir. *If I didn't have confidence in you, I would not have had you come.*
>
> Il y a dix jours que je ne l'ai vu. *I haven't seen him for ten days.*
>
> C'est lui qui a joué ce rôle, si je ne me trompe (set expression). *He's the one who played this part, if I'm not mistaken.*
>
> Voilà dix jours que je ne vous ai vu. *I haven't seen you for ten days.*

61 The Use of *ne . . . que.*

Ne . . . que is equivalent to **seulement. Que** immediately precedes the word it limits.

> Je n'ai qu'une montre. *I have only one watch.* § 197
>
> Il ne veut que vous parler. *He wishes only to speak to you.*
>
> Il n'avait d'yeux que pour elle. *He had eyes only for her.*

If <u>only</u> limits the principal verb, it must be translated by **seulement** or by such expressions as **ne faire que, se contenter de** and the infinitive.

> Elle étudie seulement (se contente d'étudier). *She does nothing but study* (Literally: *she only studies*).
>
> Il ne fait qu'étudier (se contente d'étudier *or:* se concentre exclusivement sur ses études). *He does nothing but study.*

62 The Use of *ni . . . ni.*

Neither . . . nor is regularly translated by **ne . . . ni . . . ni.**

> Il n'aime ni le thé ni le café. (Less desirable: Il n'aime pas le thé ni le café.) *He likes neither tea nor coffee.* Il ne prend ni thé ni café. (Il ne prend pas de thé ni de café.) *He takes neither tea nor coffee.*
>
> Ni ses ennemis ni ses amis ne diraient cela. *Neither his enemies nor his friends would say that.*

When verbs are co-ordinated, *neither . . . nor* is expressed in the following manner:

Il ne mange ni ne boit. *He neither eats nor drinks.*

Il ne lit, ni n'écrit, ni ne parle le français. *He neither reads, writes, nor speaks French.*

Ordinarily, negative clauses may also be co-ordinated with **et**.

Je ne le connais guère, je ne le respecte pas, et je ne l'écouterai pas. *I scarcely know him, I don't respect him, nor will I listen to him.*

63 The use of *si.*

Si is regularly used instead of **oui** to contradict a negative statement or interrogation.

Vous n'avez pas faim? Si. *Aren't you hungry? Yes.*

Elle ne nous a pas prévenus de son départ. *She didn't notify us of her departure.* Mais si (Si fait),[1] elle a téléphoné hier. *She certainly did, she telephoned yesterday.*   § 198

As **si** emphasizes a contradiction, it is sometimes preferable to use the more polite **pardon.**

64 The Use of *non plus.*

After a negative expression, *either* is translated by **non plus.**

Je n'aime pas ce roman. *I don't like this novel.* (Ni) moi non plus. *I don't either.*

65 The subjunctive after verbs of commanding and requesting.

The subjunctive is regularly used in clauses governed by verbs of *commanding* and *requesting*, such as **commander, ordonner, demander,** and **dire** [2] (to order). This construction is especially common when the subject of the subordinate clause is general or indefinite. In other cases,

---

[1] In modern French, **mais si** seems to be gaining ground at the expense of si fait.

[2] With **dire** in indirect discourse, naturally, the indicative must be used.

Il a dit qu'il prendrait toutes les précautions.

the infinitive construction (**on dit, demande, ordonne, commande à quelqu'un de faire quelque chose**) is the more usual. § 199

Le général commande, *or*, ordonne, que personne ne sorte de la ville. *The general commands that no one leave the city.*

Le médecin a demandé, *or*, a dit, qu'on prenne toutes les précautions. *The doctor asked*, or, *ordered that all precautions be taken.*

Il lui a commandé (ordonné) de rester chez lui. *He commanded him to stay at home.*

Nous leur avons demandé (dit) de suivre le régime. *We have asked (told) them to follow the diet.*

EXERCISES

I. VERBS TO REVIEW:

s'appeler,[1] **suivre, rire**

II. IDIOMATIC EXPRESSIONS:

Il croit que oui, si (in answer to a negative). *He thinks so.*

Il croit que non. *He thinks not.*

Il dit que non. *He says not* (i.e., denies a fact).

Il dit que si. *He says yes* (i.e., assertion in answer to a negative).

Il dit que oui. *He says yes* (i.e., assertion in answer to an affirmative).

Il dit oui, non. *He says yes* (i.e., gives his permission), *no* (i.e., refuses to give his permission).

pour ainsi dire, *so to speak*

Cela ne me dit rien. *That does not appeal to me; that means nothing to me.*

faire semblant (mine) de, *to pretend to*

avoir l'habitude de (plus infinitive), *to be accustomed to*

s'habituer à, *to become accustomed to, to get used to*

se faire à, *to get used to*

comme d'habitude, *as usual*

---

[1] Cf. § 246 F.

1. Is he willing to follow me to the other end of the room so that I may show him the book he spoke of? He says yes. 2. You are not accustomed to walking. Indeed I am, I walk to school every morning. 3. Although she has been here three days, she has not seen a single one of her friends. 4. She looks so young that no one would take her for a middle-aged woman. 5. When I used to meet her on the street, she always pretended not to see me.

6. Do you know Vienna? No. I regret never having visited that town. 7. Well, in spite of everything that is said about the charms of traveling in an airplane, that does not appeal to me. 8. Is it possible that he never tells anyone anything about his business? His wife says no; but I doubt it. 9. The little girl doesn't dare disobey for fear that her nurse will tell (Use *le* before verb) her parents. 10. What can we do? Some tell us to sell our cars, others tell us to keep them. Frankly, I don't know what to do. *Que faire?*

11. If I'm not mistaken, neither the book nor the magazine gives the correct solution of the problem. 12. I'm not surprised that she doesn't get good grades. Instead of studying, she does nothing but listen to the radio. 13. Under the spell of the imagination of the author, the cathedral becomes, as it were, the principal character of the novel. 14. She does not know any boys. She has only one sister and she hasn't any cousins (*m.*) either. 15. For hours at a time he doesn't read, nor does he write, nor does he speak.

16. As usual, she says no to all my invitations, but I believe that she will give up this way of acting some day. 17. You say that you are sure that you didn't see anyone there? Yes, but I haven't been there for ten days. 18. The mayor orders that every precaution be taken against spies. 19. The doctor asks that no one drink water without having (had) it boiled. 20. Boiled water is not palatable, but everyone can become accustomed to its taste.

21. She looks as if she were enjoying herself. She is smiling and from time to time she bursts out laughing. 22. The more one rests the more one gets used to rest and idleness, and before long one loses the habit of working. 23. He is not going to have the doctor come. He says he is, for unless the doctor comes, he's afraid he'll never get out of bed. 24. What is her name? I don't

know, because I was not paying attention when she was introduced to me. 25. If a friend of mine pretended not to recognize me, I assure you that I would get angry.

IV. Drill: Translate the words in parentheses:

1. C'est dommage qu'il (*spent only*) une journée dans cette ville. Il y a (*so many sights*) à voir qu'on ne pourrait pas les voir toutes, même si l'on (*stayed there two weeks*). 2. (*What is the name of*) cette ville où vos amis (*are accustomed to*) aller faire une cure? 3. Vous allez passer l'été au bord de la mer? (*I think so.*) Je ne vous envie pas. Passer tout l'été sur une plage! (*That does not appeal to me.*) 4. Les autorités ont commandé (*that all the lights along the coast be extinguished*). 5. On m'a dit qu'elle (*takes neither coffee nor tea*). Je ne le crois pas, mais (*it may very well be so*).

6. Ce n'est pas vous qui m'avez dit cette nouvelle. (*I certainly did*) et je vous ai même dit (*not to repeat it to anyone*). 7. (*He doesn't know what to do*); il ne veut ni rester ni partir. 8. Il regrette (*that he has seen no one*) avant son départ. 9. (*No one*) veut qu'il continue à faire son travail (*as usual*). 10. (*If she did not have confidence in* [en] *me*), elle ne m'aurait pas fait venir.

11. Je ne le demande pas, je ne le veux pas, (*and I will not accept it*). 12. (*Neither his relatives nor his friends*) lui en voudraient si cela ne lui disait rien. 13. (*He pretends to say yes*) à toutes nos demandes, mais en réalité (*he does nothing but oppose our plans*). 14. Le médecin défend (*the patient to receive visitors*). 15. Avez-vous dit que vous n'aimiez pas cette pièce? Oui. (*I don't either.*)

V. Verb Exercise:

A. Translate the English words:

1. Je regrette qu'il *is following me*. 2. De peur que vous en *will laugh*, je ne vous le dirai pas. 3. Elle veut que nous *follow her*. 4. C'est dommage que *her name is* Suzy. 5. Cela ne m'étonne pas *that she is laughing*. 6. Quoique *we are laughing*, nous ne sommes pas contents. 7. Si elle *laughed*, on la *would follow*. 8. Quand *will they follow* l'officier? 9. *Our name is* Durand. 10. Si *your name is* Blanchard, pourquoi faites-vous la queue ici? 11. *I am following* la foule. 12. Nous disons des bêtises pour

qu'elle *may laugh at them* (en rire).   13. *They followed* (*past def.*) l'agent.   14. *Follow me!* dit-il.

B. Put the verbs of the following sentences in the third person plural.

1. Nous nous appelons Bonnard.   2. Suis ce chemin.   3. Pourquoi rit-il (*past def.*)?   4. Je riais souvent.   5. Suivra-t-il ce monsieur? 6. Elle rit tout le temps.   7. Il s'appelait Charles.   8. Je suivis la conversation.   9. Qu'il me suive!   10. Je rirai.

XIV.

THE SUBJUNCTIVE: REVIEW & NEW USES

The subjunctive contrasted with the infinitive; sequence of tenses

66 The Subjunctive in Subordinate Clauses.

In French the subjunctive is regularly used in subordinate clauses dependent on verbs or conjunctions which indicate the *attitude* or *feeling* of the speaker. The action or state expressed by the verb in the subordinate clause is presented as necessary or unnecessary; possible, impossible, improbable, uncertain, or doubtful; desirable or undesirable, etc. § 200

67 Review.

In the preceding lessons the following uses of the subjunctive have been treated:

A. After certain conjunctions of time (**jusqu'à ce que, avant que**)[1]; of concession (**quoique, bien que, encore**

---

[1] The conjunction **après que** should always be followed by the indicative.

Après qu'il eut fini son travail, nous sortîmes. *After he had finished his work, we went out.*

que); of purpose (**pour que, afin que**); of condition (**sans que, à moins que, pourvu que**). § 201

1. The subjunctive with **avant que, afin que, pour que,** and **sans que** is regularly replaced by the infinitive with **avant de, afin de, pour,** and **sans** when there is no change of subject. Similarly, **à moins que** is often replaced by **à moins de.**

> Je suis sorti sur la pointe des pieds pour (afin de) ne pas vous réveiller. *I went out on tiptoe in order not to wake you up.*
> Avant de sortir, il a pris congé de son hôte. *Before going out, he took leave of his host.*
> Il est entré sans rien dire. *He came in without saying anything.*
> A moins d'être certain de votre concours, il ne marchera pas. *Unless he is certain of your co-operation, he won't go along with us.*

B. After expressions of necessity (**il faut, il est nécessaire**); fitness, advisability (**il est important, il convient, mériter**); possibility (**il est possible, il est impossible**), etc.

C. After expressions of emotion (**craindre, avoir peur, de peur que, de crainte que, regretter, être heureux, être content, c'est dommage**); willing, wishing, preferring (**aimer, aimer mieux, désirer, vouloir**); ordering, commanding, requesting (**commander, ordonner, dire, demander**), etc.; and in a main clause to express a wish or command in the third person.

1. Verbs of *wishing, desiring, willing,* and *preferring,* always, expressions of *fearing* and *regretting,* regularly, are followed by the infinitive if there is no change of subject. In the latter case, the use of a clause instead of the infinitive after verbs of *fearing* and *regretting* is generally quite colloquial.

(*cont.*)

> Après qu'elle a fini de laver la vaisselle, nous allons toujours au cinéma. *After she has finished (finishes) washing the dishes, we always go to the movies.*
> Après qu'il aura fini son travail, je le retrouverai ici. *After he has finished his work, I shall meet him here.* § 202

Il veut partir demain. *He wants to leave tomorrow.*
Il veut que nous partions. *He wants us to leave.*
Je crains de l'avoir offensé. *I'm afraid I offended him.*
Je crains que vous ne l'ayez offensé. *I'm afraid that you have offended him.*
Je regrette de l'avoir dit. *I'm sorry I said it.*
Je regrette qu'il l'ait dit. *I'm sorry he said it.*
Je n'ai pas bougé de crainte de vous réveiller. *I didn't move for fear of waking you up.*
Il ne veut pas rentrer de crainte que son père ne le punisse. *He doesn't want to come back for fear his father will punish him.*

68 Other Uses of the Subjunctive.

A. After expressions of *forbidding, preventing, avoiding,* and *permitting* (**défendre, empêcher, éviter, permettre,** etc.).

1. Verbs of *permitting* and *preventing* are followed by the infinitive if the subject does not change. If the subject does change, these verbs, as well as those of *forbidding,* may be followed by the subjunctive or by the infinitive. The construction with the infinitive is generally preferred, unless the subject of the subordinate clause is a thing or an indefinite person.

Je me suis permis de vous écrire. *I permitted myself to write to you.*
Il n'a pas pu s'empêcher de rire. *He couldn't keep from laughing.*
Je ne permets pas qu'on dise des bêtises. *I do not allow stupid remarks to be made.*
Je lui ai permis d'entrer. *I permitted him to enter.*
Il ne permet pas que les fenêtres soient ouvertes. *He doesn't permit the windows to be open* (or *opened*).
Empêchez-le de sortir! (Empêchez qu'il ne [1] sorte!) *Keep him from going out!*
Le médecin défend qu'on transporte le malade. *The doctor forbids moving the patient.*
Je lui ai défendu de sortir. *I forbade him to go out.*

---

[1] A redundant **ne** is regularly used after verbs of *preventing* and *avoiding* when the main clause is affirmative.

2. The verb **éviter**, *to avoid*, is followed by the infinitive if there is no change of subject. If there is a change of subject, the subjunctive is used.

> Evitez de lui parler. *Avoid speaking to him.*
> Il aura fait cela pour éviter que vous ne le soupçonniez. *He probably did that to avoid your suspecting him.*

B. After **non (pas) que, ce n'est pas que, qui que, quel que, quelque . . . que, si . . . que, quoi que, où que.**

> Non (pas) que je tienne à le faire . . . *Not that I'm anxious to do it . . .*
> Ce n'est pas qu'il soit content d'accepter cette tâche . . . *It's not that he's glad to accept this task . . .*
> Qui que vous soyez [1] . . . *Whoever you are . . .*
> Quelles que soient vos raisons . . . *Whatever your reasons are . . .*
> Quelque décision qu'il prenne . . . *Whatever decision he may make . . .*
> Quelque fort qu'il soit . . . (*or more commonly:* Si fort qu'il soit [2] . . .) *However strong he may be . . .*   § 203
> Quoi que vous fassiez . . . *Whatever you do . . .*
> Où que vous alliez . . . *Wherever you go . . .*

C. Regularly after expressions of *knowing*, *thinking*, *believing*, *hoping*, and expressions of *certainty* or *probability*, when they are used <u>*interrogatively*</u> or *negatively*. When such expressions are employed <u>affirmatively, the</u> indicative is used.[3]

> Je crois (je suis sûr) qu'il viendra. *I believe (I am sure) he will come.*
> Alors vous croyez qu'il a dit cela? (The indicative is used as the verb is *not* in the interrogative form, and since it is

---

[1] In modern French, **quel**, not **qui**, is used before a subject in the third person: **quel qu'il soit, quelle qu'elle soit.**

[2] In less formal style, **quelque . . . que** and **si . . . que** are generally replaced by **avoir beau:** Il a beau être fort, il ne pourra pas soulever cela. *No matter how strong he is, he won't be able to lift that.* (The construction with **avoir beau,** which is equivalent to a subordinate clause, is always followed by a restrictive statement, expressed or implied.)

[3] <u>**Il me semble** is generally followed by the indicative</u>, **il semble,** by the subjunctive.

Il paraît takes indicative.

110

evident that an affirmative reply is expected.) *So you believe that he said that?*

J'espère qu'il réussira à son examen. *I hope he will pass his examination.*

Il est probable qu'il acceptera. *It is probable that he will accept.*

Croyez-vous qu'elle soit ici? *Do you think she is here?*

Etes-vous sûr qu'elle vienne? *Are you sure that she is coming?*

§ 204

Est-ce que vous croyez qu'il ait dit cela? *Do you think that he said that?*

Je ne crois pas (Je ne suis pas sûr) qu'il l'ait dit. *I don't believe (I'm not sure) he said it.*

Il n'est pas probable qu'il finisse son travail cette année. *It is not likely that he will finish his work this year.*

1. If the verb in the English subordinate clause is in the conditional, or expresses an action which has already taken place, the subjunctive is generally not used in the French translation. The subjunctive is replaced by the indicative when the subordinate clause expresses a general truth.

Croyez-vous qu'il réussirait? *(or more commonly:* pourrait réussir?*) Do you believe that he would succeed?*

Saviez-vous qu'il était arrivé? *Did you know that he had arrived?*

Il ne savait pas que j'étais arrivé. *He didn't know I had come.*

Je ne croyais pas qu'il réussirait. *I didn't believe that he would succeed.*

Espériez-vous qu'il viendrait? *Were you hoping that he would come?*

Ils ne savent pas que l'or et l'argent sont des éléments. *They don't know that gold and silver are elements.*

2. In familiar French, especially when the expressions mentioned in § 67 **C** are followed by a verb of future time, the indicative frequently replaces the subjunctive in interrogation. In negation, however, educated speakers generally hesitate to make this substitution.

Croyez-vous qu'il a dit cela? *Do you think he said that?*

Croyez-vous qu'il viendra? *Do you think he will come?*

111

Etes-vous (bien) sûr qu'il viendra, qu'il a dit cela, etc.? *Are you (quite) sure that he will come, that he said that, etc.?*

Espérez-vous qu'il réussira? *Do you hope that he will succeed?*

3. Frequently, verbs of *thinking, believing, hoping,* may be followed either by the infinitive or by a clause introduced by **que,** when there is no change of subject.

Il croit avoir réussi. Il croit qu'il a réussi. *He thinks he has succeeded.*

J'espère réussir. J'espère que je réussirai. *I hope to succeed.*

Whether or not a clause is used is sometimes a matter of euphony. One would not say, for instance, **Nous espérons que nous viendrons.** The infinitive after **croire, espérer,** etc., is, in general, more frequent in literary style, whereas the clause is essentially colloquial. The latter should be used, however, to avoid a succession of infinitives. For example, **J'espère pouvoir vous faire voir mes photos,** should be replaced by: **J'espère que je pourrai vous faire voir mes photos.**

The rules just given with regard to the use of the subjunctive or indicative after verbs of *thinking, believing,* etc., represent, in general, the average modern tendency. In conservative speech, the encroachment of the indicative has been more effectively resisted; in careless speech, this encroachment is much more extensive.

D. Regularly after verbs of *doubting* or *denying.* A redundant **ne** is generally used with the subjunctive after **douter** when the main clause is negative.

Je nie (ne nie pas) qu'il soit venu. *I deny (don't deny) that he has come.* § 205

Je doute fort qu'il y réussisse. *I doubt very much that he will succeed in it.*

Doutez-vous qu'il vienne? *Do you doubt that he will come?*

Je ne doute pas qu'il n'y réussisse (*or:* qu'il y réussisse). *I don't doubt that he will succeed in it.* §§ 206, 207

69 Sequence of Tenses.

A. The verb of the subordinate clause is in the present or perfect subjunctive when the verb of the main clause is in the present or future. The subordinate verb is in the *present* subjunctive when the verb of the corresponding English clause is present or future; it is in the *perfect* subjunctive when the corresponding English verb is in the present perfect, or the future perfect.

The following examples show the relation between the tenses in a simple statement and those in the subordinate clause of a complex sentence.

SIMPLE STATEMENT	COMPLEX STATEMENT
Il ne vient pas. *He isn't coming.*	Je ne crois pas qu'il vienne. *I don't think he is coming.*
Il ne viendra pas. *He will not come.*	Je ne crois pas qu'il vienne. *I don't think he will come.*
Il n'est pas arrivé. *He hasn't come.*	Je ne crois pas qu'il soit arrivé. *I don't think he has come.*
Il l'a dit. *He said it.*	Je regrette qu'il l'ait dit. *I'm sorry that he said it.*
Il finira son devoir. *He will finish his exercise.*	J'attendrai qu'il finisse son devoir. *I shall wait until he finishes his exercise.*
Il a fini (aura bientôt fini) son devoir. *He has finished (will soon have finished) his exercise.*	J'attendrai qu'il ait fini son devoir. *I shall wait until he has finished (shall have finished) his exercise.*

B. The verb of the subordinate clause is regularly in the imperfect or the pluperfect subjunctive when the verb of the main clause is in a past tense or the conditional.

SIMPLE STATEMENT	COMPLEX STATEMENT
Il ne réussirait pas. *He would not succeed.*	J'avais peur qu'il ne réussît pas. *I was afraid that he would not succeed.*
Il avait dit cela. *He had said that.*	Je regrettais qu'il eût dit cela. *I was sorry that he had said that.*

SIMPLE STATEMENT	COMPLEX STATEMENT
Il avait terminé son travail. *He had finished his work.*	J'avais attendu qu'il eût terminé son travail. *I had waited until he had finished his work.*

In familiar spoken and written French, the imperfect subjunctive is regularly replaced by the present subjunctive and the pluperfect by the perfect. In the spoken language, only the third person singular of the imperfect subjunctive of **être** and **avoir** still appears with some frequency. There are, of course, some persons who insist on employing the imperfect subjunctive, even in the archaic forms of the first conjugation, wherever it is required by the rule stated in § 69 **B**.

> Je voudrais qu'il vienne. *I should like to have him come.* (This use of the present subjunctive is quite logical, as the conditional in this instance is merely a softened form of the present.)
>
> J'avais peur qu'il ne réussisse pas. *I was afraid that he would not succeed.*
>
> Je regrettais que vous n'ayez pas terminé votre travail. *I was sorry that you had not finished your work.*
>
> Il fallait que je vienne. *I had to come.*

EXERCISES

I. VERBS TO REVIEW:

boire, battre

II. IDIOMATIC EXPRESSIONS:

> avoir beau (plus infinitive), *to be useless, to do in vain, no matter how much . . ., etc.*
> sur la pointe des pieds, *on tiptoe*
> prendre congé, *to take leave*
> faire la cuisine, *to cook*
> faire le ménage, *to do the housework*
> faire le (son) marché, *to do the (one's) marketing*
> faire part à quelqu'un de quelque chose, *to announce something to someone*

de temps en temps, *from time to time*
avoir de la chance, *to be lucky*

III. Sentences for Translation:

1. Although I am very tired, I'm going to stay here until he comes back. 2. She went out without (*sans que* and clause) my having seen her. 3. However stupid she may be, she will pass this examination. 4. Whoever he is and whatever his reasons may be, I doubt if he is right. 5. We have done our best to keep him from leaving college.

6. He will work day and night in order that his parents may be satisfied with (*content de*) him. 7. After going downstairs,[1] he went out on tiptoe in order not to wake his child. 8. He wants to see us before we leave. 9. We don't want him to leave before tomorrow. 10. We don't allow people to laugh here.

11. Do you think that they will announce their wedding to their host before taking leave of him? 12. From time to time, when the maid does the marketing, I have to do the housework. 13. Unless you make your purchases early, you won't have time to buy everything. 14. I don't deny that even brave people are afraid when a town is bombed. 15. I hope to pass my examination; but I am afraid that I shall not get a good grade.

16. After it has rained, it is wise for the beginner to drive slowly. 17. I don't believe they have come. At any rate, I haven't seen them yet. 18. I didn't think that she would come without having told me (it). 19. It's too bad that she isn't lucky. 20. On the first day of May, thousands of workmen go on strike.

21. It's useless for you to study more, you will never understand it better. 22. Mary has the best maid in the town. She can cook and do the marketing, and she is absolutely honest. 23. I am willing to go there; but the doctor forbids her to have visitors. 24. I am sorry she has already left. I should have liked to see her. 25. Unfortunately, it seems they both arrived at the same time.

IV. Drill: Translate the words in parentheses:

1. Est-il possible qu'il (*has gone out without my having noticed it*)?
2. Croyez-vous qu'il (*will come*) demain? 3. Je sais qu'ils (*have*

---

[1] Use **après** and the past infinitive.

115

taken leave of) leur hôte. 4. Elle espérait aller chez Marie (*after making some purchases*). 5. Pour que (*you may go out from time to time*), (*I am willing to*) m'occuper de votre petit garçon.

6. C'est dommage qu'elle (*comes*) toujours me voir au moment même où (*I should like to*) sortir. 7. Je regrette qu'ils (*are going*) en ville avant que (*I can*) les accompagner. 8. Il me semble qu'elle (*is lucky*). 9. Qui que (*you are*), je ne veux pas que vous (*enter my house*). 10. Je doute fort qu'il (*will announce to us*) son départ.

11. Il a travaillé toute l'année, de sorte qu'il (*was unable to*) faire de voyage. 12. Il croit (*he has bought*) la meilleure maison (*in the city*). 13. Bien que (*I am late*), j'espère que (*they will not prevent my entering*). 14. J'attendrai qu'il (*has finished*) son travail. 15. Il craint (*he offended her*); mais il nie qu'il (*intended*) [avoir l'intention de] le faire.

V. VERB EXERCISE:

A. Give the imperative of the verbs **boire** and **battre**.

B. Put the verbs of the following sentences in the present indicative, the imperfect indicative, and the past indefinite.

1. Elle **boire** du café.
2. Je ne **battre** pas le chien.
3. Vous **boire** cette liqueur?
4. Ils **battre** les cartes.

C. Identify the following forms:

1. Qu'il batte. 2. Nous battrions. 3. Ils battirent. 4. Vous battissiez. 5. Il but. 6. Ils bussent. 7. Buvant 8. Ils boiraient. 9. Battez! 10. Ils battront.

XV.

THE SUBJUNCTIVE: RELATIVE CLAUSES

The indefinites: *certain, divers, différent, tel, même, aucun, pas un, nul*

70 The Use of the Subjunctive in Relative Clauses.

A. The verb of a relative clause which modifies an indefinite antecedent, or an antecedent whose existence is denied or placed in doubt, is regularly in the subjunctive mode.

Je cherche une bonne qui sache faire la cuisine. *I am looking for a maid who knows how to cook.*

Connaissez-vous une bonne qui sache faire la cuisine? *Do you know a maid who knows how to cook?*

Si je pouvais trouver une bonne qui sache faire la cuisine ... *If I could only find a maid who knows how to cook ...*

Vous connaissez donc une bonne qui sait faire la cuisine? *So you know a maid who knows how to cook?* (The indicative mode is used here, as the declarative order and the adverb *donc* indicate that an affirmative answer is expected.)

Il n'y a personne ici que je connaisse. *There is no one here whom I know.*

117

Il y a peu de personnes ici que je connaisse. *There are few persons here whom I know.*

Il n'y a personne ici que je ne connaisse. *There is no one here whom I don't know.*

Il y a peu de personnes ici que je ne connaisse. *There are few persons here whom I don't know.* (Note that when the main clause expresses a negative idea, the negation in the dependent clause is expressed by *ne* alone.)

B. In modern French, the conditional replaces the older imperfect subjunctive in relative clauses of the types mentioned in § 70 A.

Il n'y a personne qui consentirait (*rather than:* consentît) à le suivre. *There is no one who would consent to follow him.*

Y a-t-il quelqu'un qui accepterait de le faire? (*rather than:* acceptât)? *Is there someone who would be willing to do it?*

C. In a relative clause, the subjunctive is regularly used after a superlative and is generally preferred to the indicative after **seul, premier, dernier.** In modern French, however, these adjectives are followed by the conditional rather than the imperfect subjunctive.

C'est le roman le plus grand qui soit. *It's the greatest novel there is.*

C'est l'homme le plus intelligent que je connaisse. *He's the most intelligent man I know.*

C'est le seul (homme) qui ne m'ait jamais demandé de service. *He's the only man who has never asked me a favor.*

C'est le premier qui s'en soit servi. *He's the first one to have made use of it.*

C'est le dernier qui en ait parlé ainsi. *He is the last one who spoke of it thus.*

C'est la seule chose qui me plairait (*rather than:* plût). *That's the only thing that would please me.*

Il a dit que ce serait le dernier service qu'il me demanderait. *He said it would be the last favor he would ask me.*

D. In a relative clause depending on **il n'y a que . . .**, the verb is regularly in the subjunctive. It may be in the indicative, if one wishes to express a strong affirmation.

118

Il n'y a qu'une pièce qui $\left\{ \begin{array}{l} \text{m'ait intéressé.} \\ \text{m'a intéressé.} \end{array} \right\}$ *There is only one play which has interested me.*

71 The Use of the Indicative in Relative Clauses.

The indicative, rather than the subjunctive, must be used:

A. When the antecedent is a definite person or thing.

Je connais une bonne qui sait faire la cuisine. *I know a maid who knows how to cook.*

Il y a plusieurs personnes ici que je connais. *There are several persons whom I know.*

Pourriez-vous trouver la bonne que Suzanne a congédiée? *Could you find the maid whom Suzanne discharged?*

Si je pouvais trouver la bonne que Suzanne a congédiée... *If I could find the maid whom Suzanne discharged ...*

B. If the antecedent is introduced by **c'est** (*it is*) merely to render it more emphatic.

C'est le plus petit qui est mon frère. *It's the smallest one who is my brother.*

C'est le plus gros que j'ai choisi. *I chose the biggest one.*

C. After **la première, seconde, troisième ... dernière fois que ...**

C'*est* la première fois que je *viens* ici. *This is the first time that I have been here.*

C'*était* la première fois qu'il me *demandait* un tel service. *It was the first time that he had asked me such a favor.*

Ce *serait* la première fois qu'il *ferait* cela. *It would be the first time that he had done that.*

C'*est* la dernière fois que nous *invitons* cet homme-là. *It's the last time that we will invite that man.* (Note that in French the tense used is regularly the same in both clauses.)

72 The Avoidance of the Subjunctive.

It is frequently advisable to avoid the subjunctive, especially when it is a question of deciding between the imperfect subjunctive and its replacement by the present. This avoidance may be obtained in several ways:

A. By omitting the verb and subject of the dependent clause;

Quoique pauvre (*instead of:* quoiqu'il fût pauvre), il n'avait jamais demandé l'aumône à personne. *Although he was poor, he had never asked anyone for alms.*

B. By substituting a phrase for the dependent clause;

Je leur ai écrit avant leur retour (*instead of:* avant qu'ils revinssent). *I wrote to them before they returned.*

C. By adding an infinitive or by using a conjunction that does not require the subjunctive.

J'ai été content d'apprendre que vous n'étiez plus malade. *I was glad to learn that you were no longer ill.*

Je suis certain que nous gagnerons la bataille si chacun de nous fait son devoir (*instead of:* pourvu que chacun de nous fasse son devoir). *I am sure that we shall win the battle if each one of us does his duty.*

J'étais certain que nous ne gagnerions pas la bataille si chacun de nous ne faisait pas son devoir (*instead of:* à moins que chacun de nous ne fasse, *or* ne fît, son devoir). *I was sure that we would not win the battle unless each one of us did his duty.*

Je ne partirai que lorsqu'il m'aura dit de partir (*instead of:* Je ne partirai pas avant qu'il m'ait dit de partir). *I shall not leave until he has told me to leave.*[1]

73 Additional Indefinites.

certain, divers, différent, tel

A. The adjectives **certain, divers, différent,** and **tel** present certain peculiarities. The first three vary in meaning depending upon their position;[2] they are really indefinites only when they precede the noun they modify. **Tel,** when

---

[1] Cf. § 201 for the use of **ne . . . que** and **avant que** for *not until.*
[2] Cf. § 37 **B.**

used with the indefinite article, must follow the article, contrary to English usage.

> Certaines personnes le croient.[1] *Certain people believe it.*
> Il en a parlé à différentes (à diverses) personnes. *He has spoken of it to various persons.*
> Je n'ai jamais vu un tel homme (un pareil homme *or* un homme pareil). *I never saw such a man.*

Certains and **tels** may be used as pronouns.

> Certains le croient. *Certain people believe it.*
> Tel est pris qui croyait prendre. *He fell into his own trap.*
> Monsieur un tel, madame une telle, *Mr. So-and-so, Mrs. So-and-so*

même

B. The adjective **même,** meaning *same*, regularly precedes the noun it modifies. When it means *very* or *itself, himself,* etc., it follows the noun.

> la même chose, *the same thing*
> les mêmes livres, *the same books*
> Il a dit la même chose que vous. *He said the same thing that you did.*
> Les élèves mêmes l'ont demandé. *The pupils themselves asked it.*
> Il est entré au moment même où nous parlions de lui. *He came in at the very moment we were talking about him.*

When **même** is used as an adverb, it regularly precedes the words to which it refers.

> Même les élèves l'ont demandé. *Even the pupils asked it.*
> Il l'aurait dit même devant vous. *He would have said it even in front of you.*

aucun

C. The indefinite adjective and pronoun **aucun** is used with **ne** to express more emphatic negation than **ne . . . pas.** As

---

[1] In the older language, a partitive **de** was frequently used before **certains** and **différents.** This use of **de** is obsolete with **différents** and practically obsolete with **certains.**

a pronoun, it always has a complement, expressed or implied. The use of **aucun** is restricted today almost entirely to the singular.

> Aucun élève ne pourrait faire ce travail-là. *No pupil could do that work.*
>
> Je n'ai aucune envie de travailler. *I have no desire at all to work.* (Cf. Je n'ai pas envie de travailler. *I don't feel like working.*)
>
> Aucun de vos amis n'est venu. *Not one of your friends came.*
>
> Combien de mes amis sont venus? Aucun. *How many of my friends came? Not one.*
>
> J'en ai parlé à plusieurs de mes amis, mais aucun ne m'a donné une explication satisfaisante. *I talked about it to several of my friends, but not one gave me a satisfactory explanation.*

pas un

D. Pas un, *not one*, *not a single one*, is about equivalent to **aucun,** but it may be used only where it is a question of numbers.

> Pas un de nos amis n'est venu. *Not one of our friends came.*

nul, nulle

E. In general, the use of **nul, nulle,** as a synonym of **aucun** and **personne** is obsolescent or literary. The expression **nulle part,** however, is in current use.

> Je ne l'ai vu nulle part. *I didn't see him anywhere.*
>
> Nul n'est censé ignorer la loi. *No one is supposed to be ignorant of the law.*

EXERCISES

I. VERBS TO REVIEW:

vécu

vivre, servir

II. IDIOMATIC EXPRESSIONS:

se servir de, *to use* or employer

faire bon ménage (ensemble), *to live happily together, to get along well*

à voix basse, *in a low voice*
chemin faisant, *on the way*
rendre visite à quelqu'un, *to make a call on someone* ♦
rendre une visite, *to return a call*
visiter, *to visit* (*a thing*, or, in an official capacity, *a person*)

III. SENTENCES FOR TRANSLATION:

1. Do you know anyone who knows how to use a typewriter?
2. This is the first time that the doctor has visited his patients in the morning. 3. It's the oldest boy (*l'aîné*) whom I like best. Certain friends of mine prefer the youngest (*le cadet*). 4. To hear you talk (*A vous en croire* or: *A vous entendre*) there are few married people who live happily together, even for a very short time. 5. I am very glad that you made a call on our friends.

6. If they could only find the remedy which you used! I have various remedies in my medicine chest (*pharmacie*, f.). 7. Do you by any chance know the man who wrote this book? 8. I should like to teach a student who can talk French like that. None of my students speak French. 9. You ought to have spoken in a low tone if you wanted to ask him such a favor. 10. I spoke to them about it before they left. Not a one knew it.

11. They are the last ones who called on Mrs. Brown before her death. I am very sorry now that I didn't return her call. 12. It's the last time I shall ask you that favor. 13. Although he was rich, he was very stingy. I had never seen such a miser. 14. He said that he wouldn't leave till he had been told to leave (one told him to leave). 15. There is no one who believes what (*ce que*) you say.

16. There is only one thing which pleases him. 17. I know several people who could make the same speech. 18. On the way, I asked him if he knew someone who could help me. 19. He must have known that it was the first time that I had used that machine. 20. I have heard that John and his wife are not getting along very well.

21. There are few people who know how to express themselves. 22. I know someone who could send it to you. 23. Use it! (polite and familiar forms) Don't use it! (polite and familiar forms) Let's not use it! 24. Stay here until I come back. 25. Al-

123

though he is very intelligent, he will have to work very hard in order to pass all his examinations.

◆

IV. Drill: Translate the words in parentheses:

1. C'est l'homme le plus grand que (*I know*). 2. Voilà la bonne que Suzanne (*sent me*). (*She's the same maid*) qu'elle envoie à tout le monde. 3. Nous ferons de notre mieux pour que chacun (*know*) la vérité. 4. Si je peux trouver une robe qui (*pleases me*), je (*will send it to you*). 5. C'est la première fois que je (*have seen you here*).

6. Etes-vous abonnés à (*various magazines*)? Non, c'est la seule revue que nous (*receive*). 7. C'est le plus petit qui (*is*) le plus sympathique. 8. J'irai les voir aussitôt que possible (*after they return*). 9. Quoi que vous (*do*), ne manquez pas de (*call Mrs. So-and-so*). 10. (*I am sorry*) que (*he had to*) partir de si bonne heure.

11. (*He is the first one*) qui (*thought of*) cela. (*None of my students*) n'y aurait pensé. 12. J'attendrai qu'il (*has finished his work*). 13. Je lui ai demandé d'y aller avec moi, mais il (*wouldn't*). 14. Il est très content que (*you left without their having seen you*). 15. Pourvu que (*he isn't late*)! Je ne le vois (*anywhere*).
il ne soit pas en retard.   *nulle part*

V. Verb Exercise:

A. Translate the English words: *s'il vit*
1. *Had he lived* longtemps à Paris? 2. *If he is living, he will serve you.* 3. J'attends que la bonne *serves* le café. 4. Faut-il que *we live* seuls? 5. *By serving* plusieurs maîtres, on apprend beaucoup. 6. *He was still living*, quand son fils est revenu. 7. Voilà la maison où *I lived* heureux pendant de longues années. 8. Je doute *that he will live* longtemps. 9. *He used* un mot français pour se faire comprendre. 10. Il fait signe à la bonne pour qu'elle *serve* les invités. 11. Comment *will they use* ceci? 12. *Shall we be living* à ce moment-là? 13. François Ier *lived* à l'époque de la Renaissance. 14. Autrefois *we served* du café à tout le monde.
nous servions

B. Give the following forms in all the simple tenses:

1. *servir*, first person singular. 2. *vivre*, second person plural.

124

XVI.

DEMONSTRATIVES; THE INDEFINITES:

N'importe qui, n'importe lequel, n'importe quoi, n'importe quel [1]

74 The Demonstrative Adjective.

The demonstrative adjective must be repeated before each noun that it modifies.

cet homme et cette femme, *this man and woman*

-ci, -là

When it is necessary to distinguish between *this* and *that*, *these* and *those*, **-ci** and **-là** are added to the noun (or pronoun).

Cet élève-ci est plus intelligent que cet élève-là. *This pupil is more intelligent than that pupil.*

Ces dictionnaires-ci sont plus gros que ceux-là. *These dictionaries are larger than those.* § 208

---

[1] Cf. § 352 for forms of adjectives and pronouns.

75 Demonstrative Pronouns.

ceci, cela

A. Ceci and **cela** are regularly used when no definite antecedent has been mentioned or when the antecedent is an idea.

> Comment trouvez-vous cela? Je ne l'aime pas, je préfère ceci.
> *What do you think of that? I don't like it, I prefer this.*
>
> Vous croyez que votre père aimerait aller au théâtre? Mais oui, cela lui ferait plaisir. *Do you think that your father would like to go to the theater? Why yes, he'd like that* (literally: *that would please him*).
>
> Cela me met toujours en colère de me mettre en smoking. *It always makes me angry to put on a tuxedo.*

Colloquially **cela** (**ça**) is frequently used with a specific antecedent. This use is especially common when the antecedent is thought of in a general sense, as in the last of the following examples.

> — *Les Misérables?* — Non, monsieur, nous n'avons pas ça.
> — *Les Misérables? No, sir, we don't have that.*
>
> Prenez encore un peu de ce homard. Non? Vous n'aimez pas ça? (i.e., Vous n'aimez pas le homard?) *Do take a little more of this lobster. No? You don't like it?*

celui, celle

B. The pronouns **celui, celle,** etc., always refer to a definite antecedent. They must be accompanied by **-ci** or **-là** unless they are immediately followed by a phrase regularly introduced by **de,**[1] or by a clause.

> Voici des livres. Ceux-ci sont à vous, ceux-là sont à moi.
> *Here are some books. These are yours, those are mine.*
>
> Si vous ne pouvez pas trouver votre raquette, prenez celle de votre frère. *If you can't find your racket, take your brother's.*
>
> Ce livre, et celui dont je vous ai parlé, sont nouveaux. *This book, and the one I talked to you about, are new.*

---

[1] In spite of the opposition of purists, **celui, celle,** etc., are frequently followed by phrases introduced by prepositions other than **de.**

Cette dame, et celle que j'ai rencontrée hier, sont parentes. *This lady and the one I met yesterday are related.*

Celui à qui je parlais était mon professeur de français. *The one to whom I was talking was my French professor.*

Celui-ci, celle-ci, ceux-ci, celles-ci are equivalent to *the latter*, i.e., the nearer. **Celui-là, celle-là, celles-là, ceux-là** are equivalent to *the former*.

Victor Hugo et Sainte-Beuve sont de célèbres écrivains du dix-neuvième siècle; celui-ci était un critique, celui-là, un poète. *Victor Hugo and Sainte-Beuve are famous writers of the nineteenth century; the former was a poet, the latter, a critic.*

ce + être

C. The use of **ce,** of things, as subject of **être** (or **devoir, pouvoir,** plus **être**) followed by an adjective or a phrase.

1. *It* or *that,* plus the verb *to be* and an adjective, is translated by **ce** when it refers to an idea. §§ 209, 210

Je vous ai prévenu, n'est-ce pas? Oui, c'est vrai. *I notified you, didn't I? Yes, that's true.*

Il travaille nuit et jour à sa thèse. Ce doit être bien fatigant (ça). *Day and night he works on his thesis. That must be very tiring.*

2. When the antecedent is a definite object, **il** or **elle** generally replaces **ce** as subject of **être** followed by an adjective. When the location of a definite object is given, only **il**(s) or **elle**(s) may be used. §§ 211, 212

Comment trouvez-vous mon chapeau? Il est très joli. *How do you like my hat? It's very pretty.*

Où est mon mouchoir? Il est dans votre tiroir. *Where is my handkerchief? It's in your drawer.*

Ce is sometimes used, however, even when the predicate adjective refers to a definite object. This use is especially frequent when there is a question of identification.

Tiens! c'est la première fois que je vois ce petit chapeau. C'est nouveau? Oui, je l'ai acheté hier chez Françoise.[1]

---

[1] Adapted from *Les Noces d'argent,* by Paul Géraldy.

Il est très joli. Well, this is the first time I have seen that little hat. Is it new? Yes, I bought it yesterday at Fran-çoise's. It's very pretty.

When the verb (**être,** plus an adjective) is plural, **ils** or **elles must be** used, as the predicate adjective modifying **ce** can be only masculine singular.

> Comment trouvez-vous mes robes? Elles sont très belles. *How do you like my dresses? They are (very) beautiful.*

Ce followed by the verb **être** and an adjective cannot ordinarily stand for a person.

D. The use of **ce** for persons or things, as subjects of **être** (or **devoir, pouvoir,** plus **être**) when followed by a noun or pronoun.

1. *It* as subject of the verb *to be,* followed by a predicate noun referring to a person or thing, or by a pronoun, is expressed by **ce.**

> Qui est à la porte? C'est une petite fille qui a sonné. *Who is at the door? It's a little girl who rang the bell.*
> C'est mon meilleur dictionnaire que je vous ai prêté. *It's my best dictionary that I lent you.*
> Qui est-ce? C'est moi. C'est vous. Ce sont eux. Ce ne peut être que lui. *Who is it? It's I, you, they. It can be only he.*
> Il y a quelqu'un à la porte. Ce doit être votre ami. *There is someone at the door. It must be your friend.*

2. *He, she, they* as subject of the verb *to be* plus a predicate nominative are translated by **il, elle, ils, elles,** or by **ce.** §§ 213, 214

a. The personal pronouns are used when the predicate nominative is unmodified or when the modifier forms a unit with the predicate noun.

> Il est médecin. *He is a doctor.*
> Elle est religieuse. *She is a nun.*
> Il est beau garçon. *He is a handsome man.*
> Ils sont bons catholiques. *They are good Catholics.*

128

b. If the predicate nominative is modified (by an article, an adjective, or a clause), **ce** is regularly used as the subject.

C'est un médecin (célèbre). *He is a (famous) doctor.*
Ce sont des religieuses. *They are nuns.*
Ce sont de beaux garçons. *They are handsome men.*
C'est un jeune homme qui a bien réussi dans sa carrière.
　He's a young man who has been quite successful in his career.
C'est le meilleur avocat que je connaisse. *He is the best lawyer
　I know.*

c. In indirect discourse, when the subject of the main clause is the same as that of the subordinate clause, the personal pronoun must be used.

Il dit qu'il est votre ami. *He says that he is your friend.*

In: **Il dit que c'est votre ami,** the ever-present demonstrative value of **ce** would indicate a change of subject.

Il dit que c'est votre ami (qui a fait cela). *He says that it
　was your friend (who did that).*

The general rules given above for the use of **ce** and **il** are true in principle. Exceptions to them, however, are not infrequent even in the works of the best writers.

3. When the predicate nominative precedes the real subject, the verb *to be* is regularly preceded by **ce.**

Sa meilleure qualité, c'est la loyauté. *His best quality is
　loyalty.*
Celui à qui je parlais, c'était mon professeur de français.
　The one to whom I was talking was my French professor.
Son principal défaut, c'était de priser. *His chief fault was
　taking snuff.*
Ce que j'aime en elle, c'est qu'elle ne se vante jamais. *What
　I like about her is that she never boasts.*

76 Additional Indefinites

Anyone, meaning *anyone whatsoever*, is translated by **n'importe qui.**　　　　　　　　　　　　　　　　　　　§ 215

N'importe qui aurait fait la même chose. *Anyone would
have done the same thing.*

Adressez-vous à n'importe qui. *Apply to anyone.*

Any one, meaning *it doesn't matter which one*, is trans
by **n'importe lequel (laquelle)**.

Laquelle dois-je prendre? N'importe laquelle. *Wh
should I take? Any one (It doesn't matter).*

Lequel dois-je inviter? N'importe lequel. *Which one
I invite? It doesn't matter.*

Anything, equivalent to *anything whatsoever*, may be
lated by **n'importe quoi**.

Il a dit qu'il accepterait n'importe quoi. *He said t
would accept anything.*

The adjective *any*, equivalent to *any . . . whatsoever*, may
be translated by **n'importe quel**.

N'importe quel Français aurait fait la même chose. *Any
Frenchman would have done the same thing.*

EXERCISES

I. VERBS TO REVIEW:

dormir, s'endormir, cueillir.

II. IDIOMATIC EXPRESSIONS:

dormir debout, *to be very tired, to sleep standing up*
avoir l'oreille dure, *to be hard of hearing*
savoir vivre, *to be sophisticated, to have good manners*
le savoir-vivre, *sophistication, good manners*
le savoir-faire, *cleverness, ability to succeed in what one under-
takes* (frequently derogatory)
apprendre à vivre à quelqu'un, *to teach one how to act* (by cor-
rective punishment, etc.), *to give one a lesson in manners*
vivre de ses rentes, *to live on one's income*
entre la vie et la mort, *at death's door*
faire le mort, *to be dummy* (at cards)
donner les cartes, *to deal the cards*
Qu'est-ce que cela me fait? *What does that matter to me?*

Que voulez-vous que j'y fasse? *What do you expect me to do about it?*

laisser faire, *not to interfere with, to let (one) have one's way.*

faire (la) queue, *to stand in line.*

III. SENTENCES FOR TRANSLATION:

1. Are you tired? Yes, I'm very tired (I'm asleep standing up).
This is no time to go to sleep. 2. You are right. If I should go
to sleep now, my wife would not fail to *give* me a lesson in manners.
3. What did the woman say? I'm a little hard of hearing, you
know. 4. She said that, in order to succeed in this world, cleverness is as necessary as good manners (it takes as much cleverness
as good manners). Well, what do you expect me to do about it?
5. Who is that old gentleman who is dealing the cards? He's a
former banker who has retired from business and is living on
his income.

6. And that tall young man who is "dummy," do you know
him? Do I know him (If I know him)? I should say I do know
him. He's a doctor. At least, he told me that he was a doctor.
7. And that tall old man with a gray beard who has just picked
up his hand? Ah, that's one I don't know (that one, I don't
know him). He must be some professor or other. 8. I'm going
to have to stand in line for at least a half-hour. Well, what's
that to me? 9. There he comes. What must I tell him? Tell
him any old thing. 10. You are certainly not hard to please.
In fact, your principal fault is indifference.

11. Any fool could have told you that. Really? In that case,
I'm surprised (*Cela m'étonne*) that you didn't tell me (it).
12. Someone is knocking at the door. Go (2nd pers. sing.) see who it
is. I think it's the milkman. It can't be the milkman. He never
comes by (*passer*) before noon. 13. Here are your suitcases.
All right (*Bon*). But where are my brother's? I don't know
(*Je n'en sais rien*). Ask (*à*) the concierge. He is the one who
brought them up. 14. Although Jeanne and Louise are twin
sisters, they don't look at all alike. The former is very pretty,
the latter is frightfully ugly. 15. Someone must have informed
the police. Very likely (*Sans doute*). It seems (*Il paraît*) that it's
your very (*bien*) dear friend, Jules Leblanc, who let the cat out
of the bag.

131

16. If I had let the doctors have their way, you would have been dead long ago. 17. You didn't sell my old blue suit to that beggar, did you? 18. No, I couldn't sell that one (That one, I couldn't sell it); I had to give it to him. 19. Is Maurice sick? Is he sick? Why, he's been at death's door for two days. The doctors have given him up. 20. What's that? An airplane? No, it's Daddy (*papa*). He goes to sleep every evening in his armchair.

s'il →
depuis

21. To whom do you want me to put this question? It's all the same to me. Ask (*la*) anyone. 22. In that case, I'm going to ask *you*. Do you think you can answer it? 23. I don't know. It's always easier to ask questions than to answer them. 24. Where are my new (*neuf* after the noun) gloves? They are in the top (*premier*) drawer of the chiffonnier. 25. Which one of these rackets do you want? Any one. Take this one. I think it's the best. It's too heavy. I'll take yours.

IV. DRILL: Translate the words in parentheses:

ce crayon et ce stylo   *ces crayons*

1. (*This pencil and pen*) sont à moi. A qui sont (*those pencils*)?
(*Those*) sont à vous. 2. (*Does it give you pleasure*) de tourner un élève en ridicule? 3. Mais oui, (*anyone*) ferait la même chose.
4. Voyez-vous ce petit chapeau vert là-bas dans le coin? Oui, (*it is very pretty*), ne trouvez-vous pas? 5. Je ne trouve pas mes chaussettes. (*They are on the bed.*)

C'est →   *Elles sont sur le lit.*

6. Comment trouvez-vous les fleurs qu'il m'a envoyées? (*They are exquisite.*) 7. Il m'a demandé de lui prêter une grammaire. (*Is this the one he wants? Yes, it must be that one.*) 8. Est-il communiste? Non, (*he's a conservative and a good Catholic*). 9. Il est avocat, n'est-ce pas? Oui, (*he's a very famous lawyer*). 10. Il y a un jeune homme à la porte qui dit (*that he is your son*)

Il doit être fou.   *qu' il est votre fils* C'est

11. (*He must be crazy.*) Je n'ai pas de fils. (*That's what I told him.*) 12. Qui m'a envoyé ces fleurs? (*I think it was [est] your son-in-law.*) 13. Ce que j'aime en lui (*is that he never forgets his mother-in-law*). 14. Je dors debout. (*I've been standing in line for an hour and a half.*) 15. (*What do you want me to do about it?*)
Tout ce que je veux (*is that you do not interfere* [1] *with me*).

---

[1] Use subjunctive.

Je crois que c'est votre

132

V. Verb Exercise:

A. Rewrite the following sentences, using a plural verb:

1. Il dort toute la nuit. 2. Je m'endors de bonne heure.
3. Cueille les fleurs! 4. L'officier s'endormit. 5. Dors-tu, mon enfant?

B. Rewrite the following sentences, using a singular verb:

1. Il faut que nous dormions huit heures. 2. Si vous vous endormiez, vous manqueriez le train. 3. Ils cueilleront les fleurs demain. 4. Quand se sont-ils endormis? 5. C'est dommage que vous ayez cueilli toutes les fleurs.

C. Translate:

1. Let's go to sleep. 2. Don't sleep. 3. Would he sleep? 4. While picking . . . 5. She has gone to sleep. 6. After picking . . . 7. He had slept. 8. You (*Tu*) were sleeping. 9. They were gathering flowers. 10. I am very tired.

XVII.

Use of the indefinite *autre*

77 Relative Pronouns.

A. The relative pronoun agrees with its antecedent in gender, number, and person.

> C'est vous qui avez dit cela. *It's you who said that.*

B. In French, the relative pronoun is never omitted.

> La jeune fille que j'ai connue... *The girl (that) I knew...*
> §§ 216, 217
> La dame à qui j'ai parlé... *The lady (that) I spoke to...*

lequel; dont

C. The forms **lequel, lesquels,** etc., which refer usually to things but sometimes to persons, must have a definite antecedent and are regularly used as the object of a preposition.
§§ 218, 219

---

[1] Cf. § 243 for forms of pronouns.

134

Voilà les outils avec lesquels il a construit le modèle. *There are the tools with which he built the model.*

Duquel, de qui are regularly replaced in modern French by **dont**.

Voilà le vieillard dont je vous ai parlé. *There is the old man I spoke to you about.*

C'est justement ce dont j'ai besoin. *That's exactly what I need.*

Je connais les élèves dont vous vous moquiez tout à l'heure. *I know the pupils you were making fun of just now.*

La femme dont je soigne le fils m'a déjà téléphoné trois fois. *The lady whose son I'm taking care of has already telephoned me three times.*

La femme dont le fils vient d'être opéré est dans la salle d'attente. *The lady whose son has just been operated on is in the waiting room.*

Note that the direct object modified by **dont** must follow the verb (Example 4). When the word modified by *whose* or *of which* is the object of a preposition, the relative must be translated by the appropriate form of **lequel,** or **qui,** and *not* by **dont.** The translation should be made by **qui,** less frequently **lequel,** etc., of persons, and by **lequel,** etc., of things. This construction is generally avoided in spoken French by recasting the sentence.

La femme au fils de qui j'étais en train de parler a été tuée dans un accident d'auto. *The woman to whose son I was talking was killed in an automobile accident.*

Cette femme — c'est à son fils que j'étais en train de parler — a été tuée dans un accident d'auto. *That woman — it was to her son that I was talking — was killed in an automobile accident.*

De la maison sur le balcon de laquelle nous étions assis, on voyait tout ce qui se passait dans la rue. *From the house, on the balcony of which we were sitting, one could see everything that was going on in the street.*

Nous étions assis sur le balcon de la maison. De là, on voyait tout ce qui se passait dans la rue. *We were sitting on the balcony of the house. From there, one could see everything that was going on in the street.*

Although **lequel, lesquels,** etc., are used in formal style as subject and direct object to prevent ambiguity, this construction is generally avoided in ordinary familiar spoken and written French.

> L'auteur de cette proposition de loi, laquelle n'a jamais reçu l'approbation de la Chambre, vient d'être nommé chef de bureau. *The author of this bill, which has never received the approval of the House, has just been named head of a department.*

quoi, ce qui, ce que

D. Quoi, ce qui, ce que.

1. In modern French, the relative **quoi** is regularly used only as the object of a preposition other than **de.** It is generally used with a neuter antecedent. The antecedent may be understood. **De quoi** is generally replaced by **dont** except in certain fixed expressions. § 220

> Vous croyez qu'il sera nommé? C'est en quoi vous vous trompez. *You think he will be appointed? In that you're mistaken.*
> Ce à quoi je pense ... *What I'm thinking of ...*
> Ce sur quoi il frappe ... *What he is knocking on ...*
> Ce à quoi il faut résister ... *What you must resist ...*
> Ce contre quoi il a parlé ... *What he talked against ...*
> Ce dont vous avez besoin ... *What you need ...*
> Vous travaillerez tant que vous pourrez. Faute de quoi vous ne réussirez pas. *You will work as much as you can. If you don't, you will not succeed.*
> Son adversaire commença à le combler d'injures. Sur quoi il se retira doucement. *His adversary began to overwhelm him with insults. Whereupon he withdrew quietly.*

2. The compound English relative *what* is translated in French by **ce qui** and **ce que. Ce qui,** equivalent to *that which,* is used when *which* is the subject of the verb, **ce que** when *which* is the direct object of the verb.

> Dites-moi ce qui vous amuse. *Tell me what amuses you.*
> Ce que je n'aime pas, c'est que vous fumez trop. *What I don't like is that you smoke too much.*

78 Use of the Indefinite *autre*.

A. Autre and **autrui.** **Autre**(s) is used as an adjective and pronoun with the meaning of *other, others, another*, etc. **Autrui** (*others, other people*) is almost never used except as the object of a preposition and then only in literary language.

> Donnez-moi un autre stylo. *Give me another fountain pen.*
> Avez-vous d'autres raisons? *Have you other reasons?*
> Il ne faut pas prendre (le bien d'autrui) le bien des autres.
>   *You must not take what belongs to others* (lit., *the property of others*).

When the pronoun **autre** is the direct object, predicate nominative, or the real subject of an impersonal verb, **en** must be used before the verb.

> J'en ai trouvé d'autres. *I have found others.*
> J'en ai deux autres. *I have two others.*
> J'en suis un autre. *I am another.*
> Il y en a d'autres. *There are others.*

When the pronoun **autre** is the object of a preposition, no **en,** of course, is used.

> Je l'ai demandé à d'autres. *I asked others for it.*
> Je l'ai demandé à quelques autres. *I asked a few others for it.*
> Il s'agit d'un autre. *It is a question of another.*

When there is a contrast, expressed or implied, the first and second person plural pronouns are frequently followed by **autres.**

> Nous autres Américains (nous) avons la passion des sports.
>   *We Americans are passionately fond of sports.*   § 221

When the indefinite adjective *another* has the meaning of simply *an additional,* it is regularly translated by **encore** plus the indefinite article. When it means *different*, it is translated by **un autre,** or, **une autre.**

> Donnez-moi encore un verre de vin. *Give me another glass of wine.*
> Je vais mettre une autre robe. Celle-ci est déchirée. *I am going to put on another dress. This one is torn.*   § 222

137

l'un . . . l'autre

B. L'un . . . l'autre, les uns . . . les autres.

Les uns le félicitaient, les autres le sifflaient. *Some were congratulating him, others were hissing him.*

Ils ont besoin les uns des autres. *They need one another.*

§ 223

Elles étaient fières l'une de l'autre (les unes des autres). *They were proud of each other.* § 224

L'un et l'autre s'emploient. *Both are used.*

L'un et l'autre viendront, *or, more commonly:* Ils viendront l'un et l'autre. *Both will come.*

Je les ai salués l'un et l'autre. *I greeted them both.*

Il (leur) a répondu à l'un et à l'autre. *He answered both.*

§§ 225, 226

Il s'est moqúe de l'un et de l'autre. *He made fun of both.*

L'un et l'autre as subject, direct object, or indirect object is less frequent than **tous les deux, les deux,** etc. Cf. § 36 D.

C. Ni l'un ni l'autre may be used as subject, direct object, indirect object, or object of a preposition.

Ni l'un ni l'autre ne se marieront (*preferably:* Ils ne se marieront ni l'un ni l'autre). *Neither one will get married.*

Je n'ai vu ni l'un ni l'autre. *I saw neither one.*

Je n'ai répondu ni à l'un ni à l'autre. *I answered neither one.*

When **l'un** and **l'autre** of **ni l'un ni l'autre** are mutually exclusive, this expression is followed by a singular verb.

Ni l'un ni l'autre ne l'épousera. *Neither one will marry her.*

EXERCISES

I. VERBS TO REVIEW:

construire, acquérir

II. IDIOMATIC EXPRESSIONS:

l'un près de l'autre, *near each other*
tout près l'un de l'autre, *quite near each other*

138

weak

Il n'y a pas de quoi. *Not at all. Don't mention it. You're welcome.*

De rien. *Not at all. You're welcome.*

Il me faut de quoi écrire. *I need something to write with (writing materials).*

de temps à autre, *from time to time* (or: de temps en temps)
faute de, *for lack of*
il s'agit de . . ., *it is a question of . . .*
répondre de, *to answer for, to be responsible for*
marier, *to marry (to perform the ceremony, to marry off)*
se marier, *to get married*
se marier avec (épouser), *to marry (to take as husband or wife)*

III. Sentences for Translation:

1. The tales we are reading are those we are concerned with (it's a question of) in our literature course. 2. The two boys sat down near each other in order better to examine the map they had just received. 3. If you want her to write the letter, she must have something to write with. 4. He promised to do his best to help us. For lack of something better, I accepted his proposition. 5. The minister who married them is the man we were talking about just now.

avoir fait l'impasse ← or p

6. What he is ashamed of, is of not having finessed. 7. Which of these dresses should I put on? Neither one. They are both too dressy for such a simple occasion. 8. The author whose book has just appeared is the best-known French novelist. 9. We Americans are not very clever at foreign languages, a fact which often discommodes us in our traveling abroad. 10. I have seen his hotel, the façade of which he has reconstructed. I'm no longer satisfied with our plans.

11. It is only in the old quarter that houses are quite close together; in the other sections and in the suburbs, all the houses are surrounded by gardens. 12. I'm very thirsty. Will you give me another cup of tea? Of course; and do you want some sugar? Thank you very much. Not at all. 13. You will have to buy another dress for Mary. She will never consent to wear that one, since it is exactly like her sister's. 14. From time to time the town has acquired citizens who resist all progress. 15. They say that Mrs. Leblanc is going to get married. Do you know if she is

139

going to marry that widower? No, it's another man, whom I do not know.

16. If you continue to resist the boss, I won't answer for him any longer. 17. If you had to choose between these two expressions, which one would you use? It doesn't matter which one, since both are used. 18. Although the whole audience approved of the overture, at the end of the first act some applauded and others hissed the opera. 19. I am very sorry that neither one has accepted my invitation. I should have liked to see them both again. 20. What could I do? I need something to live on; so I accepted the first job that presented itself.

21. So you have dismissed your cook? Yes, it wasn't a question of her cooking, for she was a first-rate cook. She was simply too wasteful. 22. If he should acquire that castle, would he consent to leaving it in its present condition? 23. I doubt it. It's quite possible that he will have it done over completely and even that he will add a wing. 24. All that you say is true; but I still fear that he will not succeed in his undertaking. 25. It may be that she has announced her marriage to her intimate friends.

IV. DRILL: Translate the words in parentheses:

1. Si mes deux frères demeuraient (*quite near each other*), ils se verraient plus souvent. 2. La dame (*I spoke to*) est celle qui (*is going to get married*). 3. (*What he is thinking of*) c'est qu'il doit (*answer for*) la loyauté de son ami. 4. Je vous remercie mille fois de toute votre bonté. Mais, (*you're welcome*), mademoiselle. 5. Lequel de ces messieurs (*is going to marry*) votre sœur? (*Neither one.*) 6. C'est là une idée (*about which he is very emphatic*). Use insister sur. 7. Quand je les ai vus, (*they were congratulating each other*). 8. Ce sont de drôles de gens. (*They are always making fun of each other.*) 9. Vous m'avez donné précisément (*what I need*). 10. Savez-vous (*what*) m'amène ici? Oui, vous voulez savoir (*what*) Jean m'a dit l'autre soir.

11. Voilà la montagne (*at the foot of which*) on a trouvé le cadavre. 12. C'est une histoire (*of which I don't know the first word*). 13. Ce ne sont pas les ouvriers (*who build*) les maisons (*who acquire*) les grandes fortunes.

140

V. VERB EXERCISE:

A. Rewrite the following sentences, placing the verbs in the singular and the plural of the imperative.

1. Tu ne construis pas la maison. 2. Tu la construis. 3. Acquérez-vous la pharmacie? 4. Vous n'acquérez pas le piano.

B. Rewrite the following sentences, placing the verbs in the other simple tenses of the indicative.

1. Nous acquérions le camion. 2. Tu construis la phrase. 3. Il acquerra de la gloire. 4. Que construisit-on?

C. Translate:

1. He had acquired. 2. We had built. 3. They would acquire. 4. While constructing... 5. We acquired (*past def.*). 6. It is important that he acquire that castle. 7. It is a pity that they will not build the house.

à quoi pense-t-il
what is he thinking of?

mad-moi-sel

necessary
what
besoin ou ce qu'il me faut

XVIII. INTERROGATIVES: PRONOUNS & ADJECTIVES

Interrogative word order

79 Interrogative Pronouns and Adjectives.[1]

qui?

A. Qui is used of persons both as subject and object of a verb, and as the object of a preposition, in both direct and indirect interrogation.

Qui va là? *Who goes there?*
Qui avez-vous vu? *Whom have you seen?*
De qui est-il le fils? *Whose son is he?*
Il m'a demandé qui serait là. *He asked me who would be there.*
Il m'a demandé qui j'avais vu. *He asked me whom I had seen.*
Il m'a demandé à qui j'avais parlé. *He asked me to whom I had spoken.*
Savez-vous qui sont ces gens-là? *Do you know who those people are?* (Note inverted order.)

[1] Cf. § 244 for list of interrogatives.

142

que? qu'est-ce qui?

B. Que [1] is used of things as <u>the object of a verb, as a</u>
<u>predicate nominative,</u> and as <u>the logical subject of certain</u>
<u>impersonal verbs.</u>   *What,* as the subject of other verbs, is
expressed by **Qu'est-ce qui.**   The form with **est-ce que,**
except in the case of *qu'est-ce qui,* is more colloquial than the
short one.   § 227

Qu'avez-vous vu ?   Qu'est-ce que vous avez vu ?   *What have*
  you seen?
Que pense-t-il de votre situation ?   Qu'est-ce qu'il pense de
  votre situation ?   *What does he think of your situation?*
Qu'est-il devenu ?   Qu'est-ce qu'il est devenu ?   *What has*
  become of him?
Que vous faut-il ?   Qu'est-ce qu'il vous faut ?   *What do you*
  need?
Qu'en reste-t-il ?   Qu'est-ce qui en reste ?   *What is left?*
Qu'arrive-t-il ?   Qu'est-ce qui arrive ?   *What is happening?*
Qu'est-ce qui vous amène ici ?   *What brings you here?*   § 228

qu'est-ce que?

What in asking for a definition or a detailed explanation
is translated by **Qu'est-ce que,** or, more familiarly, by
Qu'est-ce que c'est que.

<u>Qu'est-ce que (c'est que) la philosophie ?</u>   *What is philosophy?*
<u>Qu'est-ce que (c'est que) ce livre-là ?</u>   *What is that book?*
Cf.: Je ne sais pas ce que c'est que la philosophie.   Je ne sais pas
  ce qu'est la philosophie.   *I don't know what philosophy is.*

Note that **que** is never used as the object of a preposition.

quel?

C. Quel.   The interrogative adjective *what* is **quel** in direct
and indirect interrogation.

Quel âge avez-vous ?   *How old are you?*
Dites-moi quel âge vous avez.   *Tell me how old you are.*

---

[1] The pronoun *what* (*that which*) in indirect interrogation is regularly
translated in the same manner as the relative *what.* Cf. § 76.

*Il m'a demandé ce que c'était que la
philosophie.   He asked me what philosophy was.
Memorize this !*

A quelle heure arrive-t-il? *When (At what hour) does he arrive?*

Dites-moi à quelle heure il arrivera. *Tell me when he arrives.*

The pronoun *what*, as subject of the verb *to be*, when no definition or detailed information is asked, is expressed by **quel.**[1]

Quel est ce livre? (i.e., Quel livre est ce livre?) C'est le livre que vous m'avez prêté. *What is this book? It's the book you lent me.* § 229

Je vois des livres nouveaux sur le bureau. Quels sont-ils? (*equivalent to:* Quels livres sont-ils?) *I see some new books on the desk. What are they?*

Quel is also used as the equivalent of *who*.[2]

Quel est cet homme? *Who is that man?*

quoi?

D. Quoi. The pronoun **quoi** (*what*) is used in elliptical expressions when <u>no verb is expressed</u>, and <u>as the object of a preposition</u> when no definite word is referred to, in both direct and indirect interrogation.

Quoi de nouveau? *What's new?*

Quoi de plus agréable? *What's more agreeable?*

A quoi bon? *What's the use?*

A quoi pensez-vous? *What are you thinking of?*

Savez-vous de quoi il a parlé? *Do you know what he talked about?*

Je lui ai demandé sur quoi il fondait ses espérances. *I asked him what he based his hopes on.* § 230

---

[1] In familiar French, **Qu'est-ce que c'est que** is frequently used in place of **Quel.**

[2] Generally, when it is a question of ascertaining the identity of a *person*, either **qui** or **quel** may be used with the verb **être.** If the subject is a personal pronoun, or the demonstrative **ce,** however, **quel** should not be so used.

Qui (Quel) est cet homme? *Who is that man?*

Qui êtes-vous? Qui suis-je? Qui est-ce? *Who are you? Who am I? Who is it?*

In certain cases, **quel** retains the meaning of its Latin ancestor, **qualis.**

Quel homme est-ce? *What sort of man is he?*

144

lequel?

E. Lequel. In direct and indirect interrogation, the pronoun **lequel** is used as subject or object, or object of a preposition when there is a comparison between two or more persons or things, i.e., with the meaning *which one.*

> Laquelle des deux femmes préférez-vous? *Which of the two women do you prefer?*
>
> De laquelle votre ami voulait-il parler? *Which one did your friend want to talk about?*
>
> Lequel de vos amis n'est pas arrivé? *Which one of your friends did not come?*
>
> Lequel aimez-vous mieux? *Which one do you prefer (like better)?*
>
> Lequel aimez-vous le mieux? *Which one do you prefer (like the best)?*
>
> Il m'a demandé lequel je préférais. *He asked me which one I preferred.*
>
> Il m'a demandé auquel je pensais. *He asked me which one I was thinking of.*

80 Interrogative Word Order.

Regular Order; Order with "Quel"

A. When the subject is a noun, or a pronoun other than a personal or interrogative pronoun, the regular order is: noun or pronoun, verb, personal pronoun. This order is obligatory: 1. when there is no interrogative word; 2. when the interrogative **pourquoi** is used; 3. regularly when the verb has a complement, or when a compound tense is used. When the complement is modified by **quel,** simple inverted order *may* be used provided there is no ambiguity. If there is a direct object not modified by **quel,** however, the order must be that of the eighth example.

> Les élèves sont-ils arrivés en retard? *Did the pupils come late?*
>
> Les vôtres sont-ils déjà dans la salle? *Are yours already in the room?*
>
> Cela vous convient-il? *Does that suit you?*

Pourquoi votre petit garçon ne reste-t-il pas tranquille? *Why doesn't your little boy sit still (stay quiet)?*

Combien votre frère a-t-il payé ces livres? *How much did your brother pay for these books?*

Comment les étudiants peuvent-ils consacrer tant de temps aux sports? *How can the students devote so much time to sports?*

Quand vos parents vont-ils à la campagne? *When are your parents going to the country?*

Chez quelle modiste la dame a-t-elle acheté son chapeau? *At what milliner's did the lady buy her hat?*

Quel âge a votre père? *How old is your father?*

Quelle influence exerça en Europe la littérature française? *What influence did French literature have in Europe?*

A quel étage est la salle à manger? *On what floor is the dining room?*

Inversion versus Regular Order

B. Except in the cases mentioned in **A, 3,** simple inversion is frequently used when the question is introduced by the interrogative words **comment** and **combien.**

Comment va ton frère? (*instead of* Comment ton frère va-t-il?) *How is your brother?*

Combien vaut ce billet? (*instead of* Combien ce billet vaut-il?) *How much does this ticket cost?*

Similarly, such inversion may be used after **où,** and, less frequently, after **quand.** When a compound tense is used, this order seems permissible only with an intransitive verb conjugated with **être.**

Où habite votre ami? *Where does your friend live?*

Quand part votre train? (*or, better:* Quand votre train part-il?) *When does your train leave?*

Interrogations with **qui** and **que** are expressed thus:

Qui est venu? (*colloquially:* Qui est-ce qui est venu?) *Who came?*

Qui êtes-vous? *Who are you?*

Qui sont ces gens-là? *Who are those people?*

Qui demande votre père ? (*colloquially:* Qui est-ce qui demande votre père ?) *Who is asking for your father?*

Qui votre père demande-t-il ? (*colloquially:* Qui est-ce que votre père demande ?) *Whom is your father asking for?*

Que dit le professeur ? (*never:* Que le professeur dit-il ?) (*colloquially:* Qu'est-ce que dit le professeur ?) *What is the professor saying?*

Et le professeur, qu'en dit-il ? (*not infrequent in colloquial French*). *And what does the* professor *say about it?*

Que dit-il ? (*colloquially:* Qu'est-ce qu'il dit ?) *What does he say?*

Que signifie ce titre ? (*colloquially:* Qu'est-ce que ce titre signifie ?) *What does this title signify?*

est-ce que ?

C. Interrogation may always be expressed by **Est-ce que** with the declarative word order. This form of question is regularly employed in interrogations of the first person and is practically obligatory with the first person of the present tense, especially in the first conjugation. Fairly common monosyllabic exceptions are: **ai-je, suis-je, dis-je, puis-je, sais-je, dois-je,** and **vais-je.**   § 231

Est-ce que vos parents habitent la campagne ? *Do your parents live in the country?*

Est-ce que je ne pense pas à tout ? *Don't I think of everything?*

Est-ce que je dois (*or:* dois-je) mettre la table ? *Should I set the table?*

Est-ce que je peux (*or:* puis-je) partir ? *May I leave?*

Pourquoi [1] est-ce que votre ami est parti ? *Why did your friend leave?*

Où est-ce que votre père a trouvé cette gravure ? *Where did your father find this engraving?*

N'est-ce pas que vous avez dit cela ? *Didn't you say that?*

D. Questions are very frequently asked, especially in conversation, by *keeping the voice up* to the end of a declarative sentence.

---

[1] Except when the verb is in the first person, the combination of **est-ce que** and interrogative words such as **pourquoi, où, quand,** etc , is considered very colloquial. It may be added that in general **est-ce que** is most frequent in informal style.

Vous descendez, madame? *Are you getting off, madame?*
Vous n'avez pas deux sous, madame? *Haven't you two sous, madame?*
Vous avez fini votre devoir? *Have you finished your exercise?*
Votre ami est parti? *Has your friend left?*

E. The interrogative word order is obligatory in interjected remarks, in direct quotation, and is regularly used when certain adverbs or conjunctive adverbs such as **peut-être, sans doute, à peine, aussi, encore,** etc., stand at the beginning of the sentence.[1]

Le coût de la vie, dit-on (m'a-t-on dit), a quadruplé. *The cost of living, they say (I've been told), has quadrupled.*

— Vous n'avez pas deux sous? me demanda le receveur. *"Haven't you two sous?" the conductor asked me.*

A peine avions-nous le dos tourné, qu'il recommença de plus belle. *Hardly had we turned our backs, when he began again worse than ever.*

— Peut-être s'est-il trompé d'adresse, suggéra-t-elle. *"Perhaps he made a mistake in the address," she suggested.*

Sans doute est-il déjà parti. *He has doubtless already gone.*

Hier il a plu à verse. Aussi a-t-elle renoncé à sa promenade. *Yesterday it poured rain; so she gave up her walk.*

EXERCISES

I. VERBS TO REVIEW:

préférer,[2] **valoir**

II. IDIOMATIC EXPRESSIONS:

valoir mieux, *to be worth more, to be better*
tourner le dos à quelqu'un, *to turn one's back on someone*
faire une bêtise, des bêtises, *to do a stupid thing, stupid things*
dire des bêtises, *to say stupid things, to talk nonsense*

---

[1] **Peut-être que** and **sans doute que** are followed by normal order.
Peut-être qu'il s'est trompé d'adresse.
Sans doute qu'il est déjà parti.

[2] Cf. § 246 **E.**

148

se faire inscrire, *to register, to enroll (one's self)*
féliciter quelqu'un de quelque chose, *to congratulate someone on
    something*
recommencer de plus belle, *to begin again worse than ever*
de nouveau, *again*
Cela ne vaut pas la peine, ce n'est pas la peine. *It isn't worth
    the trouble, it isn't worth while.*
coûter les yeux de la tête à quelqu'un, *to cost one a pretty penny,
    no end of money*

III. SENTENCES FOR TRANSLATION:

1. "Who lives next door to you?" the policeman asked. "On which
side," I asked. "On the right." 2. I don't know. It would be
better to ask my son who knows all my neighbors. 3. What
happened when she asked you who had told you that? 4. What
is that thingumagig (*ce machin-là*)? It is a little gadget to open
canned goods. 5. What is the use of gathering information if there
is no longer any means of transmitting it to the general staff?

6. Do you know whom I saw yesterday at Mme Leblanc's? No.
Well, it was that woman who said so many stupid things at the
last meeting of our club. 7. That one? You don't mean it. How
does it happen that she was (Use perfect subjunctive.) among the
guests? 8. Why do you ask me what an instrument board
(*planche de bord*) is? I know nothing about it. 9. You say that
he has done something stupid? Don't scold him! It isn't worth
the trouble. He will begin again worse than ever. 10. Which is
the book you told me about? Is it one of these?

11. How much did your father pay for that car? That make, they
say, costs (you) no end of money. 12. How old is your grandmother? She must be at least eighty years old, for she was born
during the Civil War. 13. Why does that little girl turn her
back to the maid? She is ashamed, or else she is angry. 14. Do
John's parents congratulate him on the good marks he gets?
15. Good morning, Mrs. Leblanc. How are you? Very well,
thank you. And how is Mr. Leblanc? I was told that he had hurt
himself last week when he fell.

16. When does the train leave for New York? Every morning at
a quarter past eleven. 17. Where do students register if they
plan to attend summer school? 18. Whom should I ask for when

j'irais

I go to the information bureau? I should prefer to speak to a friend of yours. 19. Don't I live in the country? Why can't I use my car to go to work? 20. I don't understand why he hasn't come (*arriver*) yet. Perhaps he made a mistake in the hour of the meeting.

21. The bus had hardly stopped when *qu'il* he said to me: "Are you getting off, sir?" (Do not invert.) 22. Which one of his novels do you like best? I hadn't thought of that; but I believe that it's the one which has just come out. 23. Undoubtedly he is "well up on" linguistics. However, unless his students understand philology, do they know what he is talking about? 24. What can (*pouvoir bien*) be amusing her? I hear her burst out laughing every ten minutes. 25. Tell me when she arrives and I shall tell you where she's coming from.

IV. DRILL: Translate the words in parentheses:

1. Bien qu'il (*registers*) dans toutes les agences de placement, il ne trouve pas d'emploi à son goût. 2. (*What is electricity?*) Ce n'est pas à moi qu'il faut poser cette question. (*It would be better*) la poser à mon frère (*who knows all about it*). 3. Elle m'a demandé (*who that lady was*) et j'ai dû lui demander (*which one*) elle voulait dire. 4. Savez-vous (*what that man is talking about?*) (*Whom*) voulez-vous dire? 5. Elle se demandait (*what had become of me*) quand je suis arrivée.

6. (*What is that dress on the bed?*) C'est celle que j'ai achetée l'autre jour quand je suis allée (*to town*). 7. Dites-moi (*how old your sister [1] is*). (*She looks so bad*) qu'on dirait qu'elle est très âgée. 8. C'est un scélérat invétéré. A peine (*has he come out of prison*) qu'il est condamné (*again*). 9. (*What did he ask you?*) Il m'a demandé: ("*Why does your son always do stupid things?*") 10. (*What do you think of*) notre piano à queue? (*It must have cost you a pretty penny*.) Comment trouvez-vous

11. Toutes les fois que je commençais (*to congratulate him on his success, he would turn his back on me*). 12. Quand je lui ai demandé (*what he was thinking of*) il a commencé (*to talk nonsense*). 13. A peine étiez-vous parti, (*when he began to cry again worse than ever*). 14. Je lui ai demandé (*if I should go to see the dean*) et elle m'a

---

[1] Place subject after verb.

ce n'est pas la peine   Qu'est-ce qu'elle est devenue?

répondu que (*it wasn't worth while*).   15. (*What has become of her?*)
Je n'en sais rien.

V. Verb Exercise:

A. Give the first person singular and plural of all the simple tenses of the verb **préférer.**

B. Give the third person singular of the simple and compound tenses of the verb **valoir.**

Qu'est-ce que c'est que l'electricité (?)
il faudrait mieux (?)

indirect question — use ce que
direct   "   — use qu'est-ce que

Que vous a-t-il demandé?
pourquoi votre fils fait-il toujours des bêtise?

XIX.

REFLEXIVE VERBS
PASSIVE VOICE

Exclamations: *Que! Combien! Comme! Quel(le)!*

81 Exclamations.

que! comme! combien!

A. Exclamatory **Que! Comme! Combien!** In exclamations **que and comme** are regularly preferred to **combien**.[1] **Que** is limited to direct discourse in which it may be used adverbially or as subject or direct object. **Comme** is never followed by a noun complement. Only **combien** may be used as the object of a preposition.

> Qu'elle (Comme elle) est jolie! *How pretty she is!*
> Que de (Combien de) gens ont souffert à cause de lui! *How many people have suffered because of him!*

---

[1] Where no verb is present, **combien** must be used.
Combien précieuse! *How precious!*

Que d'argent vous avez gaspillé! *How much money you have wasted!*

A combien de gens il a porté malheur! *To how many persons he has brought misfortune!*

In indirect discourse only **comme** and **combien** (only **combien** after a preposition) may be used.

Vous ne savez pas comme (combien) vous lui manquez. *You do not know how much he misses you.*

Vous ne savez pas combien (comme) ce problème est difficile. *You do not know how difficult this problem is.* § 232

Si vous aviez su à combien de gens il avait dit cela! *If you had only known to how many people he had said that!*

quel!

B. Quel is used to express the English exclamatory *What a...!*

Quelle surprise! *What a surprise!*
Quelle bêtise! *What a stupid thing!*

82 Reflexive Verbs.

A. A reflexive verb is a verb that has a direct or an indirect object which is the same person as the subject. Some verbs, such as **s'écrier, se moquer, se souvenir,** are always reflexive. All transitive verbs and some intransitive verbs may become reflexive. Many French transitive verbs when used reflexively are equivalent to English intransitives, such as **s'ouvrir,** *to open,* **se fermer,** *to close,* **se noyer,** *to drown,*[1] etc.

Elle se promène tous les jours. *She takes a walk every day.*

Nous nous levons toujours de bonne heure. *We always get up early.*

Elle s'est procuré plusieurs exemplaires de ce livre. *She got herself several copies of this book.*

Elle s'est lavé les mains et la figure. *She washed her hands and face.*

---

[1] For the agreement of past participles, cf. Chapter II.

Elle s'est blessée à la main. *She hurt her hand.*
— Voilà mon ami, s'écria-t-il. *"There's my friend," he cried.*
Il ne se plaît pas ici. *He doesn't like it here.*

moi-même, lui-même

B. When the reflexive object is emphasized, the disjunctive pronoun with **même** follows the verb.

Il s'est inscrit lui-même. *He enrolled himself.*

l'un l'autre

C. The reciprocal pronoun is the same in form as the reflexive. If the sense does not make it clear that the pronoun used is reciprocal, **l'un l'autre, les uns les autres** may be added.

Elles se sont parlé pendant quelques instants. *They talked to each other for a few moments.*
Elles se sont félicitées les unes les autres. *They congratulated each other.*
Elles se plaisaient les unes aux autres. *They liked each other.*
Ils se souvenaient les uns des autres. *They remembered each other.*

83 The Passive Voice.

A. Formation. The passive voice is formed as in English by adding the past participle of the verb to the verb **être**.

Elle a été tuée sur le coup. *She was killed outright.*
Il a été blessé au pied. *He was wounded in the foot.*

B. Translation of *by* after a passive.

1. If there is any physical action or suggested physical action, literal or figurative, by the agent on the subject, the preposition *by* must be translated by **par**.

Le voleur a été vite entouré par les agents. *The thief was quickly surrounded by the policemen.*
Le chien fut suivi de près par le loup. *The dog was closely followed by the wolf.*

Les fenêtres étaient toujours fermées par la bonne. *The windows were always closed by the servant.*

Elle a été emportée par la grippe. *She was carried off by the grippe.*

2. If there is no physical action by the agent, the preposition **de** is frequently used. This is especially common when the verb *describes* a *state* which is habitual or permanent.

Elle est aimée de tout le monde. *She is loved by everyone.*

Le professeur est entouré de ses élèves. *The professor is surrounded by his pupils.*

La maison était entourée d'un jardin. *The house was surrounded by a garden.*

Elle était terrifiée des suites de cette affaire. *She was terrified by the consequences of that affair.*

Par, however, is generally used when the verb *narrates* a *specific action*, or when the agent is emphasized.

Elle a été terrifiée par l'explosion. *She was terrified by the explosion.*

Elle est aimée de tout le monde, même par sa belle-mère. *She is loved by everyone, even by her mother-in-law.*   § 233

There are certain cases in which either **de** or **par** may be used, but the modern tendency is toward the more frequent use of **par.**

84 Substitutes for the Passive.

A. The passive voice is not so frequently used in French as in English. It may be replaced by the reflexive, or by an active construction.

1. The reflexive construction is generally used to denote what is usual or customary, or what can or cannot be done.

Cela se dit un peu partout. *That is said almost everywhere.*

Cela ne se dit pas. *That is not said.*

Les appartements meublés se louent très cher. *Furnished apartments rent very high.*

Ce vin-là ne se sert jamais avec le poisson. *That wine is never served with fish.*

La langue maternelle ne s'oublie pas de si tôt. *One's mother tongue is not forgotten so quickly.*

Sa voix s'entendait à une lieue.[1] *His voice could be heard a mile away.*

a. The reflexive construction cannot be used if the active or actual agent is expressed. If **par** may be translated as *by means of, through (the medium of)*, the reflexive may be used.

> Cette décision a été prise par votre père. *Or:* C'est votre père qui a pris cette décision. (Reflexive construction not possible.) *This decision was made by your father.*
>
> Quelquefois *cela* se traduit par *this. Sometimes* cela *is translated by (means of) this.*
>
> Sa décision s'explique par son manque de caractère. *His decision is explained by his lack of character.*

2. The reflexive is also frequently used with a figurative subject to express one act.

> La livraison des marchandises s'était effectuée sans le moindre délai. *The delivery of the merchandise had been effected without the slightest delay.*
>
> Le problème s'est résolu d'une façon inattendue. *The problem was solved in an unexpected fashion.*

3. When the passive voice denotes one act on a concrete thing as subject, the passive is regularly replaced by **on** and the active voice.[2,3] This construction cannot be used when the agent is expressed with the passive.

> On lui a envoyé les livres. *The books were sent to him.*
>
> On a mis les lettres à la poste. *The letters were mailed.*

4. When the agent is expressed, English passives are frequently best translated by an active construction.

---

[1] In familiar French, **lieue** is frequently used with the indefinite meaning of *a great distance, a long way.*

[2] **On** may also be used in the cases mentioned in A 1 and 2.

> On ne dit pas cela. *That is not said.*
> On a résolu le problème. *The problem has been solved.*

[3] This rule does not apply to reflexive verbs which are equivalent to an English intransitive.

> La porte s'est ouverte. *The door opened (was opened).*

C'est la bonne qui ferme les fenêtres. *The windows are closed by the* maid.

C'est le professeur qui a résolu le problème. *The problem was solved by the* professor.

Le professeur a résolu le problème. *The problem was solved by the professor (The professor solved the problem).*

EXERCISES

I. VERBS TO REVIEW:

vêtir, suffire

II. IDIOMATIC EXPRESSIONS:

porter malheur à quelqu'un, *to bring bad luck to someone*
porter bonheur à quelqu'un, *to bring good luck to someone*
sur le coup, *outright, instantly*
dans un délai de, *in a period of*
{ dire des injures à quelqu'un, *to insult someone*
{ injurier quelqu'un, *to insult someone*
mettre une lettre à la poste, *to mail a letter*
Cela va sans dire. *That goes without saying.*
Cela m'est égal. *It's all the same to me.*
Cela ne fait rien. *That doesn't matter.*
Cela ne me regarde pas. *That's not my affair. That's not my business.*
se mêler de ses affaires, *to mind one's own business*

III. SENTENCES FOR TRANSLATION:

1. How much time you have wasted listening to the radio! Well, well, how nice you are! 2. You don't know how astonished I was (how that astonished me) to find him so affable. 3. What an imbecile! He asked that the work be finished within a period of two months. 4. Do those two women know each other? I should say so. They insulted each other yesterday for half an hour. 5. He said that he had got up early, that he had brushed his hair, and that he had washed his face and hands.

6. He was knocked down by a truck and instantly killed. 7. The professor was surrounded by a group of students who were con-

gratulating him on his promotion.   8. The professor was quickly surrounded by a crowd of angry students who would have done him bodily injury if the police had not kept them from it.   9. Do you want him to mail this letter?   It's all the same to me.   10. You mustn't insult your friends.   That isn't done.   Mind your own business.

11. Does he like it in Paris?   Oh yes, of course.   12. Who knocked over the bottle of ink?   The cat knocked it over (It is the cat who . . .).   13. Well, I'm not surprised.   I told you a black cat would bring you bad luck.   14. I was told that you didn't like cats.   That's true.   I don't like either cats or dogs.   That's quite evident.   15. Was that book sent you by a publishing house?   No, it was the author himself who made me a present of it.

16. We now have a siren, the shrill sound of which can be heard in all quarters of the town.   17. Fine!   At the time of the last black-out there were many people who did not hear the alarm (the alarm signal).   18. That man is admired by everyone, even by his employees.   19. Whom were they making fun of?   They were making fun of each other.   How stupid that is!   20. The door opens and then closes without anyone's being seen.

21. What happened then?   I don't know (*Je n'en sais rien*).   I must have fainted.   22. Perhaps it was just a draft.   No, all the windows had been closed by the maid and there wasn't a breath of air.   23. He injured his right foot when he fell from the ladder.   24. That isn't said.   That is said by some Frenchmen.   25. The fall of the cabinet is explained by the opposition of the radical-socialist party.   26. He spent five days on a raft without food or water.   "How he must have suffered!" she cried.

IV. DRILL: Translate the words in parentheses:

1. Si vous saviez (*how he had suffered*) vous auriez pitié de lui.
2. En France (*cigarettes are not sold*) dans les pharmacies.   3. Je lui ai demandé (*if she had washed her hands and face*).   4. Si je vous dis (*how much he likes it in Paris*) vous ne me croirez pas.   5. Sans le maître-nageur (*he would have drowned*).

6. La ville était entourée (*by a wall*).   7. Le tailleur (*was followed by*) sa femme et (*by*) ses filles.   8. (*She was followed*) jusque chez elle (*by a plain-clothes man*).   9. Elle a été réveillée au milieu de la

158

nuit (*by an unusual noise*).   10. Elle est adorée (*by all those*) qui
la connaissent.
11. Les lettres (*were mailed*) hier.   12. (*The American child is
seldom asked*) où il a été.   13. Si on lui demandait cela, il répondrait
probablement: "Mind your own business!"   14. Nous nous
sommes bien rencontrés, (*but we did not talk to each other*).   15. Ça
m'étonne.   J'aurais cru (*that you would have insulted each other*).

V. VERB EXERCISE:

A. Rewrite the following sentences, placing the verbs in the
past definite, the imperfect indicative, the conditional, and
the past indefinite.

1. Cela ne suffit pas.   2. On ne vêt pas les pauvres.[1]   3. Vous ne
vêtez pas l'enfant.   4. Cette somme ne suffit pas.   5. Nous ne
nous suffisons pas.

B. Place the expression **Je regrette que** before each of the
sentences in **A,** and make the necessary changes in the verb
forms.

[1] In informal language, **vêtir** is practically always replaced by **habiller.**

XX.

PRESENT PARTICIPLE
USE OF INFINITIVES

The infinitive as a noun; in comparisons; with *pour*; with modal auxiliaries

85 The Present Participle.

A. The present participle is used with **en** to express relationship of simultaneous time, means, condition, and with **même en** or **tout en,** concession. **Tout en** is also used with the participle to emphasize the idea of simultaneity. It cannot be used, moreover, to express concession, if the idea of simultaneity is not present.

Il est sorti en riant. *He went out laughing.*   § 234
Il parlait en mangeant. *He talked as he ate.*
Il m'a vu en partant. *He saw me as he was leaving.*
En forgeant on devient forgeron. *Practice makes perfect.*
  (*By means of forging one becomes a blacksmith.*)
En faisant cela, vous aurez des chances de réussir. *If you do that, you will have a good chance to succeed.*

Même en travaillant nuit et jour, il ne finira pas sa thèse. *Even if he works night and day, he will not finish his thesis.*

Tout en mangeant, elle bavardait avec tout le monde (two simultaneous actions). *While eating (Though she was eating) she chatted with everyone.*

Tout en sachant qu'il m'attendait je n'y suis pas allé (two simultaneous actions and a result). *Though I knew he was expecting me, I didn't go.*

But: Bien qu'il ait travaillé dur, il va échouer à son examen (no idea of simultaneity). *Though he has worked hard, he is going to fail in his examination.*

The present participle with **en** must always refer to the subject.[1] When it refers to the object, no preposition is used.[2]

Je l'ai vue en sortant. *I saw her as I went out.*
Je l'ai vue sortant de l'hôtel. *I saw her going out of the hotel.*

B. The present participle is used without **en** to indicate relationship of cause or anteriority. The present participle of the auxiliary, plus a past participle, may also be used in this way.

Craignant de déranger mon père, il est parti sans sonner. *Fearing that he would disturb my father, he went out without ringing.*

Croyant qu'il n'y avait personne dans la chambre, il y est entré. *Believing there was no one in the room, he entered it.*

Ramassant (Ayant ramassé) ses gants, il est sorti. *Picking up (Having picked up) his gloves, he went out.*

N'ayant pas lu ma dépêche, il est parti à l'heure habituelle. *Not having read my telegram, he left at the usual hour.*

Etant sortie trop tôt, elle a eu une rechute. *Having gone out too soon, she had a relapse.*

---

[1] Occasional violations of this rule are found in proverbs and in the colloquial language.

L'appétit vient en mangeant.
C'est la première porte à gauche, en montant.

[2] **En** is generally repeated before each participle which it governs. **It** is not repeated, however, in the set expression **en allant et venant,** and need not be repeated when the participles are closely connected in meaning, or when its repetition would result in awkwardness of style.

C. When the English verbal form in *–ing* is the object of a preposition, it is translated by the present participle only if the preposition may be rendered by **en.** In all other cases, this form in *–ing* is translated by the infinitive. *Note that:*

1. **en** is the only preposition which is followed by the present participle.
2. **après** must be followed by the perfect infinitive. *avoir fini*
3. **avant** must be followed by **de,** plus the infinitive.
4. **par** may be used before the infinitive only after verbs of beginning and ending.

> En arrivant à la gare, il s'est aperçu qu'il avait oublié ses billets. *On arriving at the station, he noticed that he had forgotten his tickets.*
> Après s'être habillé, il a descendu l'escalier quatre à quatre. *After dressing, he ran down the stairs (four steps at a time).*
> Après avoir travaillé dur, il veut toujours s'amuser. *After working hard, he always wants to have a good time.*
> Avant de prendre une décision, il faudra que je consulte un avocat. *Before making a decision, I shall have to consult a lawyer.*
> J'ai commencé par faire mes devoirs. *I began by writing my exercises.*
> Il a fini par tout avouer. *He ended by confessing everything.*

86 Further Uses of the Infinitive.

Cf. the Appendix for lists of verbs that require **à** and **de** with the dependent infinitive and verbs which require no preposition.

A. The infinitive may be used as subject, predicate nominative, or object.[1]

> Vouloir c'est pouvoir. *Where there's a will there's a way.*
> Voir c'est croire. *Seeing is believing.*

---

[1] In traffic signs and other impersonal directions, the infinitive is used with the force of an imperative.

Ralentir *Slow*
Voir au dos *Over* (lit., *See on the back*)
Tourner, s.v.p. *Over* (lit., *Turn, if you please*)

Promettre n'est pas tenir. *It's one thing to make a promise and another to keep it.*

Je veux sortir. *I want to go out.*

1. In most cases the infinitive as real subject is introduced by the impersonal **il,** plus the verb *to be.* In colloquial French, **il** is frequently replaced by **ce.**

Il est (C'est) agréable de fumer un bon cigare après le dîner. *It is pleasant to smoke a good cigar after dinner.*

Il n'est pas nécessaire de partir demain. *It is not necessary to leave tomorrow.*

Il est impossible d'entendre ce qu'il dit. *It is impossible to hear what he says.*

When the infinitive is *not* the real subject but the complement of the adjective, it is preceded by **à. Il** is then replaced by **ce.**

Cette leçon est facile à apprendre. *This lesson is easy to learn.*

Ça, c'est facile à lire. *That is easy to read.*

C'est difficile à croire. *It's (That's) hard to believe.*

Vous êtes facile à tromper. *You are easy to deceive.*

a. Many adjectives, such as **heureux, content, sage, fou, prudent,** take **de** before the infinitive, when the sentence has a personal subject.

Je suis très heureux de pouvoir passer l'hiver dans le Midi. *I am very glad to be able to spend the winter in the south (of France).*

Vous êtes fou de croire cela. *You are foolish to believe that.*

Je suis très content de vous revoir. *I am very glad to see you again.*

b. If the infinitive subject has a predicate nominative, it is regularly separated from it by **que** in sentences introduced by **ce** and the verb *to be.*

Ce serait une folie que de faire cela. *It would be a foolish thing to do that.*

Cf. Faire cela? Ce serait une folie. *Do that? It would be folly.*

2. **A** is also used in elliptical sentences before an infinitive with a passive meaning.

> C'est un devoir (qui est) à remplir. *It is a duty to be performed.*
> Voilà une maison à louer. *There's a house for rent (to be rented).*

B. When the second member of a comparison is an infinitive, it is regularly preceded by **que de.**

> Il est plus facile de parler que d'agir. *It is easier to talk than to act.*
> J'aimerais mieux partir que de lui obéir. *I would rather leave than obey him.*
> Il mourrait plutôt que de se rendre. *He would die rather than surrender.* § 235

C. The infinitive with **pour.**

1. Verbs of motion which ordinarily are followed by an infinitive without a preposition may take **pour** if the idea of purpose is stressed, or if the purpose has not been fulfilled.

> J'irai chez elle (pour) lui en parler. *I shall go to her home to talk to her about it.*
> Je suis allé chez elle pour lui parler de cette affaire, mais elle était sortie. *I went to her house to talk to her about this matter, but she had gone out.*

2. **Pour** is also used before the infinitive after adverbs of quantity, such as **assez, trop,** etc., provided that the subject of the main clause is also the subject of the infinitive and that the action of the infinitive is dependent upon the adjective modified by the adverb of quantity.

> Il est trop fatigué pour y aller à pied. *He is too tired to walk there.*
> Il est assez grand pour savoir se tenir à table. *He is big enough to know how to act at the table.*

But note:

> C'est trop long à expliquer. *It's too long to explain.*
> Elle est vraiment trop lente à se décider. *She is really too slow in making up her mind.*
> Je ne serai que trop content de vous rendre ce service. *I shall be only too glad to do this favor for you.*

3. Pour is also used with the past infinitive to express cause.

> Pour avoir crié « Vive le roi ! » il a été mis en prison. *He was imprisoned for having shouted: "Long live the king!"*
>
> §§ 236, 237

D. The infinitive with modal auxiliaries.

1. The infinitive with **faire.**

a. Faire should regularly be separated from the infinitive only by its own pronoun subject (in interrogation), by a conjunctive pronoun object (affirmative imperative), by certain adverbs, by the indefinite **tout,** or by a reflexive object of the infinitive.

> Il a fait venir le médecin. *He sent for the doctor* (lit., *He had the doctor come*).
>
> Il a fait bâtir plusieurs maisons. *He had several houses built.*
>
> Elle faisait beaucoup parler d'elle. *She got herself talked about a lot.*
>
> Je les ai fait [1] sortir. *I had them go out.*
>
> Faites-le entrer. *Have him come in.*
>
> Faites-en monter. *Have some sent up.*
>
> Ne la faites pas pleurer. *Don't make her cry.*
>
> Vous faites-vous toujours gronder par votre mère ? *Do you always get scolded by your mother?*
>
> Faites-le s'asseoir. *Have him sit down.*
>
> Je l'ai fait s'asseoir. *I had him sit down.* § 238
>
> Il m'a fait tout dire. *He made me tell everything* (or *He had everything told me*).

b. If the infinitive has a non-reflexive direct object, the direct object of **faire** becomes indirect.[2] A non-reflexive pronoun object of the infinitive has the same position as if it were an object of **faire.**

> Je lui ai fait sortir l'auto du garage. *I had him take the car out of the garage.*
>
> Il a fait passer à ses élèves un examen des plus sévères. *He had his students take a most difficult examination.*

---

[1] The past participle of **faire,** when followed by an infinitive, is invariable.

[2] The object of **faire** may also be considered as the subject of the infinitive.

165

Faites-le-moi voir. *Show it to me.*

Ne le lui faites pas envoyer. *Don't have it sent to him* (or: *Don't make him send it*).

Je lui ai fait enlever son veston. Je le lui ai fait enlever. *I had him take off his coat. I had him take it off.*

c. Par replaces **à** in the following cases:

(1) Frequently when ambiguity might result from the use of the latter preposition.

Il a fait porter le paquet par la bonne. *He had the maid carry the package* (**à la bonne** might mean *to the maid*).

Voilà le jeune homme par qui j'ai fait envoyer l'argent. *There is the young man by whom I had the money sent* (**à qui** would mean *to whom*).

(2) Regularly when the agent is emphasized, i.e., when a passive construction with *by* could be used in English. This replacement is obligatory when both objects are persons.

Il s'est fait faire deux complets par mon tailleur.[1] *He had two suits made (for himself) by my tailor.*

Si tu ne te tiens pas bien à table, tu vas te faire gronder par ta mère. *If you don't behave at the table, you're going to get scolded by your mother.*

Il a fait réprimander le lieutenant par son colonel. *He had the lieutenant reprimanded by his colonel.*

d. If the object of the infinitive is first or second person, it is generally preferable to replace **faire** by some other verb.

Il m'a obligé à vous voir (*rather than:* Il m'a fait vous voir). *He made me see you.*

Il vous a forcé à nous trahir (*rather than:* Il vous a fait nous trahir). *He made you betray us.*

Il m'a obligé à vous parler (*rather than:* Il m'a fait vous parler). *He made me speak to you.*

2. Laisser, voir, entendre. These verbs are frequently followed by the infinitive with the same construction as with **faire.** They may, however, retain the direct object, even if the infinitive dependent upon them has a direct object.

---

[1] One could also say, **chez mon tailleur,** *at my tailor's.*

166

Whether they take the **faire** construction or not is frequently a question of the proper balance of the sentence.

> Laissez entrer tout le monde. *Let everyone come in.*
> Je l'ai entendu frapper à la porte. *I heard him knocking at the door.*
> Nous l'avons vu partir. *We saw him leave.*
> Il les (*better:* leur) laisse faire tout. *He lets them do everything.*
> Nous l'avons entendu réciter par votre mère. *We heard your mother recite it.*
> Nous avons entendu votre mère la réciter. *We heard your mother recite it.*
> Nous l'avons entendu appeler par votre mère, qui venait de rentrer de la gare. *We heard your mother, who had just returned from the station, call her.*

When there are two pronoun objects, the construction used with **faire** is generally preferred.

> Je le lui ai laissé dire. *I let him say it.*
> Je le lui ai entendu dire. *I heard him say it.*   § 238

EXERCISES

I. Verbs to Review:

vaincre, coudre

II. Idiomatic Expressions:

il y a des chances pour que (plus subjunctive), *there is a good chance that . . ., the chances are that . . .*
avoir la chance de, *to have the good luck to*
insister sur quelque chose, *to emphasize something*
insister pour que (plus clause with subjunctive), *to insist upon*
insister pour (plus noun), *to insist upon*
prendre son parti de quelque chose, *to resign one's self to something*
tenir (sa) parole, *to keep one's word*
Cela ne sert à rien. *That is useless.* that does not serve any purpose
faire quelque chose de parti pris, *to do something deliberately*
prendre le parti de quelqu'un, *to take a person's side*

167

III. Sentences for Translation:

1. By constantly mending our clothes, we shall be able to make them last longer.   2. If you read that book now, you will save yourself the trouble of reading it during the vacation.   3. He must have seen me taking (Use *sortir . . . de.*) the car out of the garage one day.   Since then he has insisted upon the chauffeur's driving.   4. You always get up early, but that doesn't serve any purpose if you do not get to class on time.   5. While emphasizing [1] the importance of intelligence, she did not succeed in interesting her intelligent students.

6. It is astonishing to note that few women after winning the right to vote choose politics as a career.   7. That isn't difficult to explain.   Many people after surmounting obstacles lose interest in their projects.   8. I am glad to announce to you that my brother has had the good luck to have his first novel accepted.   9. Is it a well-known publisher who is going to bring it out?   No, all the famous publishers are too cautious to try to launch a novice.   10. If his novel is successful, there is a good chance that his publisher will become famous also.

11. He came to see me only in order to keep his word.   12. While walking down the street, I saw Mary come out of her house.   13. You would be foolish to give up your studying before getting (*passer*) your A.B.   14. In Washington it is almost impossible to find a room to rent.   15. Picking up his valise, he went out into the night; and no one has heard of him since (Omit *since* and use *on ne . . . plus jamais . . .*).

16. For having told the truth he lost the esteem of all his colleagues. 17. It is more difficult to speak a foreign language than to read it. 18. It is folly to spend all one's money without putting aside a few dollars for an emergency.   19. If her dress arrives after she has left, we shall have it sent to her.   20. I am not surprised that she is a spoiled child.   Her mother lets her do everything she wishes.

21. She is devoted to her father.   For her, living is giving up all her own plans.   22. In this war against fascism, we are taking the side of all the conquered peoples.   23. If you insist upon the protection of the workingmen, you will have forced the employers to give up their excessive demands.   24. The workingmen are

---

[1] Use a clause with the subjunctive.

striking deliberately because they do not approve of the law which has just been passed. 25. I'm going to give you some good advice. When one is poor, one should resign one's self to poverty.

IV. DRILL: Translate the words in parentheses:

1. Si vous insistez pour l'application de vos principes, (*you will take the side of the ignorant*) contre les gens cultivés. 2. Allez-vous violer la loi (*in order to succeed in your enterprise*)? (*That will be useless.*) 3. Bien que d'abord elle ne fût pas très forte en science, (*she finally did research in chemistry*). 4. (*Not wishing to wake you up*) je ne suis pas entrée dans votre chambre. 5. Avant de lui donner la photo, (*we shall show* [faire voir] *it to him*).
6. Il est plus facile de faire la critique littéraire (*than to write something original*). 7. (*If she works hard*) elle pourra réussir à l'examen. 8. (*After deliberately refusing to help me*) elle a consenti à aider mon frère. 9. Connaissez-vous cette *aria*? Oui. La dernière fois que je suis allée au concert, (*I heard Melchior sing it*).
10. Cette *aria* est difficile (*to sing*). Bien qu'il soit artiste, (*there's a good chance that he won't succeed* [*in it*]).
11. La voyez-vous (*coming up the stairs*)? On ne dirait jamais (*that she had broken her leg*) il y a deux mois. 12. Elle n'est que trop contente (*to keep her word*). 13. (*By not resisting the enemy*) le vrai pacifiste croit (*that he will conquer him*). 14. Vous m'avez dit que (*you had a dress made by that dressmaker*), n'est-ce pas? 15. Il est trop intelligent (*to make such a blunder*).

V. VERB EXERCISE:

A. Translate the English words:

1. *After sewing* la robe, elle l'a essayée. 2. Ils *have never conquered* ce pays-là. 3. Tout en *sewing* nous écoutions la radio. 4. Autrefois, *we used to sew* beaucoup. 5. Nous doutons qu'on *will ever conquer them*. 6. Si elle *sewed well*, elle pourrait se faire des robes. 7. Nous vînmes, nous vîmes, *we conquered*. 8. Si vous *should overcome* cet obstacle, vous réussiriez. 9. Elle *had not sewed* depuis des années. 10. *When shall we conquer them?*

B. Give the imperative of the verbs **vaincre** and **coudre**.

C. Conjugate the verb **coudre** in the past definite and the present subjunctive.

169

XXI.

SPECIAL VERBS
USE AND MEANING

Ecrire, dire, lire, écouter, vivre, habiter, demeurer,
apercevoir, approcher, porter, coucher, prendre, etc.

87 Equivalents of: *"to write of, about,"* etc.

To write of, or *about, to tell of,* or *about,* should not be translated by **écrire de** [1] or **dire de.** [2]

She wrote him about that.	{ Elle lui a écrit cela.
	{ Elle lui a dit cela (a parlé de cela) dans sa lettre.
She told him about that.	{ Elle lui a parlé de cela.
	{ Elle lui a raconté cela (*a detailed narration*).

---

[1] This use of **de** after **écrire** is practically obsolete.
[2] *To say* (or *tell*) something *about* is translated by **dire de.**

Savez-vous ce qu'elle m'a dit de votre mariage ? *Do you know what she said to me (told me) about your marriage?*

170

88 Equivalents of: *"to read (of, about)."*

To read about someone or *something* is translated in various ways.

> Il a lu l'histoire de Jeanne d'Arc, des anecdotes sur Jeanne d'Arc. *He has read about Jeanne d'Arc.*
>
> J'ai lu dans le journal d'hier la nouvelle du désastre dont vous m'aviez parlé. *In yesterday's paper I read about the disaster of which you had spoken to me.*
>
> J'ai lu un article sur la découverte de l'uranium. *I read (an article) about the discovery of uranium.*

When in English there is a personal indirect object and no direct object, *to read* is translated by **faire la lecture.**

> Je vais te faire la lecture pendant une heure. *I am going to read to you for an hour.*
>
> se faire faire la lecture par quelqu'un, *to have someone read to you*

In the ending of a commercial letter, **lire** is often used transitively with the meaning of *to hear from.*

> Espérant vous lire bientôt... *Hoping to hear from you soon ...*

89 Omission of Prepositions with Equivalents of Certain English Verbs.

Unlike their English equivalents, **écouter, chercher, demander** (= *ask for*), **attendre, payer, regarder,** require no prepositions since they are transitive verbs.

> Vous n'écoutez pas ce que je vous dis. *You are not listening to what I am telling you.*
>
> Je l'ai cherché partout. *I have looked for him everywhere.*
>
> On demande votre père. *They are asking for your father.*
>
> Il attend le train transatlantique. *He is waiting for the boat train.*
>
> C'est vous qui payez le dîner. *You are the one who is paying for the dinner.*
>
> J'ai payé ce vin cinquante francs la bouteille. *I paid fifty francs a bottle for this wine.*
>
> Qu'est-ce que vous regardez? *What are you looking at?*

90 *Vivre, habiter, demeurer.*

The English verb *to live* may be translated by **vivre, habiter, demeurer.** While these verbs are often synonymous, they cannot always be used interchangeably.

A. *To live* = *to exist*, or, regularly, *to live in a certain manner*, is translated by **vivre.**

> Ce vieillard vit toujours? *Is that old man still living?*
> Elle vit toute seule. *She lives all alone.*
> vivre aux dépens d'autrui, *to live at the expense of others*
> Elle vit avec ses parents. *She lives with her parents.*
> Ces hommes vivaient il y a 200.000 [1] ans. *These men lived 200,000 years ago.*

B. *To live* = *to reside*, may be translated by **vivre,** or, more frequently, by **habiter, demeurer.**

> vivre à Paris, demeurer à Paris, habiter (à) Paris, *to live in Paris*
> Elle habite (demeure) chez sa tante. *She lives at her aunt's (with her aunt).*
> habiter (dans) la banlieue, *to live in the suburbs*

If a definite address is given, **vivre** cannot be used.

> Elle habite (demeure) 75, avenue de Wagram.

91 *Apercevoir, s'apercevoir.*

Apercevoir means *to perceive*, or *notice*, a person or a concrete object; **s'apercevoir,** *to perceive* or *notice* a fact or state. The latter verb should be used when the object is a clause.

> Je vous ai tout de suite aperçu. *I noticed you at once.*
> J'ai aperçu une petite maison grise au bout de l'avenue. *I noticed a little gray house at the end of the avenue.*

---

[1] With numerals, the use of the period and the comma is the reverse of English practice: 200.000 = 200,000; 9,5 = 9.5. A blank space sometimes replaces the period: 200 000.

172

Elle ne s'est pas aperçue de mon embarras. *She didn't notice my difficulty.*

Tout à coup je me suis aperçu qu'elle ne m'écoutait plus. *All of a sudden I noticed that she was no longer listening to me.*

Je me suis aperçu que j'avais oublié mon mouchoir. *I found that I had forgotten my handkerchief.*

92 S'approcher, approcher.

In actual practice, **s'approcher de** is regularly used to indicate immediate proximity, **approcher,** less immediate proximity. With **s'approcher** there is generally the idea of action or conscious effort. With **approcher** the state, rather than the action, is emphasized.

Il s'est approché du feu. *He approached the fire.*

Approchez-vous de la table. *Come closer to the table.* (*Pull your chair up to the table.*)

Le train approchait de Paris. *The train was nearing Paris.*

Malgré l'obscurité je me suis aperçu que nous approchions de Marseille. *In spite of the darkness I noticed that we were approaching Marseilles.*

93 Equivalents of: "to hear," "to hear of."

To hear followed by a clause is translated by **entendre dire;** *to hear of,* or *about,* by **entendre parler de.**

J'ai entendu dire que Madame une telle va divorcer. *I've heard that Mrs. So-and-so is going to get a divorce.*

Oui, j'ai beaucoup entendu parler de cela. *Yes, I've heard a lot about that.*

94 Equivalents of: "to take," "to bring," "to carry."

The verbs *to take* and *to bring* are translated by a verb of the **porter** group (**apporter, emporter, reporter,** etc.), only if the object of the verb is actually carried (literally or figuratively).

Portez ce paquet chez moi. *Take this package to my house.*
Il a apporté son violon. *He brought his violin.*
On a porté le blessé à l'hôpital. *They took (carried) the wounded man to the hospital.*
Il a apporté de bonnes nouvelles. *He brought good news.*

If the object is not actually carried, a verb of the **mener** group (**amener, emmener, ramener**), or sometimes **conduire**, is used. **Mener** is used especially where the person taken is more or less under the authority of the subject of the verb.

C'est la bonne qui mène les enfants à l'école. *It's the maid who takes the children to school.*
Je vous emmènerai au théâtre. *I shall take you to the theater.*
Il m'a promis de me ramener. *He promised to bring me back.*
Qu'est-ce qui vous amène ici ? *What brings you here?*
Il a amené son chien. *He brought his dog.*
Le dénouement est savamment amené. *The dénouement is cleverly brought about.*
Il m'a conduit dans tous les endroits intéressants de la capitale. *He took me (acting as a guide) to all the interesting places in the capital.*

When it is a question of transportation by vehicles, verbs of the **mener** group (*or* **conduire**) are regularly used for persons, those of the **porter** group for things.

Il monta dans l'autobus qui devait le conduire à X. *He got into the bus which was to take him to X.*
Le paquebot amène beaucoup de réfugiés. *The steamship brings many refugees.*
C'est le petit camion qui apporte les bagages de la gare. *It's the little truck which brings the baggage from the station.*

If the action of carrying away a person is stressed, **emporter** replaces **emmener**.

Parmi les passagers que l'avion allait emporter, il y en avait un qui ne devait jamais revenir. *Among the passengers whom the airplane was going to carry away, was one who was never to return.*

95 *Coucher* and *Dormir*.

In correct French, **coucher** means *to sleep habitually* or *to spend the night*, while **dormir** means *to sleep*, i.e., *to be asleep*. **Dormir** is sometimes loosely used in the sense of **coucher**.

> Nous allons coucher à Paris. *We shall spend the night in Paris.*
> Mon père couche dans cette chambre. *My father (habitually) sleeps in this room.*
> Ne faites pas tant de bruit. Mon père dort dans la chambre à côté. *Don't make so much noise. My father is asleep (is sleeping) in the next room.*

Se coucher means *to lie down;* it also means *to go to bed*, if there is no idea of going elsewhere to do so, or if it is a question of habitual action. If *to go to bed* contains the idea of going to one's bedroom to go to bed, it is translated by **aller se coucher**. An **aller** of futurity may, of course, be used before either **se coucher** or **aller se coucher**.[1]

se coucher

> Couchez-vous! *Lie down!*
> Il se couche toujours très tard. *He always goes to bed very late.*
> A quelle heure vous êtes-vous couché? *What time did you go to bed?*
> Je vais me coucher (= je me coucherai) ici sur le canapé. *I'm going to go to bed right here on the sofa.*

aller se coucher

> Allez vous coucher, mes enfants. *Go to bed, children.*
> Je vais aller (= j'irai) me coucher. *I'm going (to go) to bed.*

96 Prendre.

Prendre, which is regularly not used as the equivalent of the English *take* when this verb expresses motion, frequently translates the English *to get*.

---

[1] For reasons of euphony, one avoids **allez aller**. **Vous allez aller vous coucher** would, therefore, be shortened to **Vous allez vous coucher**.

Prenez ce paquet chez moi. *Get this package at my house.*

Passez au bureau prendre votre père. *Stop at the office to get your father.*

But: Il a pris l'enfant sur ses genoux. *He took the child on his lap.*

EXERCISES

I. VERBS TO REVIEW:

fuir, s'enfuir, conclure

II. IDIOMATIC EXPRESSIONS:

vivre aux dépens de quelqu'un, *to live at the expense of someone*

Vous m'en direz des nouvelles. *You'll be delighted with it.*

faire la lecture à quelqu'un, *to read to someone*

se faire faire la lecture, *to have someone read to you*

vivre au jour le jour, *to live from hand to mouth*

entendre dire, *to hear (it said)*

entendre parler de, *to hear about*

avoir des nouvelles de, *to have news of, from*

recevoir des nouvelles de, *to hear from*

faire le tour de, *to go around*

III. SENTENCES FOR TRANSLATION:

1. That's news to me. Have you ever heard about it? Yes, my mother wrote me about it in her last letter. 2. Now that I've told you that story, I'd like you to tell us about your trip. 3. I'm going to ask him to read to me every night. 4. He said that you were the one who was to pay for the dinner. Really? I was not listening to him. 5. Does Mrs. Durand live in this neighborhood? Why yes, there she is waiting for the bus.

6. What is his address? He lives at 85 Avenue Bosquet. 7. On arriving at the college she discovered (*s'apercevoir*) that she had forgotten her books. 8. Well, Mr. Dulac, don't you recognize me? Why yes, my boy, I did not notice you in the midst of all those young men. I was looking at that pretty brunette on the other side of the street. 9. After having got the habit of living at the expense of one's friends, it isn't easy to earn one's living. 10. I prefer to live alone rather than to live with my mother-in-law.

11. Does he live in the country? *la compagne* No, he lives in Paris. 12. Do you think that he noticed your nervousness? Why no, he doesn't suspect anything. 13. Say, old man, we are approaching New York. I can clearly see the silhouette of the Statue of Liberty. 14. As he was approaching the door, he suddenly turned around. "Sir," he exclaimed, "you don't know what it is to be obliged to live from hand to mouth!" 15. I'll take this package to Aunt Mary's and on the way back I'll stop at the office and get Daddy.

16. Françoise, it is time to take Jeannine to her class. Be sure (Don't fail) to bring her back before five o'clock. 17. How boring it is to travel on the train! How stupid I was (*past indef.*) not to bring along any books! 18. Did you bring my trunk in your car? 19. Do you know what has become of the young man who intended to go around the world? I heard that he had been obliged to postpone his plans for lack of money. 20. Did you sleep in the dormitory last night? Yes, I went to bed at 11:30. My roommate is still asleep.

21. "Well!" said the father, raising his eyes from the newspaper, *de dessus le journal* "are you (Use familiar form.) still there? Go to bed right away!" 22. He is a model husband; not only does he wash the dishes every evening, but he also takes his wife to the movies three times a week. 23. I haven't heard from him for two months. 24. I didn't hear from him for two months. 25. Just take one of these cream puffs. You'll be delighted with it.

IV. DRILL: Translate the words in parentheses:
1. (*Did she tell about that*) *a-t-ell dit cela* dans sa dernière lettre? 2. (*No, but she wrote a lot about*) son prochain mariage. 3. Avez-vous lu dans les journaux (*about* [1] *the floods in France*)? 4. J'ai les yeux si fatigués que je vais être obligé de (*have someone read to me*). 5. (*Is that man still living? I heard last week*) *J'ai entendu la semaine dernière dire que* qu'il était sur le point de mourir.

6. (*I've heard so much about you*) *tant* que j'ai l'impression de vous connaître depuis longtemps. 7. Prenez garde de laisser tomber ces œufs! (*I paid a franc apiece for them.*) 8. (*Coming near the door*), il m'a fait signe de le suivre. 9. Nos invités désirent (*to go* [2] *to bed*). *se coucher*

---

[1] Translate *the articles on* or *what one says about* (**sur**) . . .
[2] Use **aller**.

177

qu'ils couchent

Dans quelle chambre (*do you want them to sleep*)? 10. Qui est-ce qui ronfle? C'est votre père (*who is asleep*) dans le salon.

11. Si vous allez au cinéma, (*who is going to bring you back*)?
12. Passez chez l'épicier (*and get a pound of tea*). 13. Qu'est-ce qu'elle fait? (*She is reading to her little son* [**petit garçon**]). 14. Il faudra nous lever de bonne heure (*if we wish to go around the lake*) avant le déjeuner. 15. En ouvrant ma malle, (*I noticed*) que j'avais oublié (*to bring along*) des pantoufles.

si nous voulons faire la tour du lac

V. Verb Exercise:

A. Rewrite the following sentences, placing the italicized verbs in all the simple tenses of the indicative.

1. Mon stylo *fuit*. 2. Ils *s'enfuirent* de la ville. 3. *Concluons* l'affaire. 4. *Fuirez-vous* le danger? 5. *J'en ai conclu* qu'il était mort.

B. Translate the English words:

1. *Before concluding* l'affaire, adressez-vous à un avocat. 2. Le temps *passes quickly*. 3. *Let's flee!* 4. Sa tristesse *will disappear quickly*. 5. J'ai peur *that he will not finish* l'affaire avant la semaine prochaine. 6. *If he had concluded* l'affaire l'année dernière, il aurait eu des chances de réussir. 7. *You will not avoid the danger by fleeing.* 8. *Does that bottle leak?* 9. *On concluding* son discours, l'avocat a demandé la peine de mort. 10. *After fleeing from* la ville, ils se sont cachés chez un vieux paysan.

XXII.

An, année; jour, journée; matin, matinée;
soir, soirée, nuit

97 *An* and *Année.*

A. An is used primarily in dates, especially in the far-distant past and future; after cardinal numeral adjectives; and in expressions of repetition.   It is used with other adjectives only in a few expressions.

> depuis l'an 1500 av. J.-C. (avant Jésus-Christ), *since the year 1500 B.C.*
> (en) l'an 2000,[1] (*in*) *the year 2000*
> Il a vingt ans. *He is twenty years old.*
> Il travaille à sa thèse depuis trois ans. *He has been working on his thesis for three years.*

---

[1] As in English, dates are ordinarily expressed by the preposition and the year number.

> en 1936, depuis 1789, vers 1854, etc., *in 1936, since 1789, toward 1834, etc.*

deux fois par an, *twice a year*

tous les ans, tous les deux ans, *every year, every other year*

bon an, mal an (*old expression*), *year in, year out*

l'an prochain, *next year*

l'an dernier, *last year*

Il vous envoie ses meilleurs vœux de Nouvel An (du Jour de l'An). *He sends you his best New Year's wishes.*

B. In other cases, **année** is regularly used, especially *if a modifier is present.* It is sometimes used also after a cardinal numeral adjective, if one wishes to stress the idea of duration. It is used in modern dates, and when the idea of the whole year is present.

Dans les années qui précédaient la guerre ... *In the years which preceded the war* ...

Les années passent. *The years pass.*

Les saisons de l'année sont ... *The seasons of the year are* ...

Depuis quarante années environ, pas de grèves. *For forty odd years, no strikes.*

l'année prochaine (l'an prochain), *next year*

l'année dernière (l'an dernier), *last year*

Sur ces quatre années il a été pendant deux ans interne au lycée Condorcet. *Of these four years he spent two as a boarding student at the lycée Condorcet.*

L'année 1941 va bientôt prendre fin. *The year 1941 is soon going to end.*

Il a passé quinze années à étudier ce problème. *He has spent fifteen years studying this problem.*

L'année avait été bonne. *The year had been good (successful).*

l'année suivante, *the following year*

cette année, en cette année 1935, *this year, in this year 1935*

ces quatre dernières années, *these last four years*

toute l'année (*never:* tout l'an), *the whole year*

quelques années, *a few years*

plusieurs années, *several years*

une année sèche (pluvieuse), *a dry (wet) year*

Bonne Année! *Happy New Year!*

une année bissextile, *leap year*

l'année de sa mort, *the year of his death*

d'un bout de l'année à l'autre, *from one end of the year to the other (all through the year)*

180

Je vous souhaite une bonne et heureuse année. *I wish you a happy new year.*
Ils sont payés à l'année. *They are paid by the year.*
d'année en année, *from year to year*
une quinzaine d'années, *about fifteen years*

In poetic and literary language, **an** not infrequently encroaches upon **année.** In astronomy however, **année** is always used.

98 *jour* and *journée; matin* and *matinée; soir* and *soirée.*

A. The cases of **jour** and **journée, matin** and **matinée** are similar to that of **an** and **année,** except that **journée** is more frequently replaced by **jour, matinée** by **matin.**

un jour, deux jours, *one day, two days*
un beau jour, *one fine day*
la fin d'un beau jour, *the end of a perfect day*
tous les jours, chaque jour, *every day*
tous les deux jours, *every other day*
au jour le jour, *from hand to mouth*
de jour en jour, *from day to day*
du jour au lendemain, *from one day to the next*
le jour de son départ, *the day of his departure*
tout le jour, *the whole day*
jour par jour, *day by day*
jour et nuit (nuit et jour), *day and night*
il y a quelques jours, *a few days ago*
Nous ne pourrions pas voyager le jour (de jour) (dans la journée). *We couldn't travel during the day.*
C'était une belle journée de printemps. *It was a fine spring day.*
toute la journée, *the whole day*
toute la journée d'hier, *all day yesterday*
dans (pendant) la journée, *during the day*
être payé à la journée, *to be paid by the day*

Journée is also used to designate days famous in history, especially when it is a question of military action.

la journée de Valmy, *the battle of Valmy*
les trois journées glorieuses (les trois glorieuses), *the three glo-.
rious days* [1]

Cf.: journée de blanc, *white goods sale*

B. Matin, matinée.

le matin, *in the morning*
à dix heures du matin, *at ten o'clock in the morning*
deux matins par semaine, *two mornings a week*
tous les matins, chaque matin, *every morning*
un beau matin, *one fine morning*
du matin au soir, *from morning till night*
tout le matin (toute la matinée), *the whole morning*
demain matin, *tomorrow morning*
tous les mardis matin, *every Tuesday morning*
Il se sont mariés le matin (i.e., de ce jour-là) et sont partis
le soir. *They were married in the morning and left in the
evening.*
une belle matinée [2] de printemps, *a fine spring morning*
au début de la matinée, *at the beginning of the morning*
dans la matinée, pendant la matinée, *during the morning*
au milieu de la matinée, *in the middle of the morning*
à la fin de la matinée, *at the end of the morning*
dans la matinée d'hier, *yesterday during the morning*
une matinée, *a matinee* (These performances now given in
the afternoon were formerly given in the morning.)

C. Soir, soirée. In **soir,** the emphasis is on the relation
of the period of time to the day; in **soirée,** the emphasis is
on the duration of that period of time. This difference is
clearly indicated by the prepositions which may be used
with each word.

ce soir, *this evening*
tous les soirs, *every evening*

---

[1] The 27th, 28th, 29th of July, 1830. After this three-day revolution Louis-
Philippe d'Orléans became *roi des Français.*

[2] When **matinée, soirée, journée,** etc., are used, the whole period of time
is under consideration. Thus one would say with the present tense: **C'est
un beau matin** (not **matinée**) **de printemps.** But one says quite correctly: **La matinée va être,** or, **a été, très belle. Ç'a été une belle matinée de printemps.**

Le soir on allume les lampes. *In the evening the lamps are lit.*
Il est parti le soir de ce jour-là. *He left the evening of that day.*
un beau soir d'été, *one fine summer evening*
A ce soir. *Good-bye until this evening.*
demain soir, *tomorrow evening*
pendant la soirée, *during the evening*
toute la soirée, *the whole evening*
toute la soirée d'hier, *all yesterday evening*
Je vous reverrai dans la soirée. *I shall see you again in the course of the evening.*
Allez-vous au théâtre en soirée? *Do you go to the theater at night?*
donner une soirée, *to give a party* (*in the evening*)

D. *Last night,* when it refers to time before one goes to bed, is translated by **hier soir;** when it refers to time after one has gone to bed, by **cette nuit** or by **la nuit dernière. Cette nuit** may also mean *tonight.* **Cette nuit,** being easier to say, appears to be more common today than **la nuit dernière.** The latter expression should be used, however, if there is any chance of ambiguity. **Ce soir** means *this evening* (*tonight*).

A quelle heure vous êtes-vous couché hier soir? *When did you go to bed last night?*
Je suis allé le voir hier soir. *I went to see him yesterday evening.*
Cette nuit nous avons eu une tempête. *Last night we had a storm.*
A quelle heure allez-vous vous coucher ce soir? *When are you going to bed tonight?*
J'espère que vous dormirez bien cette nuit. *I hope you will sleep well tonight.*

99 Equivalents of: *"when"* after Temporal Nouns.

After a unit of time preceded by the definite article, or the plural of the indefinite article, *when* is regularly translated by **où.** If the article in question is indefinite singular, **que** is regularly used. (When **un jour** is the subject of the verb, however, **où** replaces que.) **Que** must also be used if the period of time is preceded by an ordinal.

Le jour où je vous ai rencontré ... *The day on which I met you ...*

Il y a des jours où on a envie de ne rien faire. *There are days when one doesn't feel like doing anything.*

Un jour que je passais rue des Petits-Champs ... *One day when I was going along the rue des Petits-Champs ...*

Un jour vint où il renonça à tous ses principes. *A day came when he renounced all his principles.*

Le premier soir que je vous ai vu ... *The first evening that I saw you ...*

If no definite day is indicated, *when* is translated by **quand**.

Le soir, quand j'allume ma lampe ... *In the evening, when I light my lamp ...*

Un jour, quand vous serez vieux ... *Some day when you are old ...*

EXERCISES

I. VERBS TO REVIEW:

croître, haïr

II. IDIOMATIC EXPRESSIONS:

prendre fin, *to come to an end, to end*
être payé à l'année, à la journée, *to be paid by the year, by the day*
d'année en année, *from year to year*
du jour au lendemain, *at a day's notice, overnight*
du matin au soir, *from morning till night*
aller au théâtre en matinée, en soirée, *to go to the theater for an afternoon performance, for an evening performance*
au moment où, *just as, just when*
toute la sainte journée, *the whole blessed day*
donner le jour à, *to give birth to*
mettre au jour, *to bring to light, to publish*

184

III. Sentences for Translation:

1. How old is he? He is seventy-seven. He was born in 1865.
2. Every year he says to me: "I hope that this year will be better than last year." 3. Sometimes he tells me that three or four times a year. 4. I have been trying to make you understand that for a whole year. 5. How many leap years are there in the first half of the twentieth century?

6. She was sick all day yesterday. If she is paid by the day, she will lose fifty francs. 7. The whole blessed day he has done nothing but complain. 8. Customers are requested to do their shopping in the morning (*matinée*). 9. *He* always goes to the theater in the afternoon, but *we* always go in the evening. 10. After all, you can't give a party every evening. 11. In January there are white goods sales in all the department stores. 12. That's why (*C'est pourquoi*) every Friday morning the good housekeepers flock to the *Trois Quartiers*. 13. As I had to interrupt my work in the middle of the morning, I'm going to be obliged to work during the evening. 14. Did you see him last night? No, I haven't seen him since the day you brought him to the club. 15. Did the storm wake you up last night? No, I slept soundly all night.

16. What are the seasons of the year? What a question! Do you take me for a fool? 17. There are days when I am sick and tired of studying from morning till night. 18. You've been here for about twenty years, haven't you? No, we've been here only fifteen years. 19. Just as she was getting out of the car, the chauffeur suddenly started. 20. She was thrown violently to the ground and was instantly killed.

21. You mustn't change your mind like that overnight. 22. In the course of his study he brought to light some interesting documents on the literary history of the Middle Ages. 23. The year 1941 has just ended. I firmly believe that the new year will bring us fewer misfortunes. 24. I am not so optimistic. It seems to me that from year to year the situation continues to grow worse. 25. There was (*Il y a eu*) great rejoicing in Italy when the crown princess gave birth to an heir.

IV. DRILL: Translate the words in parentheses:

1. Mon père m'avait promis que (*when I was twenty*) je pourrais passer (*a few years in France*). 2. Le soir (*after going to bed*) je lis toujours pendant une heure (*before going to sleep*). 3. Je me lève (*at 6:30 every day*) sauf le dimanche (*when I sleep late*). 4. (*A few days ago*) (*just as*) je sortais pour faire une promenade, j'ai reçu une dépêche d'un ami (*whom I hadn't seen for ten years*). 5. Il a plu (*all day yesterday*).

6. Cet élève n'a jamais appris à distinguer entre (*last year* and *the last year*). 7. Je ne peux pas vous dire ça au téléphone. Je vous le dirai (*the next time I see you*). 8. Si vous passez la nuit chez Marie, (*I'll come to see you in the course* [dans] *of the evening*). 9. (*There will come a day when*) vous regretterez ces paroles-là. 10. (*The whole situation*) avait changé (*overnight*).

11. Il est arrivé (*in the evening*) et il n'est parti que (*the next morning*). 12. (*The first evening that*) j'ai dîné avec cette femme-là, j'ai trouvé sa conversation insupportable. 13. (*For about ten years*) il est allé (*to the matinée performances every week*). 14. Je crois que je vais aller me coucher. (*Last night I didn't go to bed till 11:30.*) 15. Vous avez bien dormi? Non, (*I slept very badly last night*).

V. VERB EXERCISE:

A. Identify the following forms:

1. Haïssant.
2. Il croissait.
3. On hait.
4. Nous haïrions.
5. Haïtes-vous?
6. Ne hais pas.
7. Je crois.
8. Crû.
9. On aurait haï.
10. Qu'il haïsse.

B. Give the following forms in all the simple tenses:

1. *croître*, third person singular.
2. *haïr*, first person plural.[1]

---

[1] In familiar French, **détester** is much more frequently used than **haïr**.

186

être coucher

SUPPLEMENTARY
GRAMMATICAL NOTES

CHAPTER I

100 In French, the present tense, perhaps more frequently than in English, replaces a narrative past when it is desired to render the action more vivid. This use of the present tense is usually referred to as the *historical* or *narrative* present (**le présent historique** or **le présent narratif**).

> Tout à coup, il revient sur ses pas et rentre dans la maison. Il s'assied dans son grand fauteuil, rallume sa pipe, et, d'un geste autoritaire, nous réduit au silence. *Suddenly he retraces his steps and comes back into the house. He sits down in his big armchair, relights his pipe, and, with an authoritative gesture, reduces us to silence.*

101 The present tense with **depuis** is sometimes used even when the negation is expressed by **ne . . . pas.**

> Il n'est pas en Amérique depuis longtemps (= Il n'y a pas longtemps qu'il est en Amérique). *He hasn't been in America very long.*
> Il ne vient pas à l'école (Il n'est pas venu à l'école) depuis huit jours. *He hasn't been in school for a week.* (*He is expected to return.*)

Il ne vient plus à l'école depuis huit jours. *He hasn't been in school for a week. (He is not expected to return.)*

102 The present tense is sometimes used to express an immediate past.

Où est M. Dupont? — Il sort d'ici. *Where is Mr. Dupont? He has just gone out.*
J'apprends à l'instant que votre candidat n'a pas été nommé. *I have just learned that your candidate has not been appointed.*

103 In modern French there is a tendency to replace in non-temporal subordinate clauses the future and the future perfect by the present and past indefinite.

Je vous dirai ce qu'il faut en faire. *I shall tell you what must be done with it.*
Elle n'est pas obligée de se décider tout de suite. Vous pourrez me dire demain quelle décision elle a prise. *She doesn't have to make up her mind at once. You may tell me tomorrow what decision she has made.*

The older use in such clauses of the future and future perfect, however, is still common in French, especially in certain fixed phrases.

Comme vous voudrez. *As you wish.*
Faites ce que vous voudrez. *Do what you wish.*
Vous ferez ce qui vous plaira. *You will do what pleases you.*

104 Formerly, the conjunction **jusqu'à ce que** was followed by the indicative when it was a question of a completed past event. Today, **jusqu'à ce que** is practically always followed by the subjunctive. Careful speakers often avoid the difficulty by replacing **jusqu'à ce que** by **jusqu'au jour où** or **jusqu'au moment où**, etc.

Les sauvages se sont battus courageusement jusqu'au moment où nos avions ont commencé à les mitrailler. *The savages fought courageously until our airplanes began to machine-gun them.*

105 The object **quelqu'un** is sometimes omitted when qualified by a phrase.

Il veut trouver avec qui causer de ces problèmes. *He wishes to find someone with whom to talk about these problems.*

106 When the verb **jouer** has a direct object, the preposition **sur** is used if the instrument in question is portable.[1] If it is not portable, either **à** or **sur** is used.

jouer un morceau sur le violon, sur la flûte, etc., *to play a piece on the violin, on the flute, etc.*

jouer un morceau au (*or,* sur le) piano, *to play a piece on the piano.*

CHAPTER II

107 In the emphatic construction **ce . . . que,** the tense used after **ce** is regularly the present. However, the preterit is frequently employed if this tense is used in the clause introduced by **que.** The corresponding replacement of the present by the future or the imperfect, though rather frequent, is generally not recommended by grammarians.

C'est à cause de vous qu'il a démissionné. *It was on account of you that he resigned.*

C'est (Ce fut) Napoléon Ier qui gagna la bataille de Wagram. *It was Napoleon the First who won the battle of Wagram.*

C'est (Ce sera) lui qui s'y opposera. *He is (will be) the one who will oppose it.*

C'est (C'était) à vous qu'il parlait. *He was speaking to you.*

108 In literary style, the use of a succession of past indefinites is generally avoided.

It may be interesting to note in this connection that many French people use the imperfect in the narration of a succession of events. Whatever may be the future of this use, it is generally considered incorrect by grammarians, except when resorted to sparingly in order to render narration more vivid.

---

[1] The preposition **à** may be used if it is not separated from the verb by the direct object.

Ce morceau, joué au violon par Mlle Duval . . . *This piece, played on the violin by Miss Duval . . .*

109 The past participle regularly does not agree with **en.**

> Vous n'avez pas reçu de lettres? Eh bien, en avez-vous écrit? *You haven't received any letters? Well, have you written any?*

According to certain grammarians, the past participle should agree if **en** is preceded by an expression of number, such as **combien**(= *how many*). The habit of using a "neuter" participle after **en** is so strong, however, that the agreement just mentioned is not made by most French people whenever such agreement would bring about a change in the pronunciation of the participle.

> Il m'a dit d'écrire trois lettres. — Eh bien, combien en avez-vous écrit(es)? *He told me to write three letters. Well, how many have you written?*

110 When the subject of **naître** is a living person, the past tense regularly used is the past indefinite. In a subordinate clause, the tense to be used will be determined by the laws of the sequence of tenses.

> Je suis né en 1922. *I was born in 1922.*
> Je lui avais donné à entendre que j'étais né en 1900. *I had given him to understand that I was born in 1900.*

When the subject of **naître** is not a living person, the past indefinite, the preterit, or the pluperfect may be used. The latter tense is particularly frequent in newspaper obituaries.

> Pierre de Ronsard est né en 1525.
> Clément Marot naquit en 1497.
> Rémy Belleau était né à Nogent-le-Rotrou.
> M. X était né à Cherbourg, le 23 juin 1875.

111 When **nous** is used to refer to one person, a following past participle or adjective remains in the singular number.

> Nous sommes reconnaissant à M. X de l'aide qu'il nous a apportée dans notre travail. *We are grateful to Mr. X for the help which he has given us in our work.*
> (*Bedside manner*) Alors, mon cher monsieur, nous sommes un peu fatigué ce matin? *So we're not feeling so well this morning, sir?*

112 In familiar language **pour que** is shortened to **que.**

Viens ici que je te fasse beau. *Come here and let me fix you up.*

113 The use of **l'on** after **que** is especially frequent when one wishes to prevent the repetition of the sound **qu'on.**

Ce que l'on condamne surtout, c'est sa paresse. *What people condemn especially is his laziness.*

114 **Nous** and **vous** are frequently used in a general sense to replace a subject pronoun **on.** Provided this general sense is evident, this use is preferred when there is also an object **nous** or **vous.**

Nous aimons toujours les gens qui nous flattent. *We always like the people who flatter us.*

115 By analogy with **il fait très chaud, si chaud,** etc., where **chaud** is really an adjective, the adverbs **très, si, tellement, aussi** are commonly used in conversation to modify a noun in expressions such as **avoir chaud, froid, faim, soif, raison,** etc.[1] In this construction, however, the use of **bien,** instead of **très,** of **tant** and **autant** instead of **si, tellement,** and **aussi,** is generally preferred by grammarians. The literary expressions **avoir grand faim,**[2] **grand soif,**[2] **grand peur,**[2] etc., are primarily characteristic of the older language.

J'ai très (*or:* bien) chaud. *I am very warm.*
J'en avais si (*or:* tellement) peur que ... (J'en avais tant peur que ...) *I was so afraid of it that ...*
J'ai aussi (*or:* autant) faim que vous. *I am as hungry as you.*
Il a bien raison. *He is quite right.*
Il en a tellement (*or:* tant) besoin (*or:* envie) que ... *He needs* (or: *wants) it so badly that ...*

---

[1] The number of the expressions containing **avoir** plus a noun with which these adverbs may be used seems to be largely a matter of personal reaction. The use of **tellement,** however, appears to be more widely accepted than that of the other adverbs.

[2] The early feminine form **grand** has been maintained in certain expressions. It is still frequently written with an apostrophe (**grand'faim, grand'soif, grand'peur, grand'mère,** etc.) to indicate what was once thought to be an omission of the feminine ending **e.**

J'en ai autant besoin que vous. (J'en ai besoin autant que vous.) *I need it as much as you.*

Cf. Nous en avons (très) grand besoin, (très) grande envie. *We need it very much, want it very much.*

Il en a si grand besoin (si grande envie) que . . . *He needs (wants) it so badly that . . .*

J'en ai aussi grand besoin que vous. *I need it as badly as you.*

CHAPTER III

116 *To* or *in* with names of large islands is expressed by **à** without the article.

à Cuba, à Terre-Neuve, à Madagascar, *to* or *in, Cuba, New-foundland, Madagascar*

117 When the name of a country is masculine and begins with a vowel, *to* or *in* may be translated by **en or dans l'**.

en Afghanistan, dans l'Afghanistan, *to*, or *in, Afghanistan*
en Uruguay, dans l'Uruguay, *to* or *in, Uruguay*

118 Although in modern French one prefers **au Portugal, au Danemark, du Portugal, du Danemark,** to the older **en Portugal, en Danemark, de Portugal, de Danemark,** the article is still regularly omitted in the age-old expressions, **le roi de Portugal, le roi de Danemark.** In adjectival phrases which date back to the older language, in which the article was relatively little used, the article is still omitted: **le roi de France, les villes de France, les vins de France, l'histoire de France.** In more modern phrases, the article is used: **la géographie de la France, le gouverneur de l'Algérie, l'empereur du Japon, le président du Mexique.** The article reappears after **histoire** when a comparison is made and sometimes when it is simply a question of a country other than France.

L'histoire de la France est plus intéressante que l'histoire de la Pologne. *The history of France is more interesting than the history of Poland.*

l'histoire de la Pologne, *the history of Poland*

119 When it is not a question of literal movement, the preposition *to* is translated by **à** plus the article, the preposition *from* by **de** plus the article.

> Les Etats-Unis offrent leurs bons offices à la France. *The United States offers its good offices to France.*
> La Grèce aurait reçu de l'Italie des propositions de paix. *Greece is said to have received peace proposals from Italy.*

120 If the modifier and the name of the country form a unit, **en** without the article is regularly used.

> en Asie Mineure, *in Asia Minor*

In modern French there is a tendency to extend this unit idea to the names of many well-known geographical divisions.

> en Amérique du Sud, *in South America*
> en Afrique du Nord, *in North Africa*

121 In answering the telephone, the French doctor might say:

> « Ici le docteur Martin. » *"This is Dr. Martin."*

122 **Monsieur** is the only title the abbreviation of which is followed by a period.

M. (Monsieur)	*Mr.*
Mme (Madame)	*Mrs.*
Mlle (Mademoiselle)	*Miss*
Me (Maître)	*Title given to a lawyer or notary*
Dr (Docteur)	*Dr.*

123 Theoretically, **parler le français** means to speak the French language, i.e., to know how to speak it, **parler français,** to speak French, i.e., to be in the act of speaking. This distinction is not very frequently observed except where the name of the language is made emphatic by contrast or enumeration.

> Il parle l'anglais et l'italien aussi bien que le français. *He speaks English and Italian as well as he does French.*
> En Angleterre on parle l'anglais, en Allemagne on parle l'allemand, en Russie on parle le russe, etc. *In England English is spoken, in Germany, German, in Russia, Russian, etc.*

Parler français has also the idiomatic meaning, *to speak correct French.*

124 The older construction with the plural article is sometimes found.

> Il ne vient pas les dimanches. *He does not come on Sundays.*

If two days of the week are given, each may be used with the singular article, or the plural article may be used before the first and none before the last. When more than two days are mentioned, the latter construction is practically always used. When the plural article is used, the names of the days in the series are almost always pluralized.

> Le musée est ouvert le lundi et le jeudi (les lundis et jeudis). *The museum is open Monday and Thursday.*
>
> Le musée de minéralogie est ouvert les mardis, jeudis, samedis de 13 heures à 16 heures. *The mineralogy museum is open Tuesdays, Thursdays, Saturdays from 1 o'clock till 4 o'clock.*
>
> Ouvert au public les lundi, mardi, mercredi, jeudi et vendredi du 1er avril au 30 octobre. *Open to the public Monday, Tuesday, Wednesday, Thursday, Friday from the 1st of April to the 30th of October.*

125 When the season of a definite year is indicated, the preposition **dans** or **pendant** (**à** with **automne**) and the definite article are used.

> pendant (dans) l'été, l'hiver, de 1914, *during (in) the summer, winter, of 1914*
>
> pendant (dans *or* à) l'automne de 1924, *during (in) the fall of 1924*

In the spring of 1924 would be regularly expressed by **au printemps de 1924.**

126 The article is frequently omitted in enumerations and pairs, in order to add vivacity to the style, and is regularly omitted in signs, titles, and certain proverbs. In enumerations this omission is generally accompanied by a word which sums up everything enumerated, i.e., **tous** in the first example, **quantité** in the second.

Hommes, femmes, enfants, tous périrent. *Men, women, children, all perished.*

Sur la table il y avait une quantité d'articles: montres, pipes, canifs, encriers, crayons, plumes, livres [1] ... *On the table there was a quantity of things: watches, pipes, knives, inkstands, pencils, pens, books ...*

Les Anglais ont fait preuve de beaucoup de courage et de persévérance, mais courage et persévérance ne suffisent pas. *The English have displayed a great deal of courage and perseverance, but courage and perseverance are not enough.*

Plusieurs jeunes femmes leur offraient cigares et cigarettes.[1] *Several young women offered them cigars and cigarettes.*

maison à louer, *house for rent*

Histoire de France, *History of France*

Pauvreté n'est pas vice. *Poverty is not a vice.*

127 With **an** and **heure** one has a choice of two constructions: **deux fois par an; deux francs par heure;** or: **deux fois l'an, deux francs l'heure. Deux francs de l'heure** is frequently used in colloquial French but is not considered correct by grammarians.

CHAPTER IV

128 When both starting point and destination are street names, the prepositions are used.

Le chauffeur a affirmé qu'il vous avait conduit de la rue Cardinet à la rue de Vaugirard. *The chauffeur stated that he had driven you from Cardinet Street to Vaugirard Street.*

When the prepositions *to, till,* or *until* (used after *from*) have as their object the name of a month or year, they are regularly translated by **à,** whether the period of time in question is presented as inclusive or exclusive.

Pourriez-vous me prêter les numéros de cette revue de septembre à mai? *Could you lend me the numbers of this magazine from September to (till) May?*

---

[1] The article omitted here is **des,** the plural of the indefinite article.

Voici les chiffres pour une période de quinze mois, d'avril 1920 à juin 1921. *Here are the figures for a period of fifteen months, from April, 1920 to June, 1921.*

L'auberge est fermée de novembre à janvier. *The inn is closed from November to (till) January.*

En deux ans, de 1917 à 1919, le coût de la vie a doublé. *In two years, from 1917 to 1919, the cost of living doubled.*

When one wishes clearly to indicate the inclusion of a portion of the month or year, **à** is replaced by **en** or **jusqu'en.** When **jusqu'en** is used, *from* is regularly translated by **depuis.** If the starting point of the period of time is not given, **jusqu'en** must be used.

Il a été président du conseil de septembre en mai (depuis septembre jusqu'en mai). *He was president of the cabinet from September till (some time in) May.*

Je suis resté à Paris jusqu'en octobre, jusqu'en 1938, etc. *I stayed in Paris until October, until 1938, etc.*

If the object of the preposition is modified by the definite article, **à** or **jusqu'à** must be used.

du (depuis le) commencement de 1917 à (jusqu'à) la fin de 1919, *from the beginning of 1917 to the end of 1919*

Nous resterons à Paris jusqu'au mois de juin. *We shall stay in Paris until the month of June.*

Il a été président du conseil du 23 septembre au 17 mai (depuis le 23 septembre jusqu'au 17 mai). *He was president of the cabinet from September 23 till May 17.*

CHAPTER V

129 In exclamatory sentences introduced by **que** and **comme,** the partitive article is regularly used. This article may be reduced to **de,** however, when the emphasis is on quantity rather than on degree. When **comme** is used, the partitive phrase must follow the verb.

Que (Comme) cela m'a fait du bien! *How it did help me!*

Que de bien il fait! (Literary style: Qu'il fait de bien!) *How much good he does!*

On est très belle ce matin. *You are (She is) very beautiful this morning.*

On s'était connu jeunes filles. *We had known each other when we were girls.*

137 When the direct object other than a personal pronoun precedes the verb, it must be repeated in the form of a personal pronoun.

Ce que nous faisons, nous le faisons pour vous. *What we do, we do for you.*

Cet obstacle, nous l'avons déjà franchi. *We have already surmounted this obstacle.*

On the other hand, the English personal pronoun which anticipates a dependent infinitive or clause is not expressed in French.

Il a trouvé difficile de nier la vérité. *He found it difficult to deny the truth.*

Il trouve tout naturel qu'on lui rende tous ses biens. *He considers it quite natural that all his possessions be returned to him.*

138 After the affirmative imperative the forms **m'y, t'y** are avoided by most French people.

139 The conjunctive pronoun **je** stands without a disjunctive in the formula, **Je soussigné.**

Je soussigné déclare... *I, the undersigned, declare...*

140 The disjunctive pronoun of any person may stand before **seul** without the corresponding conjunctive's being expressed.

Toi seul me comprends. *You alone understand me.*

141 In the older language **en** was used for persons as well as for things. Except as a partitive, it is rarely used of persons in modern French.

142 These uses of **en** and **y** result from the fact that French avoids whenever possible the use of a preposition followed by a disjunctive pronoun referring to things or animals. Another way of avoiding this disjunctive is to use an appropriate adverb. In familiar French, when such an adverb cannot be found, the preposition is not infrequently used without an object.

> Vous a-t-il fait mal au pied? — Oui, il a marché dessus. (*Not:* **sur lui** which would mean *on him.*) *Did he hurt your foot? Yes, he stepped on it.*
> Voici la malle. Qu'est-ce qu'il faut mettre dedans? *Here's the trunk. What must we put into it?*
> Il y a une clôture tout autour. *There's a fence all around it.*
> Si je mets ma robe blanche, quel collier dois-je mettre avec? *If I put on my white dress, what necklace shall I wear with it?*

143 If the verb in question may be preceded by the indirect object **lui** or **leur,** this indirect object is regularly preferred to **y** unless ambiguity would result.

> Voici son complet. Je vais lui (*Popular speech:* **y**) donner un coup de fer. *Here is his suit. I'm going to press it.*
> *But:* Voici sa lettre. Y avez-vous répondu? *Here is his letter. Have you answered it?* (**Lui** avez-vous répondu *would mean: Have you answered him?*)

144 Whereas the English *to go* may have an implied destination, the French **aller** regularly requires that such a destination be expressed by **y**. In modern French, however, for reasons of euphony this **y** is not used with the future or conditional.

> Si vous y allez, je n'irai pas. *If you go (there), I shall not go.*

The **y** is also omitted after the imperative **Allez!** equivalent to **Allez-vous-en!** It may be omitted before **aller avec** equivalent to **accompagner.**

> Je (J'y) vais avec vous. *I'm going with you.*

145 Y is also used as equivalent to *in* or *at home.* In modern French this **y** is generally replaced by **là**.

> Monsieur X n'y est pas (Monsieur X n'est pas là). *Mr. X is not in.*

Je n'y suis pour personne (Je ne suis là pour personne). *I'm not at home to anyone.*

146 In modern French **il** is not used to translate *it* referring to an idea, except as a logical subject of **être** or as the subject of certain impersonal verbs. The translation must be made by **cela** (or: **ça**).

— Dis donc, André, est-ce que tu savais que Jeanne Dufour était mariée? *Say, Andrew, did you know that Jeanne Dufour was married?*
— Ça ne m'étonne pas. *It (That) doesn't surprise me (I'm not surprised).*
Cela m'amuse de vous voir travailler. *It amuses me to see you working.*
Il est (*Colloquial:* C'est) agréable de se promener à la campagne. *It is pleasant to take a walk in the country.*
J'irai s'il (si cela) me plaît d'y aller. *I shall go if it pleases me to go.*

147 This redundant **ne** is a survival of the **ne** which was used after verbs of fearing in Latin.

CHAPTER VII

148 When there is negation in the sentence, unless it is **ne . . . plus**, the tense used with **depuis, il y a . . . que** is regularly the same as in English. (Cf. **1, C**)

Je ne l'avais pas vu depuis deux jours. Il y avait deux jours que je ne l'avais (pas) vu. *I hadn't seen him for two days.*
Elle n'habitait plus là depuis longtemps. *She hadn't lived there for a long time.*

Cela fait (**faisait**) may replace **il y a, il y avait** when a more emphatic construction is desired. **Voici** and **voilà**, which are similarly employed, should not be used with a verb in the imperfect or pluperfect tense. (Cf. **1, C**)

Cela fait quinze jours qu'il est malade. *He's been sick for two weeks (That makes two weeks that he's been sick).*

Cela fait trois jours que je ne l'ai vu. *I haven't seen him for three days.*

Cela faisait trois jours que je ne l'avais vu. *I hadn't seen him for three days.*

149 We have seen in § 1, C that the present is used after **il y a . . . que** to express action or state which has not ended, or has barely come to an end. If the action of the dependent verb is clearly past, but still quite close to the present, **il y a . . . que** is followed by the imperfect. If the action occurs in a more remote past, the imperfect is used in each clause.

Il y a longtemps que je *désire* le connaître. *I've been wanting to meet him for a long time.*

Il y a longtemps que je *désirais* vous connaître, monsieur. (just after an introduction) *I've wanted to meet you for a long time, sir.*

Il y avait longtemps que je *désirais* le connaître. (a more remote past) *I had been wanting to meet him for a long time.*

Il y a longtemps que vous m'*attendez?* (just as one meets a friend) *Have you been waiting for me long?*

Il y a longtemps que vous m'*attendiez?* (just after the meetting takes place) *Had you been waiting for me long?*

Il y avait longtemps que vous m'*attendiez?* (some time later) *Had you been waiting for me long?*

In the case of a negative sentence in which a compound tense is used, the preceding remarks apply to the auxiliary.

Il y a deux ans qu'on ne s'*est* vus. (just as one meets a friend) *We haven't seen each other for two years.*

Il y a deux ans qu'on ne s'*était* vus. (just after the meeting) *We haven't seen each other for two years.*

Il y avait deux ans qu'on ne s'*était* vus. (some time later) *We hadn't seen each other for two years.*

150 In certain cases either the imperfect or the past indefinite may be used with a difference in meaning. For example, the imperfect in **Il était malade hier** pictures the state as still existing at a certain moment in past time, i.e., *when I was talking to him, when I saw him,* etc., and does not necessarily imply that he is well now. In **Il a été malade**

hier the past indefinite states a fact without connecting it with any particular moment of the period of past time, and does imply that he is well now. Of course, in **Il a été malade toute la journée d'hier** the past indefinite is obligatory, as the complete duration of the state is given.

151 The pluperfect indicative is regularly used in temporal clauses only in the following cases:

1. When the action of the main clause takes place considerably later than that of the subordinate clause.

> Vingt ans après que son père avait fini le manuscrit, Julien l'a envoyé à l'éditeur. *Twenty years after his father had finished the manuscript, Julian sent it to the publisher.*

2. When the main clause contains a verb in the imperfect tense.

> Quand il avait fini de lire son journal, il se renversait dans sa bergère et s'endormait. *When he had finished reading his paper, he would lean back in his easy chair and go to sleep.*

When the verb of the main clause is in the past indefinite, the past anterior cannot be used. Its place is frequently taken by the **passé surcomposé** (the past indefinite of the auxiliary plus the past participle). The **passé surcomposé** with **avoir** is now accepted by most grammarians; the form with **être** is still rather generally condemned. Reflexive verbs cannot be used in this tense.

> Quand il a eu fini ses devoirs, il est sorti en claquant la porte. *When he (had) finished his exercises, he went out slamming the door.*
> Après qu'elle a été partie, les autres invités sont revenus. *After she (had) left, the other guests came back.*

It is frequently possible to avoid the use of the **passé surcomposé** by changing the construction of the sentence.

> Après avoir fini ses devoirs (Ses devoirs finis), il est sorti en claquant la porte. *After finishing his exercises (His exercises finished) he went out slamming the door.*
> Après son départ, les autres invités sont revenus. *After her departure, the other guests came back.*

203

152 To express the idea *even if, even though*, the conditional and past conditional are used after **quand (même)** in the *if*-clauses of conditional sentences.

> Quand (même) il m'offrirait (m'aurait offert) sa place, je ne l'accepterais pas (l'aurais pas acceptée). *Even if he offered (had offered) me his place, I would not accept (would not have accepted) it.*

But, if the expression **même si** is used, the regular rule applies.

> Même s'il m'offrait sa place, je ne l'accepterais pas.

In literary style the pluperfect subjunctive is frequently used in one or both clauses of a contrary-to-fact conditional sentence.

> Si on lui eût offert cette place, il ne l'eût pas acceptée.

153 In colloquial French the conditional is frequently used in both clauses of the conditional sentence. No conjunction precedes the *if*-clause, but **que** may precede the result clause.

> Je le voudrais, (que) je ne pourrais pas. *If I should want to, I couldn't.*
>
> Il m'offrirait sa place (aurait offert sa place), (que) je ne l'accepterais pas (je ne l'aurais pas acceptée).

154 In certain cases even when the subject is a collective of number, the emphasis may be so strong on the collective that a singular verb has to be used.

> Un grand nombre d'admirateurs ne déplaît jamais à une jeune fille. *A great number of admirers is never displeasing to a girl.*

Fractions, such as **la moitié, le tiers, le quart,** etc., generally take a plural verb if they have a plural complement expressed or implied. Cf. § 9, D. When it is a question of an exact fraction, or of a contrast, these words require a singular verb. The singular is also required after **douzaine,** meaning *one dozen*, and **majorité** and **minorité,** when used as parliamentary terms.

> La moitié (des élèves) s'endormiront. *Half of the pupils will fall asleep.*

La moitié des élèves a voté pour la proposition, la moitié contre. *Half of the pupils voted for the motion, half against.*
La moitié ne vaut jamais le tout. *The half is never worth the whole.*
Une douzaine de petits pains ne suffira pas. *A dozen rolls will not be enough.*

But: Une douzaine de femmes ont été tuées. *About twelve women were killed.*
La majorité (des députés) s'oppose à la proposition. *The majority (of the deputies) is opposed to the motion.*
La majorité des écrivains (*Better:* La plupart des . . .) évitent cette tournure. *Most writers avoid this construction.*

The expression **plus d'un** is followed by a singular verb; **moins de deux** requires a plural verb.

Plus d'un soldat y restera. *More than one soldier will stay there* (i.e., *will not come back*).
Moins de deux siècles se sont écoulés depuis la Révolution française. *Less than two centuries have elapsed since the French Revolution.*

When a collective noun or an adverb of quantity is followed by a singular complement, the agreement of the predicate adjective or past participle is generally with the collective.

Trop d'instruction est dangereux. *Too much learning is dangerous.*
Une partie de l'or a été perdue. *A part of the gold was lost.*

When the subjects are nouns or personal pronouns of the same person used with **ni . . . ni,** they are considered together rather than separately; hence, the verb is almost always in the plural if the subjects are not mutually exclusive. Even when they are mutually exclusive a plural verb may generally be used. When the subjects are personal pronouns of different persons, the plural verb must be used.

Ni Jean ni sa sœur ne sont arrivés. *Neither John nor his sister came.*
Ni lui ni elle n'arriveront à temps. *Neither he nor she will arrive on time.*
Ni ta femme ni ta fille ne gagnera (gagneront) le gros lot.

Neither your wife nor your daughter will win the first prize (in a lottery).

Ni lui ni elle ne gagnera (gagneront) le gros lot. *Neither he nor she will win the first prize.*

Ni vous ni moi, nous ne gagnerons le gros lot. *Neither you nor I will win the first prize.*

Two singular subjects connected by **ou** are generally followed by a plural verb except when they are felt to be mutually exclusive. Even in the latter case, two pronoun subjects of different persons are followed by a verb in the plural.

La mauvaise chance ou la faiblesse font échouer bien des plans. *Bad luck or weakness causes many plans to fail.*

C'est Lucien ou Paul qui présidera (*Rather than:* Lucien ou Paul présidera) la distribution des prix. *(Either) Lucien or Paul will preside at the closing exercises (of a school)* (lit., *the distribution of prizes*).

C'est toi ou lui qui l'épouserez (Toi ou lui, vous l'épouserez) (*or:* [C'est] l'un de vous deux [qui] l'épousera). *(Either) You or he will marry her (One of you two will marry her).*

Subject pronouns of different persons are replaced by a third-person construction when the idea of exclusion is emphasized by expressions such as **le premier, le dernier,** etc. For example, to translate *You or he went out last,* one would say **(C'est) l'un de vous deux (qui) est sorti le dernier.**

155 In modern French, **la plupart,** as subject or object, is practically never followed by a singular complement. Its place, when such a complement is present, is regularly taken by **la plus grande partie.**

La plus grande partie du vin a été vendue. *Most of the wine has been sold.*

Il a déjà bu la plus grande partie du vin. *He has already drunk most of the wine.*

156 The impersonal construction is very common when the real subject expresses number or quantity. It is used with verbs expressing change of state, literal or figurative, and with **rester.**

Il en est sorti deux par la fenêtre. *Two went out through the window.*

Il nous en reste trois. *We have three left.*

Il m'est venu une idée. *An idea came to me.*

Il naît plus de personnes qu'il n'en meurt. *More people are born than die.*

CHAPTER VIII

157 After the conjunctions **si, quand, bien que,** and **quoique, devoir** or some equivalent construction must be used instead of **aller** before a dependent infinitive to express the idea of *planned* futurity. If the literal meaning *to go* is present, or if **si** (*whether*) or **quand** is used in indirect discourse, **aller** is used.[1]

> Si (Quand) nous devons (nous avons l'intention de) nous lever de bonne heure, nous nous couchons de bonne heure. *If (When) we are going to get up early, we go to bed early.*
>
> Bien que (Quoique) je doive partir demain, je tâcherai de faire votre commission. *Although I am going to leave tomorrow, I shall try to do your errand.*
>
> S'il allait s'établir en France, elle l'épouserait. *If he went to settle* (Not: *If he were going to settle*) *in France, she would marry him.*
>
> Il m'a demandé si j'allais faire un tour en ville. *He asked me if (whether) I was going to take a walk down town.*
>
> Il m'a demandé quand j'allais payer mes dettes. *He asked me when I was going to pay my debts.*

158 The conditional and past conditional of **falloir** are used to express moral obligation.

> Pour être respecté de ses amis il faudrait tenir ses engagements. *To be respected by one's friends, one should keep one's promises.*

---

[1] Except in literary style, **aller** (plus infinitive) is regularly not used to express futurity in a clause the verb of which is in the subjunctive mode.

> Je regrette qu'il parte (doive partir) demain. *I am sorry that he is leaving (is going to leave, is to leave, must leave) tomorrow.*

Ce n'est peut-être pas cela qu'il faudrait dire. *Perhaps that's not what should be said.*

Il aurait fallu commencer plus tôt. *We ought to have begun earlier.*

Il faudrait que vous étudiiez davantage. *You should study more.*

The past conditional is frequently replaced by the imperfect, especially in familiar style.

Si vous aimiez tant votre femme, il ne fallait pas la quitter. *If you loved your wife so much, you ought not to have left her.*

Falloir is also used to express probability.

Il faut que je me sois mal exprimé. *I must have expressed myself badly.*

Il fallait être fou pour faire cela. *He must have been crazy to do that.*

Je n'ai rien entendu; il a fallu qu'il sorte sur la pointe des pieds. *I heard nothing; he must have gone out on tiptoe.*

When **falloir** expresses probability, the negation is placed in the subordinate clause.

Pour ignorer cela, il faut qu'il n'ait aucune instruction. *To be ignorant of that, he must have no education.*

When there is no possibility of ambiguity, **il ne faut pas** is sometimes used in the sense of *it is not necessary to, one does not have to.*

Il ne faut pas être malin pour voir clair dans son jeu. *One doesn't have to be very smart to see through his game.*

Il ne faut pas absolument que nous partions à sept heures. *It isn't absolutely necessary for us to leave at seven o'clock.*

While the student should understand this use of **il ne faut pas,** he will do well to avoid it in his own writing.

159 The majority of French people keep the infinitive invariable after **devoir.** Some careful speakers, however, prefer to conjugate the infinitive, when **devoir** expresses moral obligation or probability.

Vous devriez l'avoir dit *instead of:* Vous auriez dû le dire. *You ought to have said it.*

Il doit l'avoir fait *instead of:* Il a dû le faire. *He must have done it.*

160 When the conditional of **devoir** (equivalent to the softened present) is used in a conditional sentence, the present must be used in the *if*-clause. When the true conditional of **devoir** is used, the imperfect must be used in the *if*-clause.

> Vous devriez aller le voir, si vous avez le temps. *You ought to go to see him if you have the time.*
>
> S'il vous disait de faire cela, vous devriez le faire. *If he told you to do that, you would have to do it.*

161 In statements with indefinite subjects, English *should* or *ought* is regularly translated by the present tense of **devoir** rather than by the conditional.

> On doit toujours faire son devoir. *One should always do one's duty.*

162 The imperfect of **devoir** is sometimes used as the equivalent of the past conditional.

> Vous deviez le faire *equals* Vous auriez dû le faire. (Vous étiez dans l'obligation de le faire.) *You ought to have done it.*
>
> Tu ne devais pas garder ce qui ne t'appartenait pas. *You ought not to have kept what didn't belong to you.*

163 Necessity is also frequently expressed by **avoir à** plus the infinitive. This use of **avoir à** is especially common when the obligation to be expressed is the result of an order or a regulation.

> Qu'est-ce que vous avez à faire? — J'ai des lettres à écrire. (J'ai à écrire des lettres.) *What do you have to do? I have some letters to write (I have to write some letters).*
>
> Si vous voulez du sucre, vous aurez à présenter votre carte. *If you want sugar, you'll have to present your card.*
>
> Si vous faites des fautes d'orthographe dans votre devoir, vous aurez à le recopier. *If you have any mistakes in spelling in your exercise, you'll have to recopy it.*

164 When **on** is used to represent a certain group of individuals or a certain individual, it may be the subject of a clause governed by **falloir.**

> Il faut qu'on finisse ce travail pour samedi prochain. *They (we or you) must finish this work by next Saturday.*

165 The construction of the indirect object with **falloir** and the infinitive is sometimes used to avoid two successive **que** clauses. A better way of avoiding this, however, is to use **devoir** and the infinitive.

> Il m'a dit qu'il lui avait fallu passer un examen. Il m'a dit qu'il avait dû passer un examen (*instead of:* Il m'a dit qu'il avait fallu qu'il passe un examen). *He told me that he had had to take an examination.*

166 **Tout** is followed by **de** when it means *everything about.*

> Il ignore tout de l'affaire. *He is ignorant of everything about the matter.*

167 The adverb **tout,** when it modifies an abstract noun, generally agrees with that noun.

> Il est toute bonté (tout courage). *He is kindness (courage) itself.*
> Elle est toute douceur et toute résignation. *She is all sweetness and resignation.*

When **tout** modifies a concrete noun, it is regularly invariable.

> Elle était tout yeux, tout oreilles. *She was all eyes, all ears.*
> Ce tissu est tout laine, tout soie. *This material is all wool, all silk.*

CHAPTER IX

168 Certain adjectives which regularly precede the noun frequently follow the noun without change of meaning when they are modified by an adverb or when they are used in the superlative.

un repas très maigre, un très maigre repas, *a very meager meal*

une colère très forte, *a very great rage*

le plus savant professeur, le professeur le plus savant, *the most learned professor*

mes livres les plus chers, *my dearest (i.e., favorite) books*
One could express the same idea by saying: Les livres auxquels je tiens le plus.

169 When it is a question of a novel, or play, etc.; **nouveau** generally follows the noun with the meaning of *recently published.*

un roman nouveau, *a new (recently published) novel*

Nouveau may precede or follow the noun when the latter is modified by a **de**-phrase. In the second case, **nouveau** *may* have also the idea of *original,* if this meaning is indicated by the context. It may also precede the noun with the meaning *recently published* when used in a contrast with another **nouveau** meaning *original.*

la nouvelle comédie de M. Sacha Guitry, *Mr. Sacha Guitry's new comedy*

la comédie nouvelle de M. Francis de Croisset, *the new (original) comedy of Mr. Francis de Croisset*

J'ai lu beaucoup de nouveaux romans mais aucun roman nouveau. (Jokingly) *I have read many new (recent) novels but not one original novel.*

If one had no idea of playing upon the position of **nouveau,** one would probably say:

J'ai lu beaucoup de nouveaux romans mais aucun roman vraiment nouveau.

Neuf means *brand-new* or *almost brand-new.* It is especially used in contrast with **vieux** expressed or implied. Whereas a man, for whom a new hat is usually an event, would say:

Je vais mettre mon chapeau neuf;

a woman who had several new hats would generally say:

Je vais mettre mon nouveau chapeau.

When *new* expresses the idea *recently occurred,* **nouveau** is less familiar than **neuf.**

> Quoi de nouveau? Quoi de neuf? *What is new?*

Colloquially **vieux** is used in comparisons when persons in question are not old at all. **Agé,** however, is preferred in these cases.

> Mon petit garçon est plus vieux (*better:* plus âgé) que le tien. *My little boy is older than yours.*

In expressions such as *You are too old to play with dolls, old* is regularly translated in French by **grand(e).**

> Tu es trop grande pour jouer avec des poupées.

170 When an adjective modifies two or more abstract nouns of similar meaning, the agreement may be with the nearest noun.

> L'accomplissement de cette tâche exigera un tact et une patience infinie (*or:* une patience et un tact infinis). *The accomplishment of this task will exact infinite tact and patience.*

171 When the two nouns indicate the same person, however, the preceding adjective is not repeated before the second.

> Mon cher collègue et ami. *My dear friend and colleague.*

172 In the case of the expression **avoir l'air,** the agreement of the adjective is with the subject if **avoir l'air** is considered as the equivalent of *to seem, to appear;* with *air* if it is given the meaning of *to have a certain air* or *appearance.* If the subject of **avoir l'air** is a thing, the adjective must agree with the subject.

> Elle a l'air heureuse. *She seems happy.*
> Ils avaient l'air coupable. *They had a guilty appearance.*
> *But:* Les pommes que vous avez achetées n'ont pas l'air mûres. *The apples you bought don't look ripe.*

CHAPTER X

173 In an emphatic comparison, **si** is replaced by **aussi.**

> Je vous dis qu'il n'est pas aussi intelligent que sa sœur. *I tell you that he is not as intelligent as his sister.*

174 Many grammarians prefer to omit this **ne** after most negative or interrogative clauses, especially in literary style.

175 This use of **le** appears to be especially frequent when the **ne** is omitted.

> Elle n'est pas aussi forte que vous le pensez. *She is not as strong as you think.*

176 When one phase of a person or thing is compared with another phase of the same person or thing, the masculine singular article must be used.

> C'est quand elle est en colère, qu'elle est le plus charmante. *She is most charming when she is angry.*

177 According to the rule of grammar, the adjective **pis** regularly replaces **pire** when it modifies an indefinite pronoun or the demonstrative **ce,** or a relative **ce que, ce qui. Pire,** however, is not infrequently met with in such cases.

> C'est pis que cela. *It's worse than that.*
> Il a fait quelque chose de pis. *He did something worse.*
> Ce qu'il a fait de pis . . . *The worst thing he did . . .*
> Il n'y a rien de pis que cela. *There is nothing worse than that.*

Pis is also used adverbially to replace **plus mal,** especially in set expressions. **Pire** must not be used here.

> Il a fait pis que jamais. *He did worse than ever.*
> Tant pis. *So much the worse.*
> Cela va de mal en pis. *It goes from bad to worse.*
> au pis aller, *at the very worst*

With verbs other than **faire, il y a,** and **aller** (in a few expressions) the adverb **pis** is generally replaced by **plus mal.**

178 When emphasis is placed on these words or when they are closely connected with a complement, they may follow.

Je pourrais jouer ce rôle mieux que personne. *I could play this rôle better than anyone.*

Je vais lui dire tout, vous m'entendez, tout. *I am going to tell him everything, you hear me, everything.*

Il n'a jamais fait rien d'autre.[1] *He never did anything else.*

A pronoun object may be inserted before or after these words.

Pour mieux le voir, pour le mieux voir ... *To see him better ...*

Sans rien lui dire, sans lui rien dire ... *Without saying anything to him ...*

In modern French, the pronoun is, perhaps, more frequently placed immediately before the infinitive. This order is obligatory with **tout.**

Je vais tout vous dire. *I am going to tell you everything.*

179 **Davantage** regularly expresses *more* when no complement or comparison follows. If a complement or comparison follows, **plus** is the correct word in modern French.

J'en ai davantage. *I have more.*

Il n'en a pas beaucoup et moi, je n'en ai pas davantage. *He hasn't much and I haven't any more (i.e., than he has).*

Elle a beaucoup d'esprit et encore plus d'argent. *She has a lot of wit and still more money.*

J'en ai plus que vous. *I have more than you.*

180 Even in direct address the possessive adjective of the first person is frequently used before a noun indicating relationship.

Vous avez raison, mon père. (quite formal) *You are right, father.*

Mais oui, mon oncle. *Why yes, uncle.*

Mais non, ma tante. *Of course not, aunt.*

Many French people feel that the word **oncle,** whether used in direct address or not, should be accompanied by **mon** or **l'.**

Venez ici, que je vous présente mon oncle Henri. *Come here, so that I may introduce (my) uncle Henry to you.*

Tante Hélène a suggéré d'aller au théâtre; l'oncle Henri n'a

---

[1] The same idea could be expressed thus: **Il n'a jamais fait autre chose.**

pas voulu. *Aunt Helen suggested going to the theater; Uncle Henry didn't want to (go).*

In familiar language, the possessive is frequently omitted with **père** and **mère.**

> Père ne veut pas que j'y aille. *Father doesn't want me to go there.*
> Bonjour, mère, vous avez bien dormi? *Good morning, mother, did you sleep well?*

Papa and **maman** are regularly used without possessives.

> Oui, papa. Papa et maman sont sortis.

In the army, when an equal or superior addresses another officer, the titles **lieutenant, capitaine, général,** etc., are used. An inferior speaking to a superior must prefix the possessive adjective **mon. Me voici, mon capitaine, mon général,** etc.

A civilian addressing an army officer with whom he is not on very familiar terms will generally be considered more polite if he uses the possessive adjective.

181 When each of a number of persons possesses one of a number of things or persons, the thing or person possessed is regularly placed in the singular when modified by the definite article, or in the plural when modified by a possessive adjective.

> Ils ont hoché la tête. *They shook their heads.*
> Cela nous a déchiré le cœur. *That broke our hearts.*
> Il leur a sauvé la vie. *He saved their lives.*
> Ils sont entrés l'épée à la main. *They entered with swords in hand.*
> Allez chercher vos chapeaux.[1] *Go get your hats.*

Abstract nouns, however, are regularly placed in the singular even when modified by the possessive adjective.

---

[1] As a result, possibly, of the fact that the pronunciation of **leur** and **leurs** is the same, the singular form of this pronoun frequently replaces the plural. No Frenchman, however, even though he might write **Ils sont allés chercher leur manteau,** would ever write **Nous allons chercher notre manteau.**

Ils ont passé toute leur vie à ne rien faire. *They spent their whole lives doing nothing.*

A notre âge il est dangereux de faire trop d'exercice. *At our age it is dangerous to take too much exercise.*

182 The possessive adjective must be used when the part of the body is modified, unless the adjective is an integral part of the noun.

Donnez-moi votre jolie petite main. *Give me your pretty little hand.*

Levez la main droite! *Raise your right hand!*

183 When it is a question of establishing the identity of one or more objects possessed rather than that of the possessor, the possessive pronoun is regularly used.

— Tiens, voilà ma robe de chambre. *Why, there's my bathrobe.*

— Ce n'est pas la tienne, c'est la mienne. *It's not yours, it's mine.*

CHAPTER XI

184 The word **date** is preceded by the preposition **à** with the meaning of the English *on.*

A la date indiquée... *On the appointed date...*

Quelle est la date à laquelle vous devez remettre votre manuscrit? *On what date are you to turn in your manuscript?*

185 When speaking of books, songs, plays, etc., one may use either the cardinal or the ordinal. In titles the cardinal is generally used except in the case of *first*, which is frequently expressed by either the ordinal or the cardinal.

Tome un	Tome premier
Chant un	Chant premier
Chapitre un	Chapitre premier
Acte un	Acte premier
Chapitre trois	
Scène quatre	

au premier acte, au deuxième (second) acte, à la première
scène, à la deuxième scène
à l'acte deux, à la scène deux

Note the use of the preposition **à** in the preceding examples.
If reference is made, however, to a word or expression rather
than to an event, **à** is replaced by **dans.**

Dans la troisième scène, il y a un emploi intéressant de la
préposition *à*. *In the third scene there is an interesting use
of the preposition* à.

186 When there is a plural noun subject, the adjective
both is regularly translated by **les deux,** the pronoun *both* by
tous les deux without distinction of persons or things.

Les deux sénateurs s'y sont opposés. *Both senators opposed it.*
Les sénateurs s'y sont opposés, tous les deux. *The senators
both opposed it.*
Les deux reproches sont mérités. *Both reproaches are deserved.*
Ces reproches sont mérités tous les deux. *These reproaches
are both deserved.*

With the plural noun object, **les deux** is regularly used.

J'ai vu les deux sénateurs. *I saw both senators.*
J'ai parlé aux deux sénateurs. *I spoke to both senators.*
On a coulé les deux bateaux. *They sank both boats.* (*Both boats
were sunk.*)
Il a envoyé des malades aux deux hôpitaux. *He sent patients
to both hospitals.*

187 **Second** has certain senses which **deuxième** does not
have.

Bien des gens croient que Buenos Aires est un second Paris.
Many people believe that Buenos Aires is another Paris.

Second used as a noun means *first mate,* or *second* in a duel.

188 When the ordinal is a predicate nominative, the article
may regularly be used if the sentence does not end with the
ordinal.

C'est (Il est) le premier, (le deuxième, etc.) de sa classe. *He
is first (second, etc.) in his class.*

Otherwise the article is generally omitted.

Il est premier, deuxième, troisième, etc.

189 When the cardinal adjective and the noun it modifies form a unit, the ordinal precedes the cardinal.

les premières vingt-quatre heures (*24 hours = 1 day*)

190 **Neuvaine** is used only with the meaning *novena*, i.e., prayers, masses lasting nine days.

191 The definite article is regularly used with fractions composed of cardinal and ordinal.

les neuf dixièmes, les quatre cinquièmes, *nine tenths, four fifths*

It is regularly omitted in calculations when no complement is present.

Trois cinquièmes plus trois dixièmes font neuf dixièmes.
Three fifths plus three tenths equal nine tenths.

192 Although one never says **trois et demi mètres,** one *does* say **trois et demi pour cent** (three and one-half per cent) which literally means *three and a half per hundred.*

CHAPTER XII

193 With verbs of *seeing, perceiving, hearing,* etc., **pouvoir** is regularly not used, if no effort is implied.

Un aveugle est un homme qui ne voit pas. *A blind man is a man who can't see.*
Un sourd est un homme qui n'entend pas. *A deaf man is a man who can't hear.*
Je vois bien que vous n'avez jamais été en France. *I can readily see that you have never been in France.*
De ma fenêtre, on voyait la Tour Eiffel. *From my window you could see the Eiffel Tower.*

194 **Savoir** is practically always used instead of **con-naître** when an object clause is present.

J'ai su hier qu'elle allait divorcer. *I learned yesterday that she was going to get a divorce.*

CHAPTER XIII

195 In literary style, **pas, point, plus** are frequently placed after the auxiliary of a compound infinitive.

> Elle croyait n'être pas (plus) respectée. *She thought she was not respected (any longer).*
> Je voudrais n'y être pas resté. *I should like not to have stayed there.*
> Je voudrais n'en avoir pas traité. *I should like not to have treated it.*

In literary language when the pronoun **en** is present, it is sometimes placed between the two parts of the negation which precedes the present infinitive. The pronoun **y**, however, regularly follows the negative words.

> Il me conseilla de n'en pas parler (n'en plus parler). *He advised me not to talk about it.*
> Il vaut mieux ne pas y aller. *It's better not to go.*

196 With **cesser,** the omission of **pas** is especially frequent in simple tenses. **Pas** must be used, however, if **cesser** has a specific limit.

> Il ne cessera pas d'écrire avant votre retour. *He will not stop writing until you come back.*

With **oser, pas** is generally used in compound tenses, in the past definite, and in the future. When **pas** is omitted with **pouvoir,** the negation is softened to such an extent that it no longer indicates impossibility.

> Je ne pouvais comprendre pourquoi il s'était mis en colère. *I couldn't understand why he had got angry.*
> Comme il était malade, il ne pouvait pas sortir. *As he was ill, he could not go out.*

When **pouvoir** is followed by a negative infinitive, **pas** may *not* be omitted even with the literary **je ne puis.**

> Je ne peux pas (Je ne puis pas) ne pas l'aider. *I can't keep from helping him.*

When **pas** is omitted with **savoir,** this verb expresses the idea of hesitancy or doubt rather than that of ignorance.

Je ne sais si elle consentira à être des nôtres. *I don't know whether (I doubt that) she will consent to join us.*

Je ne sais pas si elle consentira à être des nôtres. *I don't know (I have no idea) whether she will consent to join us.*

Elle ne savait quel parti prendre. *She didn't know what decision to make.*

Je ne sais pas ce qu'il a dit. *I don't know (I'm absolutely ignorant of) what he said.*

Elle ne savait pas sa leçon. *She didn't know her lesson.*

197 Colloquially **ne ... pas que** replaces **ne ... pas seulement.**

Il n'y a pas que toi qui saches le faire. *You are not the only one who can do it.*

198 In literary style, when members of a sentence are contrasted, **non** or **non pas** should replace **pas.** When the negative is not connected with a verb, *not* is translated by **non** in the expression *not far from.*

On doit tenir compte du mérite et non (non pas) de l'ancienneté. *One should take into account merit and not seniority.*

Il s'agira non de vous mais de moi. *It will not be a question of you but of me.*

Non loin de chez moi il y a un beau jardin public. *Not far from my house there is a beautiful public garden.*

199 The verb **décider** is regularly followed by the indicative.

Nous avons décidé que tu ne devrais pas y aller. *We have decided that you shouldn't go.*

CHAPTER XIV

200 The same verb may have two meanings, one of which requires that it be followed by the indicative, the other, by the subjunctive. Among such expressions are **supposer, dire, comprendre, prétendre, entendre, être d'avis.**

INDICATIVE	SUBJUNCTIVE
Je suppose qu'il y consentira. *I suppose that he will consent to it.*	Supposons qu'il n'y consente pas. (an hypothesis) *Let us assume that he doesn't consent to it.*
Dites-lui que je repasserai demain. *Tell him I'll come back tomorrow.*	Dites-lui qu'il repasse demain. (an order) *Tell him to come back tomorrow.*
Je comprenais bien que cela ne vous intéressait pas. *I realized fully that that did not interest you.*	Je comprends que ça te mette en colère. (approval) *I can understand your getting angry at that.*
Il prétend que vous lui devez cent francs. *He claims that you owe him a hundred francs.*	Je ne comprends pas qu'elle ne soit pas partie. (surprise or disapproval) *I can't understand why she didn't leave.*
Il m'a donné à entendre que je serai nommé. *He has given me to understand that I shall be appointed.*	Il prétend que vous lui rendiez ce service. (authority and desire) *He intends you do this favor for him.*
Je suis d'avis qu'il y a déjà renoncé. *It is my opinion that he has already given it up.*	J'entends que tu m'obéisses. (authority) *I intend that you obey me.*
	Je suis d'avis qu'il vous fasse des excuses. (obligation) *I feel that he should apologize to you.*

201 **Jusqu'à ce que** is generally not used after a negative clause. Its place is regularly taken by **avant que** or **ne . . . que.**[1]

Je ne partirai pas avant qu'il m'ait dit de partir. Je ne partirai que lorsqu'il m'aura dit de partir. *I shall not leave until he has told me to leave.*

---

[1] If the action of the verb of the negative clause extends to the time of the verb of the subordinate clause, **jusqu'à ce que** must be used. The preposition **jusqu'à** and a noun may take the place of a subordinate clause.

Je ne vais pas rester à Paris jusqu'à ce que l'ennemi vienne nous rendre visite. *I'm not going to stay in Paris until the enemy comes to pay us a visit.*

Vous n'y êtes pas resté jusqu'à l'arrivée de l'ennemi, n'est-ce pas ? *You didn't stay there until the enemy's arrival, did you?*

202 As a result of a confusion between the third persons singular of the past definite and imperfect subjunctive, **après que** is sometimes erroneously construed with the subjunctive.

203 By analogy with the use of the subjunctive with other conjunctions of concession, **tout ... que** is generally followed by this mode in modern French.

204 If the subordinate clause precedes the expression of certainty, probability, etc., the subjunctive must be used.

> Qu'il y ait du vrai là-dedans, c'est certain. *That there is some truth in it, is certain.*

205 In interrogatives which are purely rhetorical, the indicative must be used.

> Croyez-vous qu'elle est mignonne? *Isn't she darling?*

Douter si is followed by the indicative.

> Je doute s'il viendra. *I doubt whether he will come.*

206 Verbs construed with the expression **à ce que** regularly take the subjunctive.

> Je m'attends à ce qu'il vienne. *I am expecting him to come.*
> Je tiens à ce que tu le fasses. *I insist that you do it.*

207 When **que** replaces the conjunction **si,** it is followed by the subjunctive.

> S'il vient et que je ne le voie pas ... *If he comes and if I do not see him ...*

CHAPTER XVI

208 The suffix **–là** sometimes carries with it the idea of disparagement.

> Cette enfant est très intelligente. *That child is very intelligent.*
> Cette enfant-là est incorrigible. That *child is incorrigible.*

209 In familiar French, **ce,** even when it represents a definite noun, may be used before the verb **être** plus a past participle of a transitive verb.

C'est tout réglé. *It's all settled.*
C'est bien pesé. *It's well thought out.*
C'est vendu. *It's sold.*
Il s'agit d'un rapport très important. Je veux que ce soit étudié avec soin. *It is a question of a very important report. I want it (to be) carefully worked out.*

Cela must be used if the agent is expressed.

Cela est respecté de tout le monde. *That is respected by everybody.*

210 **Ce** may also be used with the verb **être** followed by the past participle of certain intransitives.

C'était déjà parti. *It had already gone.*
C'est arrivé poste-restante. *It arrived general delivery.*

211 When *it* refers more to the connotation of the word than to the word itself, **ce** is regularly used.

— Comment trouvez-vous ma nouvelle maison? *What do you think of my new house?*
— C'est magnifique. *It's magnificent.*
— Vous n'allez pas les loger dans la chambre d'André, n'est-ce pas? *You are not going to put them in Andrew's room, are you?*
— Mais si. Pourquoi pas? *Why yes. Why not?*
— C'est trop petit! *It's too small.*
C'est ennuyeux, les présentations. *Introductions are boring.*

In the first two sentences, the speaker is concerned with the ideas of size, appearance, and location, rather than with the object designated by the word **maison** or **chambre.** In the third, **ce** refers to everything that introductions entail.

212 When it is a question of the location of a house or place, **ce** is regularly used.

— Savez-vous où est sa nouvelle maison? *Do you know where his new house is?*

— Non. C'est loin du tramway ? *No. Is it far from the street-car line?*

Où est X ? *Where is X?*

C'est en aval de Z. *It's downstream from Z.*

213 The use of **ce** (he, she, they) as the subject of **être** followed by a modified predicate nominative is regularly obligatory when it is a question of *describing* a person. **Ce** is also commonly used to *identify* a character just introduced. If the identification is continued, the tendency is to replace **ce** by the personal pronoun.

Depuis quelques instants, je regardais, par l'entre-bâillement de la porte, une jeune personne dont le visage m'était vaguement familier. Tout à coup, elle poussa la porte et pénétra dans la salle. C'était une grande jeune fille, aux cheveux bruns, au teint mat. J'ai demandé à ma femme qui c'était. Elle me répondit que c'était la fille de M. Mével, le maire, et qu'elle était la nièce de notre hôtesse. J'ai su plus tard qu'elle était une ancienne élève de feu Grand-voisin et que j'avais dû la voir plus d'une fois à l'amphi-théâtre Michelet. *For some moments I had been looking, through the partially-opened door, at a young girl whose face seemed vaguely familiar to me. Suddenly she pushed the door open and came into the room. She was a tall girl, with dark-brown hair and a dull-white complexion. I asked my wife who she was. She replied that she was the daughter of Mr. Mével, the mayor, and that she was the niece of our hostess. I found out later that she was a former pupil of the late Grand-voisin and that I had probably seen her more than once in the Michelet lecture-hall.*

214 **Ce** as subject of the verb *to be*, plus an adjective, and **ça** (generally not **cela**) as subject of any verb other than **être** are used in very familiar French to refer to small children and in a disparaging sense to adults.

— Ça ne cause (*correct French:* parle) pas ? *Doesn't (Can't) she talk?*

— Mais non, c'est trop petit. Ça n'a pas encore dix-huit mois. *Of course not, she's too little. She isn't eighteen months old yet.*

224

C'est drôle, les femmes, ça ne nous comprend jamais. *Women are queer, they never understand us.*

When **ça** is used to refer to a definite noun, the speaker is generally thinking more of the connotation of this noun than of the word itself.

— Comment trouves-tu le salon ? *What do you think of the drawing room?*
— C'est magnifique. Ça a l'air d'une cabine téléphonique ! *It's magnificent. It looks like a telephone booth!*

215 **Quiconque** is used in literary style as the equivalent of **qui que ce soit qui, celui qui,** etc., and less frequently with the meaning of **qui que ce soit,** or **personne.**

Quiconque l'a entendu parler ne l'oubliera jamais. *Whoever has heard him talk will never forget him.*
Il le dira à quiconque voudra l'écouter. *He will tell it to whoever wishes to listen to it.*
Il le fera mieux que quiconque. *He will do it better than anyone.*

Quelconque, the adjective, is equivalent to *any whatever.*

Un homme (un livre) quelconque. *Any man (book) whatever.*

Quelconque also has the meaning of *mediocre.*

C'est un homme (un livre) très quelconque. *That's a very mediocre man (book).*

CHAPTER XVII

216 In older French **qui** was regularly used as the object of a preposition with a thing as antecedent. Although this use has survived to some extent in modern literary style, it is considered correct only where the thing in question is capable of personification, or when the author is deliberately employing archaic language.

217 Contrary to English usage, French frequently co-ordinates an adjective, or adjectival phrase, and a relative clause. This construction is sometimes used to prevent ambiguity.

Il débitait des mensonges absolument incroyables, et qui, cependant, étaient acceptés sans discussion par ses auditeurs. *He was ladling out some absolutely unbelievable lies, which, however, were accepted without argument by his listeners.*

C'était un homme de haute taille, à la voix rude, au visage perpétuellement renfrogné, et qui, au fond, était doux comme un agneau. *He was a tall man, with a harsh voice, with a perpetually frowning expression, who, in reality, was as gentle as a lamb.*

218 There are two further uses of **lequel** in literary style.

1. To avoid repetition of the relative **qui** or **que.**

Ce n'est pas le président de la République, mais le président du conseil, qui nomme les ministres, lesquels sont chargés du pouvoir exécutif. *It is not the president of the Republic, but the president of the cabinet, who names the ministers, upon whom devolves the executive power.*

2. In non-restrictive clauses.

Il va épouser la jeune Henriette Dulac, laquelle est une amie intime de votre mère. *He is going to marry young Henrietta Dulac, who is an intimate friend of your mother.*

219 The relative **où** when no other antecedent is expressed is frequently preceded by the adverb **là.** This use is especially common at the beginning of a sentence. Even in this case, however, **où** may be used alone in a figurative sense or when it is equivalent to **si.**

Là où j'ai trouvé le plus de fautes, c'est dans sa composition française. *The place I found the most mistakes was in his French composition.*

Où il excelle, c'est dans le domaine de l'abstrait. *Where he excels, is in the domain of the abstract.*

Où il y a de la fumée, il y a du feu. *Where there is smoke, there is fire.*

220 The older use of the relative **quoi** with a definite antecedent (abstract noun, person, or thing) has been revived in recent years by many well-known French writers. This use of **quoi,** however, is still condemned by grammarians, unless the antecedent is a "neuter" word, such as **ce, rien, quelque chose,** etc., or one whose connotation is vague or indefinite.

> Il n'y a rien à quoi je tienne moins qu'à cela. *There is nothing I am less fond of than that.*
>
> Quel était ce secret à quoi je songeais depuis si longtemps? *What was this secret of which I had been thinking so long?*

221 In literary style, **nous autres Américains** is replaced by **nous, (les) Américains . . .**

222 In modern French there is a growing tendency to replace **encore un** by **un autre,** i.e., to use **un autre** when *another* means *more of the same kind,* not *different.*

> Voulez-vous un autre verre d'eau (encore un verre d'eau)? *Do you want another glass of water?*
>
> Cf. Ne buvez pas cette eau tout d'un trait. Vous n'en aurez pas d'autre avant ce soir. *Don't drink that water at a draught (gulp it all down at once). You will not have any more till this evening.*
>
> Un peu plus de café, mademoiselle? (Encore un peu de café?) *(Will you have) A little more coffee, Miss . . .?*

223 **Les uns . . . les autres** should not be used when it is a question of only three persons. In ordinary speech, the reciprocal meaning of the reflexive will generally be sufficiently clear. In formal style, some such word as **mutuellement, réciproquement,** may be added to the sentence.

> Ces trois enfants s'adorent. *These three children adore each other.*

If the reciprocal pronoun is the object of a preposition, the idea may be expressed in the following manner:

> Chacun (des trois) a besoin des deux autres. *Each one (of the three) needs the other two.*

224 If more than two groups are mentioned and if all possible groups are included, the regular procedure is to use **les uns . . . d'autres . . . (d'autres) . . . (les autres) (d'autres enfin).**

Pendant les vacances, les uns étudiaient à la bibliothèque, d'autres travaillaient dans les magasins, et les autres (d'autres enfin) ne faisaient que s'amuser. *During the vacation, some studied in the library, others worked in the stores, and the others did nothing but have a good time.*

225 Prepositions and, in general, short prepositional locutions, regularly come between **l'un** and **l'autre.** Long prepositional locutions generally precede both. The prepositions **à** and **de,** of course, must be repeated before each object.

Ils ont travaillé l'un pour l'autre. *They worked for each other.*
Ils étaient assis l'un près de l'autre, tout près l'un de l'autre. *They were sitting near each other, quite near each other.*
Il (leur) a parlé à l'un et à l'autre. *He talked to both of them.*
Il s'agit de l'un et de l'autre. *It is a question of both.*

226 **L'un ou l'autre** is regularly replaced by **l'un des deux,** except in literary style.

L'un ou l'autre y consentira. L'un des deux y consentira. *One or the other will consent to it.*

CHAPTER XVIII

227 An elliptical form of indirect interrogation is frequently used in the repetition of direct interrogation.

Qu'est-ce qu'il a dit? — Ce qu'il a dit? (Vous me demandez ce qu'il a dit?) Ma foi, je ne m'en souviens plus. *What did he say? What did he say? My word, I don't remember any more.*
Il a des enfants? — S'il a des enfants? (Vous me demandez s'il a des enfants?) Il en a tant qu'il ne les connaît pas tous. *Does he have any children? Does he? He has so many that he doesn't know them all.*

228 **Qui** is still sometimes found with its older meaning **Qu'est-ce qui.** This use of **qui,** of course, should not be adopted by the student.

Qui vous amène ici? *What brings you here?*

229 There is such a strong feeling that **quel** should be followed by interrogative word order that it is frequently preferable in familiar style to use it as predicate nominative rather than as an adjective modifying a subject.

Quelles sont les difficultés qu'il a dû surmonter ? (*rather than:* Quelles difficultés a-t-il dû surmonter ?) *What obstacles did he have to surmount?*

230 In certain of these cases it is easy to distinguish between indirect interrogation and indirect relative clauses. In others, however, the clause may be considered as interrogative or relative.

Vous m'avez demandé de quoi j'avais besoin. *You asked me what I needed.*

Vous m'avez demandé à quoi il tenait le plus. *You asked me what he was most fond of.*

Vous lui avez donné ce dont il avait besoin. *You gave him what he needed.*

Vous lui avez donné ce à quoi il tenait le plus. *You gave him what he was most fond of.*

Eh bien, voilà ce dont (de quoi) je suis capable. *Well, that's what I'm capable of.*

Note that in indirect interrogation the antecedent is omitted before a preposition followed by **quoi.**

231 The forms **pensé-je, donné-je,** etc., are not used except in literary style and even then infrequently.

CHAPTER XIX

232 In familiar language exclamatory **que, combien, comme** are frequently replaced by **ce que.**

Ce qu'elle est jolie, la petite ! *What a pretty little girl she is!* (*How pretty the little one is!*)

Si tu savais ce que j'ai eu d'ennuis ! *If you knew how many troubles I've had!*

233 After **voir** and **entendre** either **de** or **par** is used, if the agent is not specific.

> Elle a été vue (entendue) de (par) tous les assistants. *She was seen (heard) by all the bystanders.*

If the agent is specific, **par** is regularly used.[1]

> Elle a été vue (entendue) par sa voisine. *She was seen (heard) by her neighbor.*

CHAPTER XX

234 The present participle is used after the verbs **aller** and **être** to express progressive action.

> La situation va empirant (*preferred to:* va en empirant). *The situation is getting worse.*
> Il est dans sa chambre, travaillant à sa thèse.[2] (*En*, of course, is not possible here.) *He is in his room, working on his thesis.*

235 In proverbial expressions and in those in which the infinitives are not mutually exclusive, **de** is not used.

> Mieux vaut plier que rompre. *Discretion is the better part of valor (It is better to bend than to break).*
> Il aime mieux priser que fumer. *He prefers taking snuff to smoking.*

236 **Pour** is used to express concession when the main clause is negative.

> Pour être riche, il n'en est pas moins serviable. *Although he is rich, he is no less obliging.*
> Pour avoir visité Paris plusieurs fois, vous ne le connaissez pas très bien. *Even though you have visited Paris several times, you do not know it very well.*

237 The infinitive with **à** is sometimes used to express a condition.

---

[1] Some French people would use **de** even in this case.
[2] The infinitive with **à** is also used in this sense.

Il est dans sa chambre, à travailler.

A vous en croire, nous allons tous faire faillite. *If we believe you, we are all going to fail (become bankrupt).*

238 In theory a certain ambiguity is possible in these constructions of **faire, laisser,** etc. with the infinitive. In practice, however, the context will generally make the meaning clear.

Je lui ferai rendre l'argent. *I shall make him return the money. I shall have the money returned to him.*

Elle le lui a laissé dire. *She let him say it. She let it be said to him.*

APPENDIX

239 Irregular Adjectives. (Cf. Chapter IX)

M.	F.	M.	F.
actif	active	cher	chère
bref	brève	léger	légère
heureux	heureuse	étranger	étrangère
blanc	blanche	(in)complet	(in)complète
franc	franche	(in)discret	(in)discrète
sec	sèche	inquiet	inquiète
public	publique	secret	secrète
long	longue	favori	favorite
doux	douce	causeur	causeuse
faux	fausse	flatteur	flatteuse
roux	rousse	menteur	menteuse
grec	grecque	rêveur	rêveuse
cruel	cruelle	trompeur	trompeuse
pareil	pareille	créateur	créatrice
ancien	ancienne	directeur	directrice
bon	bonne	gros	grosse
bas	basse	épais	épaisse
muet	muette	beau, bel *	belle
sot	sotte	fou, fol *	folle
		mou, mol *	molle
		nouveau, nouvel *	nouvelle
		vieux, vieil *	vieille

* The alternate masculine forms starred are used before masculine singular nouns beginning with a vowel or a mute *h*.

240 A. Possessive Adjectives. (Cf. Chapter X)

	M.	F.	Pl.
my	mon	ma	mes
your	ton	ta	tes
his, her	son	sa	ses
our	notre	notre	nos
your	votre	votre	vos
their	leur	leur	leurs

B. Possessive Pronouns.

mine	le mien	la mienne	les miens	les miennes
yours	le tien	la tienne	les tiens	les tiennes
his, hers	le sien	la sienne	les siens	les siennes
ours	le nôtre	la nôtre	les nôtres	les nôtres
yours	le vôtre	la vôtre	les vôtres	les vôtres
theirs	le leur	la leur	les leurs	les leurs

241 Numerals. (Cf. Chapter XI)

A. Cardinals.

1	un, une	11	onze	21	vingt et un
2	deux	12	douze	22	vingt-deux
3	trois	13	treize	30	trente
4	quatre	14	quatorze	40	quarante
5	cinq	15	quinze	50	cinquante
6	six	16	seize	60	soixante
7	sept	17	dix-sept *	70	soixante-dix
8	huit	18	dix-huit	71	soixante et onze
9	neuf	19	dix-neuf	72	soixante-douze
10	dix	20	vingt	80	quatre-vingt(s)

81	quatre-vingt-un	201	deux cent un
90	quatre-vingt-dix	1000	mille
91	quatre-vingt-onze	1001	mille un
100	cent	1,000,000	un million
101	cent un	2,000,000	deux millions
200	deux cent(s)	1,000,000,000	un milliard

PRONUNCIATION: The final consonant of **cinq, six, huit, dix,** and their compounds, is silent before the initial con-

---

* All compound cardinals under 100, except those in which **et** occurs, are hyphenated. **Et** appears regularly in 21, 31, 41, 51, 61, 71.

sonant or aspirate *h* of a noun multiplied by these numbers. If the numbers are final, or if the noun they precede is not multiplied by them, the final consonant is pronounced. The final consonant of **sept** and **neuf,** and their compounds, which formerly came under the rule given above, is now rather generally pronounced in all cases. Some French people always pronounce the final consonant of **cinq** but in the best usage the pronunciation of this word follows the general rule.

cinq (sẽ)		Le cinq (sẽk)			cinq (sẽk)
six (si)		six (sis)			six (sis)
huit (ɥi)	mois	huit (ɥit)	mai	J'en ai	huit (ɥit)
dix (di)		dix (dis)			dix (dis)
dix-huit		dix-huit			dix-huit
(dizɥi)		(dizɥit)			(dizɥit)

In liaison, **dix** is pronounced (diz). **Neuf** has the pronunciation (nøv) in **neuf ans** and **neuf heures.** While this pronunciation is occasionally met with in a few other expressions, the modern tendency seems to be to give **neuf** in liaison the same pronunciation it has when final, i.e., (nœf).

Dix (diz) ans; neuf (nøv) ans; neuf (nøv) heures; neuf (nœf) erreurs.

There is no elision in **le huit, le onze.**
The *t* of **vingt** in 21, 23, 24, 25, 26, 27, 28, 29, is pronounced. In 22, this *t* becomes a *d* by assimilation.
In 81–99, the *t* of **vingt** is silent.
In 101, 102, etc. the *t* of **cent** is silent.

B. Ordinals.

1st	premier, première	8th	huitième
2nd	second, deuxième	9th	neuvième
3rd	troisième *	10th	dixième
4th	quatrième *	11th	onzième
5th	cinquième *	21st	vingt et unième
6th	sixième	22nd	vingt-deuxième, etc.
7th	septième		

---

* **le tiers** and **le quart** are used in fractions and in a few expressions. **Quint,** for fifth, is used only in the titles, **Charles-Quint, Sixte-Quint.**

242 **A.** Demonstrative Adjectives. (Cf. Chapter XVI)

M.	M.	F.	Pl.
ce	cet *	cette	ces

B. Demonstrative Pronouns.

ceci *this*
cela *that* (regularly used with indefinite antecedents)
ce *he, she, it, they*

M.	F.	M. pl.	F. pl.	
celui	celle	ceux	celles	*this* (one), *these*
celui-ci	celle-ci	ceux-ci	celles-ci	*this* (one), *these, the latter*
celui-là	celle-là	ceux-là	celles-là	*that* (one), *those, the former*

243 Relative Pronouns. (Cf. Chapter XVII)

qui	*who, which, that; whom* (after prep.)
que	*whom, which, that*
lequel, laquelle, lesquels, lesquelles	*who, whom, which, that*
dont	*whose, of whom, of which*
quoi	*what* (object of prep.)
ce qui	*what* (subject)
ce que	*what* (object)

244 Interrogatives. (Cf. Chapter XVIII)

A. Adjectives.

Quel? Quelle? Quels? Quelles? *Which? What?*

B. Pronouns.

Lequel? Laquelle? Lesquels? Lesquelles? *Which? Which one(s)?*

Qui?	*Who? Whom?*
Quoi?	*What?* (alone or after prep.)
Que?	*What?*

245 Regular Verbs.

A. Regular verbs are classified in three conjugations, according to the ending of the infinitive: (1) donn-*er*, (2) fin-*ir*, (3) vend-*re*. The principal parts of these verbs are:

---

* This form is used before a masculine noun beginning with a vowel or mute *h*.

INFINITIVE	PRES. PART.	PAST PART.	PRES. IND.	PAST DEF.
donner	donnant	donné	je donne	je donnai
finir	finissant	fini	je finis	je finis
vendre	vendant	vendu	je vends	je vendis

B. Formation of simple tenses.

With the exception of the future and the conditional, the various tenses were not actually derived from the principal parts. As all the tenses may be worked out from the principal parts, however, a knowledge of these forms will be valuable to the student.

The infinitive, unchanged for the regular –er and –ir verbs, and the infinitive minus the final –e, for the regular –re verbs form the stem of the future and conditional tenses. To this stem are added the endings –ai, –as, –a, –ons, –ez, –ont in order to form the future tense. Note that the endings are actually the present indicative of the verb **avoir,** shortened in the first two persons of the plural.

To form the conditional, the endings –**ais, –ais, –ait, –ions, –iez, –aient,** the same endings, to be noted, as those of the imperfect tense, are added to the infinitive of the –er and –ir verbs. In the case of the –re verbs, these endings are added to the infinitive minus the final **e.**

From the present participle, the plural of the present indicative may be formed. To do this, the endings –**ons, –ez, –ent** are added to the stem of the present participle (the participle minus the –**ant**).

Since the plural imperative forms are the same as the present indicative, they too may be derived from the present participle.

The present participle may also act as a guide for the formation of the present subjunctive. For the ending –**ant** are substituted the endings –**e, –es, –ions, –iez, –ent.**

The first person singular of the present indicative sets the pattern for the singular of this tense. The first person singular of the present indicative of the –**er** verbs is identical with the third person. The second person may be formed by substituting –es for the ending of the first person. The first person singular of the –ir and –re verbs is identical with the second person. The third person of the –ir and –re verbs may be formed by substituting –it, –(t) respectively for the ending of the first person. The t in parentheses is omitted if the stem ends in –t or –d.

This principal part also indicates the form of the singular imperative. In the –er verbs the imperative drops the final –s of the second person singular present. The s is retained when y or en follow this verb form.

In the past definite of the –er verbs, the endings –as, –a, –âmes, –âtes, –èrent are substituted for the final –ai of the first person singular. The first person singular of the –ir and –re verbs is identical with the second person. The other persons of these verbs may be formed by substituting –it, –îmes, –îtes, –irent for the –is of the first person.

From the past definite is formed the imperfect subjunctive by omitting the final letter of the first person singular, whether –i or –s, and by adding to the remaining form, –sse, –sses, –ˆt, –ssions, –ssiez, –ssent. The third person singular bears a circumflex accent over the vowel which precedes the final –t.

C. Model verbs.

THE ACTIVE VOICE

INDICATIVE MOOD

PRESENT

I give, am giving, etc.	*I finish, am finishing,* etc.	*I sell, am selling,* etc.
je donne	je finis	je vends
tu donnes	tu finis	tu vends
il donne	il finit	il vend
nous donnons	nous finissons	nous vendons
vous donnez	vous finissez	vous vendez
ils donnent	ils finissent	ils vendent

IMPERFECT

I was giving, used to give, etc.	*I was finishing, used to finish*, etc.	*I was selling, used to sell*, etc.
je donnais	je finissais	je vendais
tu donnais	tu finissais	tu vendais
il donnait	il finissait	il vendait
nous donnions	nous finissions	nous vendions
vous donniez	vous finissiez	vous vendiez
ils donnaient	ils finissaient	ils vendaient

PAST DEFINITE

I gave, etc.	*I finished*, etc.	*I sold*, etc.
je donnai	je finis	je vendis
tu donnas	tu finis	tu vendis
il donna	il finit	il vendit
nous donnâmes	nous finîmes	nous vendîmes
vous donnâtes	vous finîtes	vous vendîtes
ils donnèrent	ils finirent	ils vendirent

FUTURE

I shall give, etc.	*I shall finish*, etc.	*I shall sell*, etc.
je donnerai	je finirai	je vendrai
tu donneras	tu finiras	tu vendras
il donnera	il finira	il vendra
nous donnerons	nous finirons	nous vendrons
vous donnerez	vous finirez	vous vendrez
ils donneront	ils finiront	ils vendront

CONDITIONAL

I should give, etc.	*I should finish*, etc.	*I should sell*, etc.
je donnerais	je finirais	je vendrais
tu donnerais	tu finirais	tu vendrais
il donnerait	il finirait	il vendrait
nous donnerions	nous finirions	nous vendrions
vous donneriez	vous finiriez	vous vendriez
ils donneraient	ils finiraient	ils vendraient

Subjunctive Mood

PRESENT

I (may) give, etc.	*I (may) finish, etc.*	*I (may) sell, etc.*
je donne	je finisse	je vende
tu donnes	tu finisses	tu vendes
il donne	il finisse	il vende
nous donnions	nous finissions	nous vendions
vous donniez	vous finissiez	vous vendiez
ils donnent	ils finissent	ils vendent

IMPERFECT

I (might) give, etc.	*I (might) finish, etc.*	*I (might) sell, etc.*
je donnasse	je finisse	je vendisse
tu donnasses	tu finisses	tu vendisses
il donnât	il finît	il vendît
nous donnassions	nous finissions	nous vendissions
vous donnassiez	vous finissiez	vous vendissiez
ils donnassent	ils finissent	ils vendissent

Imperative Mood

PRESENT

give, etc.	*finish, etc.*	*sell, etc.*
donne *	finis	vends
donnons	finissons	vendons
donnez	finissez	vendez

Compound Tenses

All the compound tenses are formed by adding the past participle of the verb to the proper tense of the proper auxiliary, **avoir** or **être**.

With auxiliary **avoir**   With auxiliary **être**

Infinitive

PERFECT

to have given	*to have come*
avoir donné	être venu(e)(s)

---

* This form becomes **donnes** when followed by −y or −en.

PARTICIPLE

having given	*having come*
ayant donné	étant venu(e)(s)

INDICATIVE MOOD

PAST INDEFINITE

I have given, etc.	*I have come*, etc.
j'ai donné	je suis venu(e)
tu as donné	tu es venu(e)
etc.	etc.

PLUPERFECT

I had given, etc.	*I had come*, etc.
j'avais donné	j'étais venu(e)
etc.	etc.

PAST ANTERIOR

I had given, etc.	*I had come*, etc.
j'eus donné, etc.	je fus venu(e), etc.

FUTURE PERFECT

I shall given, etc.	*I shall have come*, etc.
j'aurai donné, etc.	je serai venu(e), etc.

CONDITIONAL PERFECT

I should have given, etc.	*I should have come*, etc.
j'aurais donné, etc.	je serais venu(e), etc.

SUBJUNCTIVE MOOD

PERFECT

I (may) have given, etc.	*I (may) have come*, etc.
j'aie donné, etc.	je sois venu(e), etc.

241

PLUPERFECT

I (might) have given, etc.	*I (might) have come*, etc.
j'eusse donné, etc.	je fusse venu(e), etc.

The Passive Voice

The passive voice is formed by adding the past participle of the verb conjugated to the proper tense of the verb **être**.

Infinitive

PRESENT

être aimé(e)(s), *to be loved*

PERFECT

avoir été aimé(e)(s), *to have been loved*

Participle

PRESENT

étant aimé(e)(s), *being loved*

PERFECT

ayant été aimé(e)(s), *having been loved*

Indicative Mood

PRESENT

I am (being) loved, etc.

je suis aimé(e)
tu es aimé(e)
il (elle) est aimé(e)
nous sommes aimé(e)s
vous êtes aimé(e)(s)
ils (elles) sont aimé(e)s

PAST INDEFINITE

I have been (was) loved, etc.

j'ai été aimé(e)
tu as été aimé(e)
il (elle) a été aimé(e)
nous avons été aimé(e)s
vous avez été aimé(e)(s)
ils (elles) ont été aimé(e)s

IMPERFECT

I was loved, etc.

j'étais aimé(e), etc.

PLUPERFECT

I had been loved, etc.

j'avais été aimé(e), etc.

PAST DEFINITE

I was loved, etc

je fus aimé(e), etc.

PAST ANTERIOR

I had been loved, etc.

j'eus été aimé(e), etc.

FUTURE	FUTURE PERFECT

I shall be loved, etc.
je serai aimé(e), etc.

I shall have been loved, etc.
j'aurai été aimé(e), etc.

CONDITIONAL	CONDITIONAL PERFECT

I should be loved, etc.
je serais aimé(e), etc.

I should have been loved, etc.
j'aurais été aimé(e), etc.

SUBJUNCTIVE MOOD

I (may) be loved, etc.
je sois aimé(e), etc.

I (may) have been loved, etc.
j'aie été aimé(e), etc.

IMPERFECT	PLUPERFECT

I (might) be loved, etc.
je fusse aimé(e), etc.

I (might) have been loved, etc.
j'eusse été aimé(e), etc.

IMPERATIVE MOOD

sois aimé(e), *be loved*
soyons aimé(e)s, *let us be loved*
soyez aimé(e)(s), *be loved*

REFLEXIVE VERBS

INFINITIVE

PRESENT	PERFECT

se louer, *to praise one's self*

s'être loué(e)(s), *to have praised one's self*

PARTICIPLE

PRESENT	PERFECT

se louant, *praising one's self*

s'étant loué(e)(s), *having praised one's self*

243

INDICATIVE MOOD

PRESENT

I praise myself, etc.

je me loue
tu te loues
il se loue
nous nous louons
vous vous louez
ils se louent

PAST INDEFINITE

I praised myself, etc.

je me suis loué(e)
tu t'es loué(e)
il (elle) s'est loué(e)
nous nous sommes loué(e)s
vous vous êtes loué(e)(s)
ils (elles) se sont loué(e)s

IMPERFECT

I was praising myself, etc.

je me louais, etc.

PLUPERFECT

I had praised myself, etc.

je m'étais loué(e), etc.

PAST DEFINITE

I praised myself, etc.

je me louai, etc.

PAST ANTERIOR

I had praised myself, etc.

je me fus loué(e), etc.

FUTURE

I shall praise myself, etc.

je me louerai, etc.

FUTURE PERFECT

I shall have praised myself, etc.

je me serai loué(e), etc.

CONDITIONAL

I should praise myself, etc.

je me louerais, etc.

CONDITIONAL PERFECT

I should have praised myself, etc.

je me serais loué(e), etc.

SUBJUNCTIVE MOOD

PRESENT

I (may) praise myself, etc.

je me loue, etc.

PERFECT

I (may) have praised myself, etc.

je me sois loué(e), etc.

IMPERFECT

I (might) praise myself, etc.

je me louasse, etc.

PLUPERFECT

I (might) have praised myself, etc.

je me fusse loué(e), etc.

loue-toi	*praise thyself (yourself)*
louons-nous	*let us praise ourselves*
louez-vous	*praise yourself (yourselves)*

246 Verbs with Orthographical Peculiarities.

The following classes of verbs in –er have certain orthographical peculiarities:

A. Verbs ending in –cer, such as **commencer,** must keep the soft sound of c before all endings.   C, therefore, is replaced by ç before –a or –o.

PRES. PART.	PRES. IND.	IMP. IND.	PAST DEF.	IMP. SUBJ.
commençant	commence	commençais	commençai	commençasse
	commences	commençais	commenças	commençasses
	commence	commençait	commença	commençât
	commençons	commencions	commençâmes	commençassions
	commencez	commenciez	commençâtes	commençassiez
	commencent	commençaient	commencèrent	commençassent

B. Verbs ending in –ger, such as **manger,** keep the soft sound of g before all endings.   G, therefore, becomes ge before –a or –o.

PRES. PART.	PRES. IND.	IMP. IND.	PAST DEF.	IMP. SUBJ.
mangeant	mange	mangeais	mangeai	mangeasse
	manges	mangeais	mangeas	mangeasses
	mange	mangeait	mangea	mangeât
	mangeons	mangions	mangeâmes	mangeassions
	mangez	mangiez	mangeâtes	mangeassiez
	mangent	mangeaient	mangèrent	mangeassent

C. Verbs ending in –oyer and –uyer, such as **nettoyer** and **essuyer,** *must* change y to i whenever the ending begins with a mute e.   Verbs ending in –ayer, such as **payer,** *may* change y to i before a mute e.

PRES. IND.	PRES. SUBJ.	FUTURE	CONDITIONAL
nettoie	nettoie	nettoierai	nettoierais
nettoies	nettoies	nettoieras	nettoierais
nettoie	nettoie	nettoiera	nettoierait
nettoyons	nettoyions	nettoierons	nettoierions
nettoyez	nettoyiez	nettoierez	nettoieriez
nettoient	nettoient	nettoieront	nettoieraient
essuie, etc.	essuie, etc.	essuierai, etc.	essuierais, etc.
paie ⎱ etc. paye ⎰	paie ⎱ etc. paye ⎰	paierai ⎱ etc. payerai ⎰	paierais ⎱ etc. payerais ⎰

D. Verbs having **e** as the stem vowel, like **mener,** *to lead*, change this **e** to **è** when the following syllable contains a mute **e**. (For verbs in **–eler** and **–eter,** see below.)

PRES. IND.	PRES. SUBJ.	FUTURE	CONDITIONAL
mène	mène	mènerai	mènerais
mènes	mènes	mèneras	mènerais
mène	mène	mènera	mènerait
menons	menions	mènerons	mènerions
menez	meniez	mènerez	mèneriez
mènent	mènent	mèneront	mèneraient

E. Verbs having as the stem vowel **é** followed by a consonant, like **céder,** *to yield*, change **é** to **è** in the present indicative and subjunctive when followed by a syllable containing a mute **e,** but retain the **é** throughout the future and the conditional.

PRES. IND.	PRES. SUBJ.	FUTURE	CONDITIONAL
cède, etc.	cède, etc.	céderai, etc.	céderais, etc.

F. Verbs ending in **–eler, –eter,** like **appeler,** *to call*, **jeter,** *to throw*, usually double the **l** or the **t** before a syllable containing mute **e**.

PRES. IND.	PRES. SUBJ.	FUTURE	CONDITIONAL
appelle	appelle	appellerai	appellerais
appelles	appelles	appelleras	appellerais
appelle	appelle	appellera	appellerait

PRES. IND.	PRES. SUBJ.	FUTURE	CONDITIONAL
appelons	appelions	appellerons	appellerions
appelez	appeliez	appellerez	appelleriez
appellent	appellent	appelleront	appelleraient
jette, etc.	jette, etc.	jetterai, etc.	jetterais, etc.

A few verbs in –eler, –eter, like **acheter**, *to buy*, **geler**, *to freeze*, are conjugated like **mener**.

247 Irregular Verbs.

Acquérir, *to acquire*

1 *Infinitive* acquérir; *fut.* acquerrai; *condl.* acquerrais.
2 *Pres. Part.* acquérant; *impf. indic.* acquérais; *pres. subj.* acquière, acquières, acquière, acquérions, acquériez, acquièrent.
3 *Past Part.* acquis; *past indef.* j'ai acquis.
4 *Pres. Indic.* acquiers, acquiers, acquiert, acquérons, acquérez,
acquièrent; *impve.* acquiers, acquérons, acquérez.
5 *Past Def.* acquis, acquis, acquit, acquîmes, acquîtes, acquirent;
impf. subj. acquisse, acquisses, acquît, acquissions, acquissiez,
acquissent.

Like **acquérir**: **conquérir**, *to conquer*.

Aller, *to go.*

1 *Infinitive* aller; *fut.* irai; *condl.* irais.
2 *Pres. Part.* allant; *impf. ind.* allais; *pres. subj.* aille, ailles, aille,
allions, alliez, aillent.
3 *Past Part.* allé; *past indef.* je suis allé.
4 *Pres. Ind.* vais, vas, va, allons, allez, vont; *impve.* va, allons,
allez.
5 *Past Def.* allai, allas, alla, allâmes, allâtes, allèrent; *impf. subj.*
allasse, allasses, allât, allassions, allassiez, allassent.

Like **aller:** **s'en aller,** *to go away, to leave.* Je m'en vais, tu
t'en vas, etc.

s'appeler   (p.d. - appelèrent)

Asseoir, *to seat.*

1 *Infinitive* asseoir; *fut.* assiérai (*or* asseyerai [1]) *or* assoirai [2]; *condl.*
assiérais *or* asseyerais [1] *or* assoirais.[2]

---

[1] Obsolete form.
[2] The form with **oi** or **oy** is generally considered provincial.

2 *Pres. Part.* asseyant *or* assoyant; *impf. ind.* asseyais *or* assoyais; *pres. subj.* asseye, asseyes, asseye, asseyions, asseyiez, asseyent *or* assoie, assoies, assoie, assoyions, assoyiez, assoient.

3 *Past Part.* assis; *past indef.* j'ai assis.

4 *Pres. Indic.* assieds, assieds, assied, asseyons, asseyez, asseyent *or* assois, assois, assoit, assoyons, assoyez, assoient; *impve.* assieds, asseyons, asseyez *or* assois, assoyons, assoyez.

5 *Past Def.* assis, assis, assit, assîmes, assîtes, assirent; *impf. subj.* assisse, assisses, assît, assissions, assissiez, assissent.

Like **asseoir**: s'**asseoir**, *to sit down.*

Avoir, *to have.*

1 *Infinitive* avoir; *fut.* aurai; *condl.* aurais.

2 *Pres. Part.* ayant; *impf. ind.* avais; *pres. subj.* aie, aies, ait, ayons, ayez, aient.

3 *Past Part.* eu; *past indef.* j'ai eu.

4 *Pres. Indic.* ai, as, a, avons, avez, ont; *impve.* aie, ayons, ayez.

5 *Past Def.* eus, eus, eut, eûmes, eûtes, eûrent; *impf. subj.* eusse, eusses, eût, eussions, eussiez, eussent.

Battre, *to beat.*

1 *Infinitive* battre; *fut.* battrai; *condl.* battrais.

2 *Pres. Part.* battant; *impf. ind.* battais; *pres. subj.* batte, battes, batte, battions, battiez, battent.

3 *Past Part.* battu; *past indef.* j'ai battu.

4 *Pres. Indic.* bats, bats, bat, battons, battez, battent; *impve.* bats, battons, battez.

5 *Past Def.* battis, battis, battit, battîmes, battîtes, battirent; *impf. subj.* battisse, battisses, battît, battissions, battissiez, battissent.

Boire, *to drink.*

1 *Infinitive* boire; *fut.* boirai; *condl.* boirais.

2 *Pres. Part.* buvant; *impf. indic.* buvais; *pres. subj.* boive, boives, boive, buvions, buviez, boivent.

3 *Past Part.* bu; *past indef.* j'ai bu.

4 *Pres. Indic.* bois, bois, boit, buvons, buvez, boivent; *impve.* bois, buvons, buvez.

5 *Past Def.* bus, bus, but, bûmes, bûtes, burent; *impf. subj.* busse, busses, bût, bussions, bussiez, bussent.

Conclure, *to conclude.*

1 *Infinitive* conclure; *fut.* conclurai; *condl.* conclurais.
2 *Pres. Part.* concluant; *impf. indic.* concluais; *pres. subj.* conclue, conclues, conclue, concluions, concluiez, concluent.
3 *Past Part.* conclu; *past indef.* j'ai conclu.
4 *Pres. Indic.* conclus, conclus, conclut, concluons, concluez, concluent; *impve.* conclus, concluons, concluez.
5 *Past Def.* conclus, conclus, conclut, conclûmes, conclûtes, conclurent; *impf. subj.* conclusse, conclusses, conclût, conclussions, conclussiez, conclussent.

Conduire, *to conduct, lead,* etc.

1 *Infinitive* conduire; *fut.* conduirai; *condl.* conduirais.
2 *Pres. Part.* conduisant; *impf. indic.* conduisais; *pres. subj.* conduise, conduises, conduise, conduisions, conduisiez, conduisent.
3 *Past Part.* conduit; *past indef.* j'ai conduit.
4 *Pres. Indic.* conduis, conduis, conduit, conduisons, conduisez, conduisent; *impve.* conduis, conduisons, conduisez.
5 *Past Def.* conduisis, conduisis, conduisit, conduisîmes, conduisîtes, conduisirent; *impf. subj.* conduisisse, conduisisses, conduisît, conduisissions, conduisissiez, conduisissent.

Like **conduire : construire,** *to build;* **détruire,** *to destroy;* **instruire,** *to instruct;* **produire,** *to produce;* **réduire,** *to reduce;* **traduire,** *to translate.*

Connaître, *to know.*

1 *Infinitive* connaître; *fut.* connaîtrai; *condl.* connaîtrais.
2 *Pres. Part.* connaissant; *impf. indic.* connaissais; *pres. subj.* connaisse, connaisses, connaisse, connaissions, connaissiez, connaissent.
3 *Past Part.* connu; *past. indef.* j'ai connu.
4 *Pres. Indic.* connais, connais, connaît, connaissons, connaissez, connaissent; *impve.* connais, connaissons, connaissez.
5 *Past Def.* connus, connus, connut, connûmes, connûtes, connurent; *impf. subj.* connusse, connusses, connût, connussions, connussiez, connussent.

Like **connaître: apparaître,** *to appear;* **paraître,** *to appear;* **disparaître,** *to disappear;* **reconnaître,** *to recognize.*

Coudre, *to sew.*

1 *Infinitive* coudre; *fut.* coudrai; *condl.* coudrais.
2 *Pres. Part.* cousant; *impf. indic.* cousais; *pres. subj.* couse, couses, couse, cousions, cousiez, cousent.
3 *Past Part.* cousu; *past indef.* j'ai cousu.
4 *Pres. Indic.* couds, couds, coud, cousons, cousez, cousent; *impve.* couds, cousons, cousez.
5 *Past Def.* cousis, cousis, cousit, cousîmes, cousîtes, cousirent; *impf. subj.* cousisse, cousisses, cousît, cousissions, cousissiez, cousissent.

Courir, *to run.*

1 *Infinitive* courir; *fut.* courrai; *condl.* courrais.
2 *Pres. Part.* courant; *impf. indic.* courais; *pres. subj.* coure, coures, coure, courions, couriez, courent.
3 *Past Part.* couru; *past indef.* j'ai couru.
4 *Pres. Indic.* cours, cours, court, courons, courez, courent; *impve.* cours, courons, courez.
5 *Past Def.* courus, courus, courut, courûmes, courûtes, coururent; *impf. subj.* courusse, courusses, courût, courussions, courussiez, courussent.

Craindre, *to fear.*

1 *Infinitive* craindre; *fut.* craindrai; *condl.* craindrais.
2 *Pres. Part.* craignant; *impf. indic.* craignais; *pres. subj.* craigne, craignes, craigne, craignions, craigniez, craignent.
3 *Past Part.* craint; *past indef.* j'ai craint.
4 *Pres. Indic.* crains, crains, craint, craignons, craignez, craignent; *impve.* crains, craignons, craignez.
5 *Past Def.* craignis, craignis, craignit, craignîmes, craignîtes, craignirent; *impf. subj.* craignisse, craignisses, craignît, craignissions, craignissiez, craignissent.

Like **craindre: peindre,** *to paint;* **plaindre,** *to pity.*

Croire, *to believe.*

1 *Infinitive* croire; *fut.* croirai; *condl.* croirais.
2 *Pres. Part.* croyant; *impf. indic.* croyais; *pres. subj.* croie, croies, croie, croyions, croyiez, croient.
3 *Past Part.* cru; *past indef.* j'ai cru.

250

4 *Pres. Indic.* crois, crois, croit, croyons, croyez, croient; *impve.* crois, croyons, croyez.
5 *Past Def.* crus, crus, crut, crûmes, crûtes, crurent; *impf. subj.* crusse, crusses, crût, crussions, crussiez, crussent.

Croître, *to grow.*

1 *Infinitive* croître; *fut.* croîtrai; *condl.* croîtrais.
2 *Pres. Part.* croissant; *impf. indic.* croissais; *pres. subj.* croisse, croisses, croisse, croissions, croissiez, croissent.
3 *Past Part.* crû; *past indef.* j'ai crû.
4 *Pres. Indic.* croîs, croîs, croît, croissons, croissez, croissent; *impve.* croîs, croissons, croissez.
5 *Past Def.* crûs, crûs, crût, crûmes, crûtes, crûrent; *impf. subj.* crûsse, crûsses, crût, crûssions, crûssiez, crûssent.

Cueillir, *to gather, pick.*

1 *Infinitive* cueillir; *fut.* cueillerai; *condl.* cueillerais.
2 *Pres. Part.* cueillant; *impf. indic.* cueillais; *pres. subj.* cueille, cueilles, cueille, cueillions, cueilliez, cueillent.
3 *Past Part.* cueilli; *past indef.* j'ai cueilli.
4 *Pres. Indic.* cueille, cueilles, cueille, cueillons, cueillez, cueillent; *impve.* cueille, cueillons, cueillez.
5 *Past Def.* cueillis, cueillis, cueillit, cueillîmes, cueillîtes, cueillirent; *impf. subj.* cueillisse, cueillisses, cueillît, cueillissions, cueillissiez, cueillissent.

Like **cueillir: accueillir,** *to welcome;* **recueillir,** *to gather, collect.*

Devoir, *to owe.*

1 *Infinitive* devoir; *fut.* devrai; *condl.* devrais.
2 *Pres. Part.* devant; *impf. indic.* devais; *pres. subj.* doive, doives, doive, devions, deviez, doivent.
3 *Past Part.* dû; *past indef.* j'ai dû.
4 *Pres. Indic.* dois, dois, doit, devons, devez, doivent; *impve.* ——.
5 *Past Def.* dus, dus, dut, dûmes, dûtes, durent; *impf. subj.* dusse, dusses, dût, dussions, dussiez, dussent.

Dire, *to say, tell.*

1 *Infinitive* dire; *fut.* dirai; *condl.* dirais.
2 *Pres. Part.* disant; *impf. indic.* disais; *pres. subj.* dise, dises, dise, disions, disiez, disent.
3 *Past Part.* dit; *past indef.* j'ai dit.
4 *Pres. Indic.* dis, dis, dit, disons, dites, disent; *impve.* dis, disons, dites.
5 *Past Def.* dis, dis, dit, dîmes, dîtes, dirent; *impf. subj.* disse, disses, dît, dissions, dissiez, dissent.

Dormir, *to sleep.*

1 *Infinitive* dormir; *fut.* dormirai; *condl.* dormirais.
2 *Pres. Part.* dormant; *impf. indic.* dormais; *pres. subj.* dorme, dormes, dorme, dormions, dormiez, dorment.
3 *Past Part.* dormi; *past indef.* j'ai dormi.
4 *Pres. Indic.* dors, dors, dort, dormons, dormez, dorment; *impve.* dors, dormons, dormez.
5 *Past Def.* dormis, dormis, dormit, dormîmes, dormîtes, dormirent; *impf. subj.* dormisse, dormisses, dormît, dormissions, dormissiez, dormissent.

Like **dormir: endormir,** *to put to sleep;* **s'endormir,** *to fall asleep;* **mentir,** *to lie;* **partir,** *to set out;* **se repentir,** *to repent;* **sentir,** *to feel;* **consentir,** *to consent;* **ressentir,** *to feel, resent;* **servir,** *to serve;* **sortir,** *to go out.*

Écrire, *to write.*

1 *Infinitive* écrire; *fut.* écrirai; *condl.* écrirais.
2 *Pres. Part.* écrivant; *impf. indic.* écrivais; *pres. subj.* écrive, écrives, écrive, écrivions, écriviez, écrivent.
3 *Past Part.* écrit; *past indef.* j'ai écrit.
4 *Pres. Indic.* écris, écris, écrit, écrivons, écrivez, écrivent; *impve.* écris, écrivons, écrivez.
5 *Past Def.* écrivis, écrivis, écrivit, écrivîmes, écrivîtes, écrivirent; *impf. subj.* écrivisse, écrivisses, écrivît, écrivissions, écrivissiez, écrivissent.

Envoyer, *to send.*

1 *Infinitive* envoyer; *fut.* enverrai; *condl.* enverrais.
2 *Pres. Part.* envoyant; *impf. indic.* envoyais; *pres. subj.* envoie, envoies, envoie, envoyions, envoyiez, envoient.

3 *Past Part.* envoyé; *past indef.* j'ai envoyé.
4 *Pres. Indic.* envoie, envoies, envoie, envoyons, envoyez, en-voient; *impve.* envoie, envoyons, envoyez.
5 *Past Def.* envoyai, envoyas, envoya, envoyâmes, envoyâtes, envoyèrent; *impf. subj.* envoyasse, envoyasses, envoyât, en-voyassions, envoyassiez, envoyassent.

Like **envoyer: renvoyer**, *to send away, dismiss.*

Etre, *to be.*

1 *Infinitive* être; *fut.* serai; *condl.* serais.
2 *Pres. Part.* étant; *impf. indic.* étais; *pres. subj.* sois, sois, soit, soyons, soyez, soient.
3 *Past Part.* été; *past indef.* j'ai été.
4 *Pres. Indic.* suis, es, est, sommes, êtes, sont; *impve.* sois, soyons, soyez.
5 *Past Def.* fus, fus, fut, fûmes, fûtes, furent; *impf. subj.* fusse, fusses, fût, fussions, fussiez, fussent.

Faire, *to do, make.*

1 *Infinitive* faire; *fut.* ferai; *condl.* ferais.
2 *Pres. Part.* faisant; *impf. indic.* faisais; *pres. subj.* fasse, fasses, fasse, fassions, fassiez, fassent.
3 *Past Part.* fait; *past indef.* j'ai fait.
4 *Pres. Indic.* fais, fais, fait, faisons, faites, font; *impve.* fais, faisons, faites.
5 *Past Def.* fis, fis, fit, fîmes, fîtes, firent; *impf. subj.* fisse, fisses, fît, fissions, fissiez, fissent.

Falloir, *to be necessary*, etc. (impersonal)

1 *Infinitive* falloir; *fut.* il faudra; *condl.* il faudrait.
2 *Pres. Part.* ——; *impf. indic.* il fallait; *pres. subj.* il faille.
3 *Past Part.* fallu; *past indef.* il a fallu.
4 *Pres. Indic.* il faut; *impve.* ——.
5 *Past Def.* il fallut; *impf. subj.* il fallût.

Fuir, *to flee, fly.*

1 *Infinitive* fuir; *fut.* fuirai; *condl.* fuirais.
2 *Pres. Part.* fuyant; *impf. indic.* fuyais; *pres. subj.* fuie, fuies, fuie, fuyions, fuyiez, fuient.
3 *Past Part.* fui; *past indef.* j'ai fui.

4 *Pres. Indic.* fuis, fuis, fuit, fuyons, fuyez, fuient; *impve.* fuis, fuyons, fuyez.

5 *Past Def.* fuis, fuis, fuit, fuîmes, fuîtes, fuirent; *impf. subj.* fuisse, fuisses, fuît, fuissions, fuissiez, fuissent.

Like **fuir**: **s'enfuir**, *to flee, escape.*

Haïr, *to hate.*

1 *Infinitive* haïr; *fut.* haïrai; *condl.* haïrais.

2 *Pres. Part.* haïssant; *impf. indic.* haïssais; *pres. subj.* haïsse, haïsses, haïsse, haïssions, haïssiez, haïssent.

3 *Past Part.* haï; *past indef.* j'ai haï.

4 *Pres. Indic.* hais, hais, hait, haïssons, haïssez, haïssent; *impve.* hais, haïssons, haïssez.

5 *Past Def.* haïs, haïs, haït, haïmes, haïtes, haïrent; *impf. subj.* haïsse, haïsses, haït, haïssions, haïssiez, haïssent.

Lire, *to read.*

1 *Infinitive* lire; *fut.* lirai; *condl.* lirais.

2 *Pres. Part.* lisant; *impf. indic.* lisais; *pres. subj.* lise, lises, lise, lisions, lisiez, lisent.

3 *Past Part.* lu; *past indef.* j'ai lu.

4 *Pres. Indic.* lis, lis, lit, lisons, lisez, lisent; *impve.* lis, lisons, lisez.

5 *Past Def.* lus, lus, lut, lûmes, lûtes, lurent; *impf. subj.* lusse, lusses, lût, lussions, lussiez, lussent.

Like **lire**: **élire**, *to elect;* **relire**, *to read again.*

Mettre, *to place, put.*

1 *Infinitive* mettre; *fut.* mettrai; *condl.* mettrais.

2 *Pres. Part.* mettant; *impf. indic.* mettais; *pres. subj.* mette, mettes, mette, mettions, mettiez, mettent.

3 *Past Part.* mis; *past indef.* j'ai mis.

4 *Pres. Indic.* mets, mets, met, mettons, mettez, mettent; *impve.* mets, mettons, mettez.

5 *Past Def.* mis, mis, mit, mîmes, mîtes, mirent; *impf. subj.* misse, misses, mît, missions, missiez, missent.

Like **mettre**: **admettre**, *to admit;* **permettre**, *to permit;* **promettre**, *to promise.*

254

earn

Mourir, *to die.*

1 *Infinitive* mourir; *fut.* mourrai; *condl.* mourrais.
2 *Pres. Part.* mourant; *impf. indic.* mourais; *pres. subj.* meure, meures, meure, mourions, mouriez, meurent.
3 *Past Part.* mort; *past indef.* je suis mort.
4 *Pres. Indic.* meurs, meurs, meurt, mourons, mourez, meurent; *impve.* meurs, mourons, mourez.
5 *Past Def.* mourus, mourus, mourut, mourûmes, mourûtes, moururent; *impf. subj.* mourusse, mourusses, mourût, mourussions, mourussiez, mourussent.

Naître, *to be born.*

1 *Infinitive* naître; *fut.* naîtrai; *condl.* naîtrais.
2 *Pres. Part.* naissant; *impf. indic.* naissais; *pres. subj.* naisse, naisses, naisse, naissions, naissiez, naissent.
3 *Past Part.* né; *past indef.* je suis né.
4 *Pres. Indic.* nais, nais, naît, naissons, naissez, naissent; *impve.* nais, naissons, naissez.
5 *Past Def.* naquis, naquis, naquit, naquîmes, naquîtes, naquirent; *impf. subj.* naquisse, naquisses, naquît, naquissions, naquissiez, naquissent.

Ouvrir, *to open.*

1 *Infinitive* ouvrir; *fut.* ouvrirai; *condl.* ouvrirais.
2 *Pres. Part.* ouvrant; *impf. indic.* ouvrais; *pres. subj.* ouvre, ouvres, ouvre, ouvrions, ouvriez, ouvrent.
3 *Past Part.* ouvert; *past indef.* j'ai ouvert.
4 *Pres. Indic.* ouvre, ouvres, ouvre, ouvrons, ouvrez, ouvrent; *impve.* ouvre, ouvrons, ouvrez.
5 *Past Def.* ouvris, ouvris, ouvrit, ouvrîmes, ouvrîtes, ouvrirent; *impf. subj.* ouvrisse, ouvrisses, ouvrît, ouvrissions, ouvrissiez, ouvrissent.

Like **ouvrir: couvrir,** *to cover;* **découvrir,** *to discover, uncover;* **offrir,** *to offer;* **souffrir,** *to suffer.*

Partir, cf. dormir. *pres. part. partant*
Plaire, *to please.*

1 *Infinitive* plaire; *fut.* plairai; *condl.* plairais.
2 *Pres. Part.* plaisant; *impf. indic.* plaisais; *pres. subj.* plaise, plaises, plaise, plaisions, plaisiez, plaisent.

3 *Past Part.* plu; *past indef.* j'ai plu.
4 *Pres. Indic.* plais, plais, plaît, plaisons, plaisez, plaisent; *impve.* plais, plaisons, plaisez.
5 *Past Def.* plus, plus, plut, plûmes, plûtes, plurent; *impf. subj.* plusse, plusses, plût, plussions, plussiez, plussent.

Like **plaire: déplaire,** *to displease;* **se taire,** *to be silent* (**il se tait** has no circumflex).

Pleuvoir, *to rain* (impersonal).

1 *Infinitive* pleuvoir; *fut.* il pleuvra; *condl.* il pleuvrait.
2 *Pres. Part.* pleuvant; *impf. indic.* il pleuvait; *pres. subj.* il pleuve.
3 *Past Part.* plu; *past indef.* il a plu.
4 *Pres. Indic.* il pleut; *impve.* ——.
5 *Past Def.* il plut; *impf. subj.* il plût.

Pouvoir, *to be able.*

1 *Infinitive* pouvoir; *fut.* pourrai; *condl.* pourrais.
2 *Pres. Part.* pouvant; *impf. indic.* pouvais; *pres. subj.* puisse, puisses, puisse, puissions, puissiez, puissent.
3 *Past Part.* pu; *past indef.* j'ai pu.
4 *Pres. Indic.* peux *or* puis, peux, peut, pouvons, pouvez, peuvent; *impve.* ——.
5 *Past Def.* pus, pus, put, pûmes, pûtes, purent; *impf. subj.* pusse, pusses, pût, pussions, pussiez, pussent.

préférer

Prendre, *to take.*

1 *Infinitive* prendre; *fut.* prendrai; *condl.* prendrais.
2 *Pres. Part.* prenant; *impf. indic.* prenais; *pres. subj.* prenne, prennes, prenne, prenions, preniez, prennent.
3 *Past Part.* pris; *past indef.* j'ai pris.
4 *Pres. Indic.* prends, prends, prend, prenons, prenez, prennent; *impve.* prends, prenons, prenez.
5 *Past Def.* pris, pris, prit, prîmes, prîtes, prirent; *impf. subj.* prisse, prisses, prît, prissions, prissiez, prissent.

Like **prendre: apprendre,** *to learn;* **comprendre,** *to understand;* **entreprendre,** *to undertake;* **reprendre,** *to take back;* **surprendre,** *to surprise.*

 Cromener *manger* **256** *commencer*
Jeter *mener*

Recevoir, *to receive.*

1 *Infinitive* recevoir; *fut.* recevrai; *condl.* recevrais.
2 *Pres. Part.* recevant; *impf. indic.* recevais; *pres. subj.* reçoive, reçoives, reçoive, recevions, receviez, reçoivent.
3 *Past Part.* reçu; *past indef.* j'ai reçu.
4 *Pres. Indic.* reçois, reçois, reçoit, recevons, recevez, reçoivent; *impve.* reçois, recevons, recevez.
5 *Past Def.* reçus, reçus, reçut, reçûmes, reçûtes, reçurent; *impf. subj.* reçusse, reçusses, reçût, reçussions, reçussiez, reçussent.

Like **recevoir**: **apercevoir,** *to perceive;* **concevoir,** *to conceive.*

Résoudre, *to resolve.*

1 *Infinitive* résoudre; *fut.* résoudrai; *condl.* résoudrais.
2 *Pres. Part.* résolvant; *impf. indic.* résolvais; *pres. subj.* résolve, résolves, résolve, résolvions, résolviez, résolvent.
3 *Past Part.* résolu [1]; *past indef.* j'ai résolu.
4 *Pres. Indic.* résous, résous, résout, résolvons, résolvez, résolvent; *impve.* résous, résolvons, résolvez.
5 *Past Def.* résolus, résolus, résolut, résolûmes, résolûtes, résolurent; *impf. subj.* résolusse, résolusses, résolût, résolussions, résolussiez, résolussent.

Rire, *to laugh.*

1 *Infinitive* rire; *fut.* rirai; *condl.* rirais.
2 *Pres. Part.* riant; *impf. indic.* riais; *pres. subj.* rie, ries, rie, riions, riiez, rient.
3 *Past Part.* ri; *past indef.* j'ai ri.
4 *Pres. Indic.* ris, ris, rit, rions, riez, rient; *impve.* ris, rions, riez.
5 *Past Def.* ris, ris, rit, rîmes, rîtes, rirent; *impf. subj.* risse, risses, rît, rissions, rissiez, rissent.

Like **rire**: **sourire,** *to smile.*

Savoir, *to know.*

1 *Infinitive* savoir; *fut.* saurai; *condl.* saurais.
2 *Pres. Part.* sachant; *impf. indic.* savais; *pres. subj.* sache, saches, sache, sachions, sachiez, sachent.
3 *Past Part.* su; *past indef.* j'ai su.

---

[1] In chemistry, the past participle is **résous** (no feminine).

4 *Pres. Indic.* sais, sais, sait, savons, savez, savent; *impve.* sache, sachons, sachez.

5 *Past Def.* sus, sus, sut, sûmes, sûtes, surent; *impf. subj.* susse, susses, sût, sussions, sussiez, sussent.

 Sortir, cf. **dormir.**

 Suffire, *to suffice.*

1 *Infinitive* suffire; *fut.* suffirai; *condl.* suffirais.
2 *Pres. Part.* suffisant; *impf. indic.* suffisais; *pres. subj.* suffise, suffises, suffise, suffisions, suffisiez, suffisent.
3 *Past Part.* suffi; *past indef.* j'ai suffi.
4 *Pres. Indic.* suffis, suffis, suffit, suffisons, suffisez, suffisent; *impve.* suffis, suffisons, suffisez.
5 *Past Def.* suffis, suffis, suffit, suffîmes, suffîtes, suffirent; *impf. subj.* suffisse, suffisses, suffît, suffissions, suffissiez, suffissent.

 Suivre, *to follow.*

1 *Infinitive* suivre; *fut.* suivrai; *condl.* suivrais.
2 *Pres. Part.* suivant; *impf. indic.* suivais; *pres. subj.* suive, suives, suive, suivions, suiviez, suivent.
3 *Past Part.* suivi; *past indef.* j'ai suivi.
4 *Pres. Indic.* suis, suis, suit, suivons, suivez, suivent; *impve.* suis, suivons, suivez.
5 *Past Def.* suivis, suivis, suivit, suivîmes, suivîtes, suivirent; *impf. subj.* suivisse, suivisses, suivît, suivissions, suivissiez, suivissent.

Vaincre, *to conquer.*

1 *Infinitive* vaincre; *fut.* vaincrai; *condl.* vaincrais.
2 *Pres. Part.* vainquant; *impf. indic.* vainquais; *pres. subj.* vainque, vainques, vainque, vainquions, vainquiez, vainquent.
3 *Past Part.* vaincu; *past indef.* j'ai vaincu.
4 *Pres. Indic.* vaincs, vaincs, vainc, vainquons, vainquez, vainquent; *impve.* vaincs, vainquons, vainquez.
5 *Past Def.* vainquis, vainquis, vainquit, vainquîmes, vaniquîtes, vainquirent; *impf. subj.* vainquisse, vainquisses, vainquît, vainquissions, vainquissiez, vainquissent.

Like **vaincre: convaincre,** *to convince.*

Valoir, *to be worth.* *(compare partially with aller)*

1 *Infinitive* valoir; *fut.* vaudrai; *condl.* vaudrais.
2 *Pres. Part.* valant; *impf. indic.* valais; *pres. subj.* vaille, vailles, vaille, valions, valiez, vaillent.
3 *Past Part.* valu; *past indef.* j'ai valu.
4 *Pres. Indic.* vaux, vaux, vaut, valons, valez, valent; *impve.* vaux, valons, valez.
5 *Past Def.* valus, valus, valut, valûmes, valûtes, valurent; *impf. subj.* valusse, valusses, valût, valussions, valussiez, valussent.

Venir, *to come.*

1 *Infinitive* venir; *fut.* viendrai; *condl.* viendrais.
2 *Pres. Part.* venant; *impf. indic.* venais; *pres. subj.* vienne, viennes, vienne, venions, veniez, viennent.
3 *Past Part.* venu; *past indef.* je suis venu.
4 *Pres. Indic.* viens, viens, vient, venons, venez, viennent; *impve.* viens, venons, venez.
5 *Past Def.* vins, vins, vint, vînmes, vîntes, vinrent; *impf. subj.* vinsse, vinsses, vînt, vinssions, vinssiez, vinssent.

Like **venir: convenir,** *to agree, suit;* **devenir,** *to become;* **parvenir,** *to arrive, succeed;* **prévenir,** *to anticipate;* **provenir,** *to proceed, come;* **revenir,** *to come back;* **se souvenir de,** *to remember.*

Vêtir, *to dress.*

1 *Infinitive* vêtir; *fut.* vêtirai; *condl.* vêtirais.
2 *Pres. Part.* vêtant; *impf. indic.* vêtais; *pres. subj.* vête, vêtes, vête, vêtions, vêtiez, vêtent.
3 *Past Part.* vêtu; *past indef.* j'ai vêtu.
4 *Pres. Indic.* vêts, vêts, vêt, vêtons, vêtez, vêtent; *impve.* vêts, vêtons, vêtez.
5 *Past Def.* vêtis, vêtis, vêtit, vêtîmes, vêtîtes, vêtirent; *impf. subj.* vêtisse, vêtisses, vêtît, vêtissions, vêtissiez, vêtissent.

Vivre, *to live.*

1 *Infinitive,* vivre; *fut.* vivrai; *condl.* vivrais.
2 *Pres. Part.* vivant; *impf. indic.* vivais; *pres. subj.* vive, vives, vive, vivions, viviez, vivent.
3 *Past Part.* vécu *past indef.* j'ai vécu.

4 *Pres. Indic.* vis, vis, vit, vivons, vivez, vivent; *impve.* vis, vivons, vivez.

5 *Past Def.* vécus, vécus, vécut, vécûmes, vécûtes, vécurent; *impf. subj.* vécusse, vécusses, vécût, vécussions, vécussiez, vécussent.

Voir, *to see.*

1 *Infinitive* voir; *fut.* verrai; *condl.* verrais.

2 *Pres. Part.* voyant; *impf. indic.* voyais; *pres. subj.* voie, voies, voie, voyions, voyiez, voient.

3 *Past Part.* vu; *past indef.* j'ai vu.

4 *Pres. Indic.* vois, vois, voit, voyons, voyez, voient; *impve.* vois, voyons, voyez.

5 *Past Def.* vis, vis, vit, vîmes, vîtes, virent; *impf. subj.* visse, visses, vît, vissions, vissiez, vissent.

Like **voir: revoir,** *to see again.*

Vouloir, *to wish.*

1 *Infinitive* vouloir; *fut.* voudrai; *condl.* voudrais.

2 *Pres. Part.* voulant; *impf. indic.* voulais; *pres. subj.* veuille, veuilles, veuille, voulions, vouliez, veuillent.

3 *Past Part.* voulu; *past indef.* j'ai voulu.

4 *Pres. Indic.* veux, veux, veut, voulons, voulez, veulent; *impve.* veux, voulons, voulez; veuille, veuillons, veuillez.

5 *Past Def.* voulus, voulus, voulut, voulûmes, voulûtes, voulurent; *impf. subj.* voulusse, voulusses, voulût, voulussions, voulussiez, voulussent.

The imperative **veux, voulons, voulez** is practically obsolete except in the expression **en vouloir à.** Even in this case, the forms **veuille, veuillons, veuillez** are more frequently used. **Veuillez** followed by an infinitive is frequently equivalent to the English *please, be kind enough to,* etc.

248 The Dependent Infinitive.

In French, certain verbs are followed by the infinitive without a preposition; others require the prepositions **à or de.** Among the verbs which require no preposition are the modal auxiliaries, verbs of perception, verbs of wishing and desiring, verbs of motion, verbs of thinking and believing, and a few impersonal verbs. Verbs which express a "tendency toward," such as verbs of beginning, learning, and teaching, usually require the preposition **à**. In general, verbs which do not fall into the two groups just mentioned are followed by the preposition **de**. Lists of the most common verbs of these three groups follow.

A. The following verbs govern an infinitive without a preposition:

aimer, *to like, love* [1]
aimer mieux, *to prefer*
aller, *to go*
compter, *to expect, intend*
croire, *to believe*
désirer, *to desire*
devoir, *must, ought*
écouter, *to listen to*
entendre, *to hear*
envoyer, *to send*
espérer, *to hope*
faire, *to do, make*
falloir, *to be necessary*
laisser, *to let*

oser, *to dare*
paraître, *to appear*
penser, *to intend*
pouvoir, *to be able*
préférer, *to prefer*
prétendre, *to assert, claim*
regarder, *to watch*
savoir, *to know (how)*
sembler, *to seem*
sentir, *to feel*
valoir mieux, *to be preferable*
venir, *to come*
voir, *to see*
vouloir, *to wish*

B. The following verbs take **de** before the infinitive:

cesser, *to cease*
conseiller, *to advise*
craindre, *to fear*
décider, *to decide*
défendre, *to forbid*
demander, *to ask*
dépêcher (se), *to hurry*
devoir, *to owe*
dire, *to say, tell*
empêcher, *to prevent*
essayer, *to try*
être obligé (forcé) *to be obliged to*
éviter, *to avoid*

finir, *to finish* [2]
hâter (se), *to hurry*
offrir, *to offer*
oublier, *to forget*
permettre, *to permit*
prier, *to beg, request*
promettre, *to promise*
refuser, *to refuse*
regretter, *to regret*
remercier, *to thank*
tâcher, *to try*
venir, (= *to have just*)

---

[1] Except in the conditional, it is generally preferable to use **à** when **aimer** is followed immediately by the infinitive.
[2] Cf. § **85, C 4.**

C. The following verbs take **à** before the infinitive:

aider, *to help*

apprendre, *to learn*

chercher, *to try, seek*

commencer, *to begin* [1, 2]

consentir, *to consent*

continuer, *to continue* [1]

décider, *to persuade*

décider (se), *to make up one's mind*

engager, *to urge*

enseigner, *to teach*

forcer, *to force* [3]

inviter, *to invite*

mettre (se), *to begin*

obliger, *to oblige* [3]

penser, *to think of*

prétendre, *to aspire*

prier, *to invite*

réussir, *to succeed*

venir, *to happen to*

---

[1] Sometimes takes **de.**

[2] Cf. § 85, C 4.

[3] Takes **de** only when used in the passive with no agent expressed.

FRENCH-ENGLISH VOCABULARY

A

à at, to, in, for, into, on
abonné, –e: être — à to subscribe for
abord: d'— at first
accompagner to accompany
accuser to accuse
acheter to buy
acquérir to acquire
adorer to adore
adresser: s'— à to apply to
affaire *f.* affair, business; **homme d'—s** businessman
âge *m.* age; **quel — avez-vous?** how old are you? **moyen âge** Middle Ages
âgé, –e old, aged
agence *f.* agency; **— de placement** employment agency
aider to aid, help
aimer to like, love; **— mieux** to prefer
air *m.* air
allemand, –e German
aller to go; **— au-devant de** to go to meet; **s'en — to go away**
amener to bring
ami, –e friend
an *m.* year
anglais, –e English
année *f.* year
appeler: s'— to be called; **il s'appelle Jean** his name is John
application *f.* application
apprendre to learn, study
après after
après-midi *m. or f.* afternoon

argent *m.* money
aria *f.* aria
arriver to arrive, come
artiste *m. and f.* artist
aspirine *f.* aspirin
asseoir: s'— to sit down
attendre to wait, wait for
aussi as, also; therefore
aussitôt immediately; **— que** as soon as
auto *f.* auto, car
autorité *f.* authority
autre other
autrefois formerly
avant, before (of time)
avant que *conj.* before
avec with
avocat *m.* lawyer
avoir to have; **— besoin de** to need; **— l'habitude de** to be used to, in the habit of; **— pitié de** to feel sorry for; **qu'est-ce que tu as?** what's the matter with you?

B

battre to beat, strike; **— les cartes** to shuffle cards
beaucoup much, many, a lot
besoin *m.* need; **avoir — de** to need
bêtise *f.* nonsense, silly thing
bien very; well; many; **eh —!** well! **— que** although
boire to drink
bon, –ne good, kind; **de (si) —ne heure** (so) early

bonjour good day! good morning! good afternoon!

bonne *f.* maid

bonsoir good evening!

bonté *f.* kindness

bord *m.* edge, shore; **au — de la mer** at the seashore

bouquiniste *m.* dealer in second-hand books

bout *m.* end; **en venir à —** to succeed in (something), get the better of, accomplish

bureau *m.* desk

C

ça *contr. of* **cela** that

cacher to hide; **se —** to hide (one's self)

cadavre *m.* corpse, body

café *m.* coffee

caisse *f.* box, chest

camion *m.* truck

carte *f.* card

ce this, that; it; **— qui, — que,** what

cela that

celle this, that; this one, that one; the one

cent hundred

ces these, those

cet this, that

cette this, that

ceux these, those; the ones

chacun, –e each, each one

chambre *f.* bedroom

chance *f.* luck; chance; **avoir des —s de** to have a good chance to

changer to change

chapeau *m.* hat

chauffeur *m.* chauffeur

chaussette *f.* sock

chemin *m.* road, way

cher, chère dear; expensive, high

chercher to look for; get

chez at (to) the house of, home of, office of

chien *m.* dog

Chine *f.* China

chose *f.* thing

cigare *m.* cigar

cinéma *m.* moving-picture show, movies

coin *m.* corner

collège *m.* college

combien how much, how many; **(depuis) — de temps?** how long?

commander to command, order

comme as, like; how

commencer to begin

comment how; what

communiste *m. and f.* communist

compagnie *f.* company

comprendre to understand, realize

comprimé *m.* tablet

concentrer: se — sur to concentrate on

conclure to conclude

condamner to condemn

conduire to drive (a car); to take (a person)

connaître to know, be acquainted with; **se — à (en)** to understand, know a lot about; to be a good judge of

consentir to consent

conséquent: par — therefore, consequently

construire to build, construct

content, –e glad, satisfied

contenter: se — de to content one's self with

continuer to continue

contraire: au — on the contrary

conversation *f.* conversation

coter to grade, mark

coucher to sleep (spend the night); **se —** to go to bed

coudre to sew

courir to run
coûter to cost
craindre to fear
critique *f.* criticism
croire to think, believe
croître to grow
cueillir to pick, gather
cultivé, –e cultivated
cure *f.* treatment; **faire une (or
la)** to take treatment, take "the
cure"

D

dame *f.* lady
dans in, into
danser to dance
de of, from, in, by, with, to
debout standing; **dormir —** to be
very tired (*lit.* to sleep standing)
défendre to forbid
déjeuner *m.* lunch
demain tomorrow
demande *f.* request
demeurer to live
demi, –e half
demi-heure *f.* half-hour
départ *m.* departure
dépêche *f.* telegram
depuis since, for
déraper to skid
dernier, –ère last, latest
désirer to wish, desire
deux two; **tous (les) —** both
devant before, in front of; **aller
au– de** to go to meet
devoir *m.* duty; written work,
paper
devoir to have to, must, ought, be
to
difficile hard, difficult
dimanche *m.* Sunday
dîner *m.* dinner
dîner to dine, eat dinner
dire to say, tell; **cela ne me dit**

rien that doesn't appeal to me;
vouloir — to mean
discours *m.* speech
disparaître to disappear
distinguer to distinguish
dix ten
dommage *m.* pity; **c'est dommage!** it's a pity! it's too bad!
donner to give
dormir to sleep; **— debout** to be
very tired (*lit.* to sleep standing)
douter to doubt
drôle funny, queer, strange
dur, –e hard

E

échouer to fail
éclater to burst, break out
école *f.* school
écrire to write
électricité *f.* electricity
élève *m. and f.* pupil
elle she, it, her
emploi *m.* job
en in
en of it, of them; some, any
endormir: s'— to go to sleep
enfant *m. and f.* child
enfuir: s'— to flee; disappear;
pass quickly
ensuite next, then
entourer to surround
entre between, among
entreprise *f.* enterprise, undertaking
entrer to enter, come in
envoyer to send
épicier *m.* grocer
époque *f.* time, period, epoch
espérer to hope
essayer to try; (of clothes) to try
on
États-Unis *m.* United States
été *m.* summer

étonner to astonish, surprise; **ça ne m'étonne pas** I'm not surprised at that

étrange strange

être to be; — à to belong to; — en retard to be late

étude *f.* study; **continuer à faire ses —s** to continue one's studies (school work)

éviter to avoid

examen *m.* examination; **réussir à l'—** to pass the examination

exclusivement exclusively

excuse *f.* excuse, apology; **faire des —s** to apologize

expliquer to explain

F

faire to do, make; take; **— de son mieux** to do one's best; **continuer à — ses études** to continue one's studies (school work); **— la grasse matinée** to sleep late in the morning; **— signe à** to motion to, make a sign to; **— (une) visite à** to go to see, visit; **— un voyage** to take a trip; **— la queue** to stand in line

falloir to be necessary, need; **il me faut . . .** I need . . .

fatiguer to tire; (of eyes) to strain

femme *f.* woman; wife

fenêtre *f.* window

fille *f.* girl, daughter

fils *m.* son

fleur *f.* flower

fois *f.* time

fort, —e strong; good

foule *f.* crowd

franc *m.* franc

français, —e French; **en —** in French

frère *m.* brother

fuir to flee, avoid by fleeing; to leak; (of time) to pass quickly

fumer to smoke

G

gai, —e gay, merry

garçon *m.* boy

garde *f.* care, heed; **prendre — de** take care not to

gens *m. pl. (sometimes fem.)* people; **jeunes —** young men, young people

gloire *f.* glory; fame, renown

goût *m.* taste

grammaire *f.* grammar

grand, —e large, tall; great

gras, —se fat; **faire la —se matinée** to sleep late in the morning

gris, —e gray; drunk

gronder to scold

guerre *f.* war

H

habiller to dress; **s'habiller** to dress, get dressed

habiter to live, live in

habitude *f.* habit; **avoir l'— de** to be used to, in the habit of

haïr to hate

heure *f.* hour, time; **de (si) bonne heure** (so) early

heureux, heureuse happy

hier *m.* yesterday

histoire *f.* story

homme *m.* man; **— d'affaires** businessman

hôte *m.* host

I

ici here

idée *f.* idea

il he, it; **il y a** there is, there are; ago

imperméable *m.* raincoat
impression *f.* feeling, impression
indiquer to indicate; to choose
insister to insist; **— pour** to insist on
insu: à l'—de without the knowledge of
insupportable unbearable
intention *f.* intention; **avoir l'—de** to intend to
inutile useless
invétéré, –e inveterate
invité, –e guest

J

jamais never; ever; **ne —** never
jambe *f.* leg
je I
Jean John
jeune young
jour *m.* day; **quinze —s** two weeks
journal *m.* newspaper
journée *f.* day
jusque even, as far as; **jusqu'à ce que** until

L

la *f.* the, her, it
là there, here; **—-bas** over there; **c'est là . . .** that is . . .
laisser to leave, allow, let; **— tomber** to drop
le *m.* the, him, it
leçon *f.* lesson
lequel, laquelle, lesquels, lesquelles who, whom; which, that; which one, which ones
les *pl.* the; them
lettre *f.* letter
leur their; them, to them
lever to raise; **se —** to get up, stand

lieu *m.* place; **au — de** instead of
liqueur *f.* cordial, "liqueur"
lire to read
littéraire literary
livre *m.* book
loi *f.* law
l'on *same as* **on**
longtemps long, a long time
louer to rent
loyauté *f.* loyalty
lui he, him; to him, to her

M

M. *abbreviation* **Monsieur,** Mr.
machinalement mechanically, without thinking
madame madam, Mrs.
mademoiselle Miss
maintenant now
mais but; why
maison *f.* house
maître *m.* master, teacher; **—-nageur** lifeguard
mal *m.* pain; evil; **avoir — au pied** to have a sore foot, have one's foot hurt
malgré in spite of
malheureusement unfortunately
malle *f.* trunk
manger to eat
manquer to miss, fail; **ne manquez pas de** don't fail to, be sure to
mari *m.* husband
mariage *m.* marriage
matinée *f.* morning; matinée; **faire la grasse —** to sleep late in the morning
me me, to me; for me, from me
médecin *m.* doctor
meilleur, –e better, best
même same, even, very; **tout de — just** the same
mener to lead, take

mer f. sea, ocean; **au bord de la — at** the seashore

mère f. mother

messieurs pl. of **monsieur** gentlemen

mettre to put (of clothes, to put on); **se — to** sit down; **se — à** to begin to

mieux better; best; **aimer — to** prefer; **faire de son — to** do one's best

milieu m. middle, midst; environment, circle, "milieu"; **au — de** in the middle of

mille thousand

minute f. minute

Mme abbreviation of **Madame** Mrs., madam

moi I, me; **— -même** myself

moins less; **à — que** unless

mois m. month

moment m. moment, minute, time; **en ce — now,** at this time

mon my

monde m. world, people; **tout le — everybody**

montagne f. mountain

mot m. word

mourir to die

moyen, -ne middle; **— âge** Middle Ages

N

nageur m. swimmer; **maître- — lifeguard**

naître to be born

ne not; **— . . . pas** not; **— . . . que** only, not until; **— . . . rien** nothing

n'est-ce pas? isn't it so? won't you? doesn't he? etc.

nier to deny

Noël m. (sometimes f.) Christmas

non no, not

nous we, us; to us, for us, from us

nouveau nouvel, nouvelle, new

nouvelle f. news; story; short story

nuit f. night

O

obliger to oblige

obstacle m. obstacle

occuper to occupy; **s'— de** to occupy one's self with, look after

œil (pl. **yeux**) m. eye; **j'ai les yeux fatigués** my eyes are strained, I've strained my eyes

œuf m. egg

officier m. officer

on one, they, men, we, you, people

orage m. storm

ordinaire ordinary; **d'— ordinarily,** usually

ou or

où where; when

oublier to forget

oui yes

outre beyond; **en — in** addition, besides

ouvrier m. workman

ouvrir to open

P

pacifiste m. and f. pacifist

pantoufle f. slipper

par by, through; **deux fois — an** twice a year

paraître to seem, appear

parler to speak, talk

parmi among

parole f. word

partie f. part

partir to leave, go

pas no; **ne . . . — not**

passer to pass; spend (time); to

take (an examination); to go to, stop (in) at

pays country, nation

paysan, –ne peasant

peine *f.* trouble, difficulty; **à —
... que** hardly ... when

pendant for, during; **— que** while

penser to think; **— à** to think of, about; **— de** to think of (to have a good or bad opinion of)

père *m.* father

personne *f.* person; *m.* nobody; **ne ... —** nobody

petit, –e little, small

peu little, few

peur *f.* fear; **de — que** for fear that

pharmacie *f.* pharmacy, drugstore

phrase *f.* sentence

piano *m.* piano; **— à queue** grand piano

pièce *f.* room, piece

pied *m.* foot; **avoir mal au —** to have a sore foot, have one's foot hurt

pique-nique *m.* picnic

pitié *f.* pity; **avoir — de** to feel sorry for

placement *m.* placing; **agence de —** employment agency

plaire to please, be pleasing

pleurer to cry, weep

pleuvoir to rain

plupart *f.* most

plus more, most

plusieurs several

point *m.* point; **sur le — de** on the point of, about to

poisson *m.* fish

porte *f.* door

porter to carry, wear

poser to ask

possible possible

pour for, in order to, to; **— que** so that, in order that

pourquoi why

pourvu que provided that; if only

pouvoir to be able; can, may

précipitamment hurriedly

précisément exactly

préférer to prefer

premier, première first

prendre to take, get

présenter to introduce

presque almost

prêt, –e ready

prêter to lend

prier to ask, beg

principe *m.* principle

probable probable

probablement probably

problème *m.* problem

prochain, –e next, approaching

professeur *m.* professor, teacher

promenade *f.* walk

promener: se — to walk (take a walk)

promettre to promise

proposer to propose, suggest

puis then

Q

quand when; **depuis —?** how long? since when?

quatre four

que what; than, as, how! **qu'est-ce?** what is it?

que *conj.* that

quelque some

quelqu'un, –e someone, somebody

question *f.* question

queue *f.* tail; **piano à —** grand piano

qui who, whom, that, which; **qui que ...** whoever

quinze fifteen; **— jours** two weeks

quoi what, which; **— que** whatever

quoique although

R

ramener to bring back
réalité *f.* reality
réception *f.* reception
recevoir to receive
regretter to regret, be sorry; to miss
remercier to thank
rencontrer to meet; **nous nous sommes bien rencontrés, mais** . . . we *did* meet, but . . .
rendez-vous *m.* engagement; meeting place
rendre to give back; **— un service** to do a favor
rentrer to come back, come in, go *or* come (back) home
répliquer to reply, retort
répondre to answer
représentation *f.* performance, show
résoudre to solve; **— de** (*plus inf.*) to determine to
ressusciter to resuscitate
rester to stay, remain; **— tranquille** keep still, quiet
retard: être en — to be late
réunion *f.* meeting
réussir to succeed; **— à l'examen** to pass the examination
réveiller to awaken
revenir to come back
revoir to see again
revue *f.* magazine
ridicule ridiculous; **tourner qqn en —** to make a person appear ridiculous
rien nothing; anything
rire to laugh
rivière *f.* river
robe *f.* dress
roman *m.* novel
ronfler to snore
rue *f.* street

S

sa his, her
salon *m.* parlor, drawing room, living room
sauf except
savoir to know, know how
scélérat *m.* scoundrel
science *f.* science
semaine *f.* week
sembler to seem
service *m.* service, favor
servir to serve; **se — de** to use
ses (*pl.*) his, her, one's, its
seul, -e alone; only
si if
signe *m.* sign; **faire — à** to motion to, make a sign to
six six
sœur *f.* sister
son his, her, its
sorte *f.* kind, sort; **de — que** so (that)
sortir to go out; to take out
souffrant, -e ailing, indisposed
sourd-muet, sourde-muette deaf-and-dumb person
souvent often
stylo *m.* fountain pen
suffire to suffice, be enough; **se —** to be self-sufficient (i.e., not to need the help of others)
suite *f.* consequence, result, succession; **tout de —** immediately
suivre to follow
sujet *m.* subject
sur on, in
sympathique likable, attractive

T

table *f.* table
tâche *f.* task
tailleur *m.* tailor
taire to silence; **se —** to keep quiet, to "shut up"

tard late

téléphone *m.* telephone; **au** — on, over, the telephone

temps *m.* time, weather; **(depuis) combien de** —? how long?

terminer to end; **se** — to end

tiens! well! (*of surprise*)

tomber to fall; **laisser** — to drop

toujours always, still

tourner to turn; — **qqn en ridicule** to make someone appear ridiculous

tout, –e all; — **le monde** everybody

tout *m.* all, everything

tout *adv.* — **de même** just the same; — **de suite** immediately

tranquille quiet, tranquil; **rester** — to keep still, quiet

travail *m.* work

travailler to work

très very

trois three

trop too, too much, too many

trouver to find; **Comment trouvez-vous cela?** How do you like that?

tu you

U

un, –e a, an, one

V

vaincre to conquer, overcome

valeur *f.* value

valise *f.* valise, suitcase

valoir to be worth

venir to come; **en** — **à bout** to succeed in something, get the better of, accomplish; — **de** to have just

verbe *m.* verb

vérité *f.* truth

vert, –e green

veston *m.* coat (of a man's business suit)

vêtir to dress, clothe

ville *f.* town, city; **en** — downtown, in town

violer to violate

visite *f.* visit; **faire (une) visite à** to visit, go to see

vivre to live

voilà there is, there are

voir to see

vos *pl.* your

votre *sing.* your

vouloir to wish, be willing; — **bien** to be willing; to be kind enough to; — **dire** to mean; **en** — **à qqn** to have a grudge against, be angry with someone

vous you; to you, for you, from you

voyage *m.* trip; **faire un** — to take a trip

vrai, –e true

Y

y there, here; to it, in it, at it, etc.; **il** — **a deux mois** two months ago

ENGLISH-FRENCH VOCABULARY

A

A.B. le baccalauréat; **to get one's — ** passer son baccalauréat

**able: to be — ** pouvoir

about à propos de, de, sur, au sujet de; (**about**, *plus a pronoun referring to a thing, is often translated by* en *before the verb*); (**nearly**) à peu près, environ, dans les . . ., vers

abroad à l'étranger; **in our traveling — ** quand nous voyageons à l'étranger

absence une absence; **in the — of** en l'absence de

absolutely absolument

accept accepter

according: — to d'après

account le compte; **on — of** à cause de

accustomed: to be — to avoir l'habitude de; **to become — to** s'habituer à

acquaintance la connaissance; **influential —s** de belles relations

acquainted: to be (well) — with connaître (bien)

acquire acquérir

act un acte

act *v.* agir

active actif, –tive

add ajouter

address une adresse

admire admirer

advice le conseil; **to give good — to** donner de bons conseils à

affable affable

afraid: to be — (to) (that) avoir peur (de) (que)

Africa l'Afrique *f.*; **North — ** l'Afrique du nord

after après; *conj.* après que; **— all** après tout

afternoon l'après-midi *m. or f.*; **at three o'clock in the — ** à trois heures de l'après-midi; **in the — ** dans l'après-midi; (**theater**) en matinée

again encore une fois, de nouveau

against contre

age un âge; **the Middle Ages,** le moyen âge

ago il y a; **two weeks — ** il y a quinze jours

ahead: to go straight — ** aller tout droit; **— of time en avance

aid aider

air l'air *m.*; **there wasn't a breath of — ** il n'y avait pas un souffle d'air, de vent

airplane un avion; **in an — ** en avion

alarm une alerte

all tout, toute, tous, toutes; **not at — ** pas du tout; **not . . . at — ** pas . . . du tout; **— the time** toujours, sans cesse; **to study — the time** ne faire qu'étudier

allow permettre

almost presque

alone seul

already déjà

always toujours

America l'Amérique *f.*; **North — ** l'Amérique du nord

American *n.* un Américain; *adj.* américain

among entre, parmi; **to be — the guests** être de la partie

and et

angry en colère, fâché; furieux, furieuse; **to get —** se mettre en colère, se fâcher

animal un animal, une bête

announce annoncer

annoy ennuyer; **to be annoyed at someone** en vouloir à qqn

another autre, un autre, encore un

answer répondre à; **— for** répondre de

antiquarian un antiquaire

anxious: to be — to tenir à

any de, en; (*with neg.*) **— more, — longer** ne ... plus; n'importe quel; **— one** n'importe lequel

anyone personne, qui que ce soit; quelqu'un; n'importe qui

anything quelque chose; (*after neg.*) rien

anywhere (*after neg.*) nulle part

apiece la pièce; (*fam.*) pièce

apparently apparemment

appeal: that doesn't — to me ça ne me dit rien

appear paraître

applaud applaudir

apple la pomme

apply (to) s'adresser (à)

appointment le rendez-vous; **to make an —** prendre rendez-vous

approach s'approcher de; approcher de

approve (of) approuver

April avril

argument un argument

armchair le fauteuil

army une armée

around: to go — the world faire le tour du monde

arrival une arrivée

arrive arriver

as comme; **— soon —** aussitôt que

ashamed honteux, honteuse; **to be — of** avoir honte de; **to be quite — of** être tout honteux de

aside de côté

ask demander; **to — someone to do something** demander à qqn de faire quelque chose; **to — a question** poser une question; **to — someone for something** demander quelque chose à qqn; **to — for** demander

asleep: to be — (standing up) dormir (debout)

assure assurer

astonish étonner

astonishing étonnant, –e

at à, dans, chez; **— Mary's** chez Marie

attend assister à; **to — summer school** suivre des (les) cours de vacances

attention: to pay — to faire attention à

audience un auditoire, une assistance; (**theater**) le public

author un auteur

avenue une avenue

avoid éviter (de *before inf.*); (*by fleeing*) fuir

away: to go — s'en aller

B

back *n.* le dos; **to turn one's —** to tourner le dos à

back *adv.* de retour; **on the way —** en rentrant, en revenant; **to be —** être de retour, être rentré

bad mauvais, méchant; **It's too — that ...** C'est dommage que ...; **to go from — to worse**

aller de mal en pis; **to look —** avoir mauvaise mine

bag: to let the cat out of the — vendre la mèche

banker le banquier

be être; **aren't you? isn't he?** etc. n'est-ce pas? **to — to** devoir

beach la plage; **at** *or* **to the —** au bord de la mer

beard la barbe

beautiful beau, bel, belle

because parce que; **— of** à cause de

become devenir; **— of** devenir

becoming (to) qui va (bien) (à), sied (à), est seyant (à)

bed le lit; **to go to —** se coucher; **to get out of —** (after an illness) se relever

before *prep.* (*time*) avant; (*place*) devant; **— long** bientôt; *conj.* avant que

beggar le mendiant

begin (to) commencer (à), se mettre à; **to — again** recommencer

beginner (*fam.*) le débutant; le commençant

behind derrière

believe croire

bench la banquette; **wooden —es** banquettes de bois

beside à côté de

best *adj.* (le) meilleur; *adv.* le mieux; *n.* **to do one's —** faire de son mieux, faire (tout) son possible; **to get the — of** venir à bout de

better *adj.* meilleur; **all the (so much the) —** tant mieux; *adv.* mieux; (*health*) **to be —** se porter, aller, mieux; **to be —** valoir mieux

between entre

bicycle la bicyclette; **on a —** à bicyclette

birth: to give — to donner le jour à

black noir, –e

black-out une obscuration

blessed: the whole — day toute la sainte journée

blond blond, –e

blow *n.* le coup; **to come to —s** en venir aux mains

blow: the wind —s il fait du vent; **to — one's nose** se moucher

blue bleu, –e

blunder (*fam.*) la gaffe, la bêtise; (*gross blunder*) la bévue

boardinghouse la pension (de famille)

bodily: to do — injury to faire violence à

boil bouillir

boiled bouilli, –e

bomb bombarder; lancer des bombes sur

book le livre

boring ennuyeux, ennuyeuse

born: to be — naître; **I was —** je suis né

boss le patron

both tous (les) deux, les deux

bottle la bouteille

boulevard le boulevard

boy le garçon; **—s** (young men) jeunes gens

brave brave

bread le pain

break une gaffe; **to make a —** faire une gaffe

break casser; **to — one's leg** se casser la jambe

breath le souffle; **there wasn't a breath of air** il n'y avait pas un souffle d'air (de vent)

bridge (*game*) le bridge

brilliant brillant, –e

bring (*things*) apporter; (*persons*) amener; **to — out** (*publish*) publier, faire paraître; **to — up** monter; **to — along** (*things*) emporter; **to — back** (*things*) rapporter; (*persons*) ramener; **to — to light** mettre au jour

brother le frère

brush brosser; **to — one's hair** se brosser les cheveux

brunette la brune

build bâtir, construire

bureau le bureau; **information — bureau** de renseignements

burst éclater; **to — out laughing** éclater de rire

bus un autobus

business les affaires *f.*; **to retire from —** se retirer des affaires; **to mind one's own —** se mêler de ses affaires, de ce qui vous regarde

busy occupé, –e

but *conj.* mais; **to do nothing —** ne faire que *plus inf.*

butter le beurre

buy acheter

by par; (*beside*) à côté de; en (*plus present participle*); (*by dint of*) à force de (*plus inf.*)

C

cabinet le cabinet

call une visite; **to make a — on** rendre visite à, aller voir; **to return a —** rendre une visite

call appeler; **to -- in** appeler, faire venir; **to — on** rendre visite à, aller voir

can pouvoir

canned: *cf.* **goods**

capital la capitale

car une auto; **in a —** en auto

cards les cartes *f.*; **to play —** jouer aux cartes

care le soin

care *v.* **— to,** tenir à; **Who —s?** Qu'importe? Et après?

career la carrière

careful attention!

carry porter; **to — down** descendre; **to — up** monter; **to — out successfully** mener à bien; venir à bout de

case le cas; **in that —** dans ce cas

castle le château

cat le chat; **to let the — out of the bag** vendre la mèche

cathedral la cathédrale

cautious prudent, –e

century le siècle; **a quarter of a —** un quart de siècle

certain certain, –e; sûr, –e

certainly: I certainly did! Si fait! mais si!

chance le hasard; **by (any) —** par hasard; la chance: **there's a good — that . . .** il y a des chances pour que . . .

change changer; **to — one's mind** (*opinion*) changer d'avis; (*purpose*) changer d'idée

character (*play, movie*) le personnage

charm le charme

charming charmant, –e

chauffeur le chauffeur

chemistry la chimie; **in —** en chimie

chiffonnier la commode

child un enfant

children les enfants

choose choisir; **to — as a** choisir comme

Christmas Noël *m. or* la (fête de) Noël

church une église; **to go to —** aller à l'église

cigarette la cigarette

citizen le citoyen

city la ville; **in the —** à la ville

civil: **the Civil War** la guerre de Sécession

class la classe; (*travel*) **third —** (voyager) en troisième (classe); **a third — coach** un wagon (une voiture) de troisième (classe)

clear *v.*: **to — up** (*with* le temps *as subject*) s'éclaircir, se lever

clearly clairement, distinctement

clever habile; **to be very — at foreign languages** être très fort en langues étrangères; avoir beaucoup de facilité à apprendre les langues étrangères

cleverness l'habileté *f.*; le savoir-faire

close *v.* fermer; (*int.*, *as of a door*) se fermer, se refermer

close: **quite — together** très (*or* tout) près les uns des autres

clothes les vêtements

cloud le nuage

cloud *v.*: **to — up** (*with* le temps *or* le ciel *as subject*) se couvrir

cloudy: **it is —** le temps (le ciel) est couvert

club (*French*) le cercle (français)

coach (*railway*) le wagon; la voiture; **a third class —** un wagon (une voiture) de troisième (classe)

coffee le café

cold le froid; (*weather*) **it is —** il fait froid

colleague collègue *m. or f.*

college le collège (*approximate equivalent only*); **to, in, at —** au collège

color la couleur

comb peigner: **to — one's hair** se peigner

come venir; (*date*) tomber; **to — back** revenir; **to — home** rentrer (chez soi); **to — in**(**to**) entrer; **to — near** s'approcher de; **to — out**

sortir, (*sun*) se montrer, (*to be published*) paraître; **to — up** monter

comfortable (*persons*) bien; (*things*) confortable

complain se plaindre

completely complètement, tout à fait

concern regarder

conclude conclure

condition un état; **in very bad —** en très mauvais état

conduct conduire

confidence la confiance; **to have — in** avoir confiance en

congratulate féliciter; **to — someone on something** féliciter qqn de qqch; (*When it is a question of a state which follows an action,* féliciter *is frequently followed by* sur) féliciter qqn sur son mariage, son avancement, etc.

conquer vaincre

consent consentir (à)

conservative conservateur

constantly constamment

construct construire

continue (to) continuer (à)

convince convaincre

cook *n.* la cuisinière

cook *v.* faire la cuisine

correct correct, –e

cost coûter; **to — one no end of money** coûter les yeux de la tête à qqn

counter le comptoir

country le pays; (*not the city*) la campagne; **in the —** à la campagne

course le cours; **literature —** cours de littérature; **of —** bien entendu, naturellement; **in the — of** au cours de

cousin le cousin, la cousine

cover couvrir; (*ground in a book*) voir

crazy fou, fol, folle

cream la crème; **the — puff** le chou à la crème

creature la créature

cross traverser; **to — the ocean** faire la traversée

crowd la foule

cry pleurer; (*to exclaim*) s'écrier

cup la tasse

cure guérir

customer le client, la cliente

cut couper

D

daddy papa *m.*

dance danser

dare oser

dark sombre; **to be (get) —** faire sombre; (*after nightfall*) faire nuit

daughter la fille

day le jour, la journée; **all — yesterday** toute la journée d'hier; **by the —** à la journée; **— and night** nuit et jour; **every —** tous les jours; **the whole —** toute la journée; **What day of the week?** Quel jour de la semaine?

deal: to — (*cards*) donner

dean le doyen

dear cher, chère

death la mort; **to starve to —** mourir de faim; **to be at —'s door** être entre la vie et la mort

deliberately de parti pris

delighted enchanté, –e; **You'll be — with it** Vous m'en direz des nouvelles

demand une exigence

dentist le dentiste; **to the —'s** chez le dentiste

deny nier

department: — stores les ma-gasins de nouveautés, les grands magasins

detail le détail

devoted: to be — to adorer

die mourir

diet le régime

different différent, –e

difficult difficile

dine dîner; **to — out** dîner en ville; (*in certain parts of France*) dîner dehors

dinner le dîner

disappear (*fig.*) s'enfuir

discommode incommoder; em-barrasser; causer des ennuis à

discover s'apercevoir

dishes la vaisselle

dismiss renvoyer

disobey désobéir (à)

do faire; **doesn't it? didn't it?** etc. n'est-ce pas?; **to — one's best** faire de son mieux, faire (tout) son possible; **to — over completely** remettre à neuf; **to — without** se passer de; **to — without meat** se passer de viande, faire maigre

doctor le docteur, le médecin

document le document

dollar le dollar

door la porte; **next — to you** à côté de chez vous; **to be at death's —** être entre la vie et la mort

dormitory le dortoir; **in the —** au dortoir

doubt douter (de)

down: to take — descendre

downstairs: to go — descendre, descendre l'escalier

draft le courant d'air

drawer le tiroir

dress la robe

dressmaker (ladies' tailor) le cou-turier; (*seamstress*) la couturière

dressy habillé, –e
drink boire
drive (a car) conduire
drown (*int.*) se noyer; (*tr.*) noyer
dummy: to be — faire le mort
during pendant
duty le devoir

E

each *adj.* chaque; *pron.* chacun, –e;
— **one** chacun; — **other** se;
l'un l'autre, l'un à l'autre, etc.;
near — **other** l'un près de
l'autre
ear une oreille; **over one** —, sur
l'oreille
early (**very**) de (très) bonne heure;
so — de si bonne heure; (*equiva-lent to* **soon**) tôt
earn gagner; **to** — **one's living**
gagner sa vie
Easter Pâques *m.*
easy facile
eat manger; **to** — **meat** manger de
la viande, faire gras; **to** — **a**
(**meager**) **meal** faire un
(maigre) repas
economy l'économie *f.*
eighty quatre-vingt(s), —**-eight**
quatre-vingt-huit
either: — ... **or** (*after negative*)
ni ... ni; **I don't** — (Ni) moi
non plus
elderly d'un certain âge
electricity l'électricité *f.*
eleven onze; —**-thirty** onze
heures et demie
**emergency: to put money aside
for an** — mettre de l'argent de
côté en cas de besoin
emphasize insister (sur)
employee employé, –e
employer le patron, l'employeur,
–euse
end la fin; le bout; **to come to an**

— prendre fin; **to cost no** — **of
money** coûter les yeux de la
tête à qqn
end *v.* finir
England l'Angleterre *f.*
English anglais, –e; **the** — **lan-guage** l'anglais *m.*
enjoy one's self s'amuser
enter entrer (dans)
enterprise une entreprise
esteem estime *f.*
Europe l'Europe *f.*
evening le soir, la soirée; **in the**
— le soir; dans la soirée;
(*theater*) en soirée
ever jamais
every day tous les jours
everyone tout le monde
everything tout
everywhere partout; **practically**
— un peu partout
evident évident, –e
exactly précisément, exactement;
at — **nine o'clock** à neuf heures
précises
examination un examen; **to take
an** — passer un examen; **a
French** — un examen de fran-çais
excellent excellent, –e
excessive excessif, –sive
excited (*and showing it*) surexcité,
–e
exclaim s'écrier
exhausted: to be — n'en pouvoir
plus, être rendu
expect espérer; **What do you** —
me to do about it? Que vou-lez-vous que j'y fasse?
expense: to live at the — **of**
vivre aux dépens de
expensive cher, chère
explain expliquer
express exprimer; **to** — **one's
self** s'exprimer

expression une expression, une locution

exquisite exquis, –e

extraordinary extraordinaire

eye un œil; —s, les yeux

F

façade la façade

face la figure, le visage

fact le fait; **in** — en fait; **a** — **which** ce qui, ce que

fail manquer (de); **to** — **an examination** ne pas réussir à, échouer à, un examen

faint s'évanouir

fall la chute

fall *v.* tomber

family la famille

famous fameux, –euse, célèbre

fascism le fascisme

fashionably à la mode

fast *adv.* vite

father le père

fault le défaut

favor le service; **to ask a** — **of someone** demander un service à qqn

favorite favori, –ite; préféré, –e

fear *n.* la peur; **for** — **that** de peur (de crainte) que

fear *v.* craindre

fed: to be — **up with** avoir plein le dos de

fellow le type, le diable

fever la fièvre; **a high** — une forte fièvre

few peu (de); *adj.* **a** — quelques; (*pro.*) quelques-uns (unes)

fewer moins de

fifteen quinze; **about** — une quinzaine

fifth cinquième

finally finalement; — **to do something** finir par faire qqch

find trouver; **to** — **out,** savoir

fine! à la bonne heure!

finesse faire l'impasse

finish finir; conclure

firmly fermement

first *adj.* premier, –ière; **Napoleon the First** Napoléon premier; *adv.* d'abord

first-rate de premier ordre; **a** — **cook** un cordon bleu

five cinq

flee fuir, s'enfuir

flock se rendre en foule

flood une inondation

floor: ground — le rez-de-chaussée; **the second** — le premier (étage)

flower la fleur

foggy: to be — faire du brouillard

follow suivre

folly la folie

food la nourriture

fool un imbécile

foolish stupide, bête

foot le pied

for *prep.* pour; (*during*) pendant; (*since*) depuis; *conj.* car

forbid défendre; **God forbid that . . .** A Dieu ne plaise que . . .

force forcer

foreign étranger, –ère

forget oublier

former celui-là, celle-là, etc.; *adj.,* ancien, –ne

forty quarante

founder le fondateur

four quatre; **twenty minutes past** — quatre heures vingt

fourth le quart; **three** —**s** les trois quarts (de)

franc le franc

France la France

frank franc, franche

frankly franchement

frankness la franchise

French le français

French *adj.* français, –e

Frenchman le Français; **French-woman** la Française

Friday vendredi

friend un ami

frightfully à faire peur

from de; (*after* **raise**) de dessus

front: in — of devant

frying pan poêle à frire *f.*

fun: to make — of se moquer de

G

gadget le petit instrument, le dispositif

garage le garage

garden le jardin; **the Luxembourg** — le jardin du Luxembourg

gather: to — **information** prendre des renseignements; (*flowers or fruit*) cueillir

general le général

general *adj.* général, –e; **— staff** l'état-major

generally généralement

gentleman le monsieur

geographical géographique

get avoir; prendre; arriver; (aller) chercher; (aller) prendre; **stop at the office and get your father** passez au bureau prendre votre père; **to — along well** (**together**) faire bon ménage (ensemble); s'entendre bien; **to — good grades** avoir (recevoir) de bonnes notes; **to — in** (*come home*) rentrer; **to — one's A.B.** passer son baccalauréat; **to — off, out of** descendre (de); **to — the best of** venir à bout de; **to — up** se lever

girl la jeune fille; **little —** la petite fille

give donner; **to — back** rendre; **to — up** renoncer à; **to — up** (*a doctor of his patient*) condamner

gladly volontiers, avec plaisir

glove le gant

go aller; **to — to church** aller à l'église; **to — get,** aller chercher; aller prendre; **to — to the movies** aller au cinéma; **to — around the world** faire le tour du monde; **to — away** s'en aller; **to — on, happen** se passer; **to — out** sortir; **to — with** aller avec, accompagner

good bon, bonne; (*well behaved*) sage; **to have a — time** s'amuser (bien)

good-bye, au revoir; **to tell one —** dire au revoir à qqn

goods: canned — les conserves *f.*; (*the cans and contents*) les boîtes (*f.*) de conserves; **white — sale** une journée de blanc

grade la note; **to get good —s** avoir, de bonnes notes

grammar la grammaire; **French — grammaire française**

grandmother la grand'mère, (*new spelling*) grand-mère

gray gris, –e

great grande, –e

greet saluer, recevoir

grocer l'épicier *m.*

ground le sol, la terre; **to throw violently to the —** projeter violemment par terre

group le groupe

grow: to — worse empirer, devenir pire, plus mauvais

grudge: to have a — against someone en vouloir à qqn

guest un invité; **to be among the —s** être de la partie

H

habit une habitude; **to get the — of** prendre l'habitude de

hair les cheveux *m.*; **to brush**

one's — se brosser les cheveux; to have one's — cut se faire couper les cheveux; to wear one's — (cut) short porter (avoir) les cheveux courts

half *n.* la moitié; *adj.* (*exact mathematical term*) demi, -e

hand la main; (*cards*) le jeu; **he shook my —** il m'a serré la main; **to live from — to mouth** vivre au jour le jour; *adj.* **second- —** d'occasion

handsome beau, bel, belle

happen arriver; **How does it — that ...?** Comment se fait-il que ...?

happily heureusement; **to live — together** faire bon ménage (ensemble)

happiness le bonheur

hard *adj.* difficile, dur, -e; **to be — of hearing** avoir l'oreille dure; **to be — to please** être difficile; **it is — to ...,** il est difficile de ...

hard *adv.*: **to work —** travailler dur, bien

hardly à peine, ne ... guère

hat le chapeau

have avoir; **to — to** avoir à *plus inf.*; falloir, devoir, être obligé de *plus inf.*; **to — something done** faire *plus inf.*

headache le mal de tête; **to have a —** avoir mal à la tête

health la santé; **to be in good —** être en bonne santé

hear entendre; **to — about something** entendre parler de qqch.; **to — from** avoir des nouvelles de, recevoir des nouvelles de; **to — of** (*hear mention of*), entendre parler de; (*to have news of*), avoir des nouvelles de; **to — (it said) that** entendre dire que

hearing: to be hard of — avoir l'oreille dure

heat la chaleur; **the — of summer** les grandes chaleurs

heavy lourd, -e

heir un héritier

Helen Hélène

helpless faible

her *adj.* son, sa, ses; *pron.*, la; elle

here ici; **— is, are** voici

him le, lui

his son, sa, ses; *pron.*, le sien, la sienne, les siens, les siennes

hiss siffler

history une histoire

hit taper; **to — one for a loan** taper qqn

hockey le hockey

hold tenir

holiday le congé; **to have a —** avoir congé

home la maison; **to stay at —** rester chez soi, à la maison

honest honnête

honor un honneur; **in — of** en l'honneur de

hope espérer; **I — to the Lord that ...** Plaise à Dieu que ...

horizon un horizon; **— blue** bleu horizon

hospital un hôpital; **in, at, the — à** l'hôpital

host un hôte

hotel un hôtel

hour une heure

house la maison; **boarding—** la pension (de famille); **publishing —** une maison d'édition; **at (to) the — of** chez ...; **to leave the —** quitter la maison

housekeeper la ménagère

housework le ménage

how (*exclamation*) comme, combien, que; (*in what manner*) comment; **— do you say ...**

comment dit-on . . . ? — **long (depuis) combien de temps; — much, many** combien (de)

however cependant; *plus adj. or adv.,* si . . . que

hundred: a — cent; **—s** des centaines (de); **a few —** quelques centaines (de)

hungry: to be — avoir faim; **to make —** donner faim (à)

hurt faire mal à; **to — one's self** se faire mal; se blesser (*to wound one's self*)

husband le mari; **a model —** un mari modèle

I

I je, moi

idea une idée; **the very —!** Quelle idée!

idleness la paresse, l'oisiveté *f.*

if si; **— only** pourvu que

ignorant ignorant, –e

ill malade

illness la maladie, le mal

imagination une imagination

imbecile un (*or* une) imbécile

importance une importance

impossible impossible

in à, dans, en

income la rente; **to live on one's —** vivre de ses rentes

indeed vraiment; (*after a negative*) **— I am** si fait; mais si

indifference une indifférence

influential qui a de l'influence; **— acquaintances** de belles relations

inform faire savoir; (*to point out*) faire remarquer; prévenir (la police)

information renseignements *m. pl.;* **to gather —** prendre (se procurer) des renseignements; **—**

bureau bureau de renseignements

inhabitant habitant, –e

injure se faire mal (à), se blesser (à)

injury: to do bodily — to faire violence à

ink une encre

insist (*to emphasize*) insister (sur); insister pour (*plus inf.*), pour que (*plus clause*)

instantly sur le coup

instead of au lieu de

insult insulter, injurier; dire des injures à

intelligence une intelligence

intend avoir l'intention (de)

interest *n.* un intérêt; **to lose — in** ne plus prendre intérêt à, ne plus s'intéresser à

interest *v.* intéresser

interesting intéressant, –e

interfere: not to — with someone laisser faire qqn

interrupt interrompre

intimate *adj.* intime

introduce présenter

invitation une invitation

invite inviter

it il, elle, ce, ça; la, le, cela

Italian l'italien *m.*

Italy l'Italie *f.*

J

James Jacques

janitor le *or* la concierge

January janvier

jealous jaloux, jalouse

jewel le bijou

job la place

John Jean

judge: to be a good — of se (s'y) connaître en (*in certain cases,* à)

just (*merely, simply*) simplement, tout simplement; **— now** tout à l'heure; **to have** — venir de *plus inf.*; — **take** prenez donc

K

keep garder; (*to prevent*) empêcher; **He can't** — **from doing it** Il ne peut pas ne pas le faire; il ne peut pas s'empêcher de le faire; **to** — **one's word** tenir (sa) parole

kill tuer

kilo le kilo(gramme)

kind bon, bonne; **to be** — **enough to** vouloir bien *plus inf.* (*imperative*) veuillez *plus inf.*

kitchen la cuisine

knock frapper; **to** — **down, over,** renverser

know connaître, savoir; **to let one** — **something** faire savoir qqch à qqn; **I don't** — **anything about mathematics** je n'entends rien aux mathématiques

known: well — bien connu

L

lack: for — **of** faute de; **for** — **of something better** faute de mieux

lack *v.* manquer

ladder une échelle

lady la dame

LaFayette LaFayette

lake le lac

language la langue

last *adj.* dernier, –ière; — **night** hier soir; cette nuit, la nuit dernière; — **summer** l'été dernier; — **week** la semaine dernière; — **year** l'an dernier, l'année dernière

last *v.* durer

late tard; **to be** — (*in the day,*

evening, etc.) être tard; **to be** — (*behind time*) être en retard; (*a train, plane, etc.*) avoir du retard; **a half-hour** — en retard d'une demi-heure; (*fam.*) une demi-heure en retard

latter celui-ci, celle-ci, etc.

laugh rire

launch lancer

law la loi; **to pass a** — voter une loi

leak fuir

leap year une année bissextile

learn apprendre; **to** — **of** apprendre

learned savant, –e; instruit, –e

least: at — au moins; (*at any rate*) du moins

leave (*tr.*) quitter; (*int.*) partir, s'en aller; (*go out of*) sortir; **to** — **the house** quitter la maison; **to** — **something somewhere** (*in a certain condition, etc.*) laisser

leave: to take — **of** prendre congé de

lecture une conférence

lecturer le conférencier

left gauche; **to the** — à gauche

leg la jambe; **to break one's** — se casser la jambe

lend prêter

less moins

lesson la leçon; **the private** — la leçon particulière

let laisser; permettre (à qqn de faire qqch); **to** — **one have his way** laisser faire qqn

letter la lettre

Liberty: Statue of — la statue de la Liberté (éclairant le monde)

library la bibliothèque; **in the** — à la bibliothèque

life la vie

life guard le maître-nageur

light la lumière; **turn on (off) the**

— allumer (éteindre) l'électricité); **to bring to** — mettre au jour

likable sympathique

like aimer; vouloir; **to** — **it in Paris** se plaire à Paris

like comme, pareil, –le à

line la ligne; **to stand in** — faire la queue

linguistics la linguistique

listen (to) écouter

literary littéraire

literature la littérature; — **course** cours de littérature

liter le litre

little *adj.* petit, –e; *adv.* peu; **a** — un peu (de)

live vivre; (*reside*) generally habiter; demeurer; **to** — **at the expense of** vivre aux dépens de; **to** — **from hand to mouth** vivre au jour le jour; **to** — **happily together** faire bon ménage (ensemble); s'entendre bien; **to** — **on one's income** vivre de ses rentes; **I need something to** — **on** il me faut de quoi vivre

living la vie; vivre; **the** — **room** le salon; **to be still** — vivre toujours, (encore), être toujours vivant, en vie

loan: to hit one for a — taper qqn

London Londres

long *adj.* **a** — — **time** bien longtemps

long *adv.* longtemps; **how** — combien de temps, depuis combien de temps, depuis quand; — **ago** il y a longtemps; **no** —**er** ne . . . plus; **before** — bientôt; sous peu

look *n.* le coup d'œil; **to take a** — **at** (aller) jeter un coup d'œil sur, (aller) regarder

look *v.* regarder; sembler, paraître,

avoir l'air; **to** — **at** regarder; — **alike** se ressembler; **to** — **for** chercher; **to** — **out on** donner sur; avoir vue sur; **it** —**s as though** (if) . . . on dirait que . . .; **to** — **well (bad)** avoir bonne (mauvaise) mine

Lord Dieu, *m.*, le Seigneur

lose perdre; **to** — **interest in** ne plus prendre intérêt à, ne plus s'intéresser à

lot: a — **of** beaucoup; un tas de (a large number of); **to know a** — **about** se connaître en, être très fort en

Louvre le Louvre

low bas, –se

luck la chance; **to bring good (bad)** — **to** porter bonheur (malheur) à; **to have the good** — **to** avoir la chance de

lucky: to be — avoir de la chance

lycée le lycée

M

machine la machine

mad fâché, en colère; **to get** — se fâcher, se mettre en colère

Madam madame

magazine la revue

maid la bonne

mail *v.* mettre à la poste

make *n.* (*brand*) la marque

make *v.* faire; **to** — **a brilliant record, brilliant records** faire de brillantes études; **to** — **a break** faire une gaffe; **to** — **an appointment** prendre rendez-vous; **to** — **a tour of the United States** faire une tournée aux États-Unis

man un homme; **old man** le vieillard; (*term of affection*) **old** — mon vieux

manner la manière, la façon; **to**

give a lesson in —s to apprendre à vivre à qqn

manner: good manners (*sophistication, breeding*) le savoir-vivre

manual le manuel

manuscript le manuscrit

many beaucoup (de); a great — beaucoup

map la carte

March mars; in — en mars, au mois de mars

mark la note

marketing: to do the — faire le marché

marry se marier avec, épouser; to get married se marier; to unite in marriage marier

Mary Marie

mathematics les mathématiques *f.*

matinee la matinée; to go to — performances aller au théâtre en matinée

matter *n.* une affaire

matter *v.* importer; no — which one n'importe lequel; no — which one (*of two*) l'un ou l'autre

Maurice Maurice

May (*month*) mai *m.*

may pouvoir; it may be that . . . il se peut que . . .; that may well be so ça se peut bien

mayor le maire

me me

meal le repas; to eat a (meager) — faire un (maigre) repas

mean vouloir dire; you don't mean it allons donc; pas possible

means le moyen

meat la viande

meatless meal le repas maigre

meddle (with) se mêler (de)

meet faire la connaissance de; connaître; go to — aller chercher

meeting la réunion

Melchior Melchior

mend raccommoder

meter le mètre

Mexico le Mexique

middle: in the — of au milieu de; —-aged entre deux âges; Middle Ages le moyen âge; — class people les bourgeois

midnight minuit *m.*

midst le milieu; in the — of au milieu de

might le pouvoir; that — well be ça se pourrait bien

milkman le laitier

million le million

mind un esprit; to change one's — (*opinion*) changer d'avis, (*purpose*) changer d'idée; to — one's own business se mêler de ses affaires, de ce qui vous regarde

mine le mien, la mienne, les miens, les miennes; a friend of — un de mes amis

minister le prédicateur

minute la minute; at any — d'un moment à l'autre

miser un avare

misfortune le malheur

mistake une erreur, une faute; to make a — se tromper (sur)

mistaken: to be — se tromper

mister monsieur

model le modèle; a — husband un mari modèle

Monday (le) lundi

money l'argent; to put — aside for an emergency mettre de l'argent de côté en cas de besoin

Monica Monique

month le mois

more plus; — than one plus d'un; the — . . . the — . . . plus . . . plus . . .; (*final*) davantage; not (*plus neg. verb*) any more than ne . . pas plus que

morning le matin; la matinée;
from — till night du matin au
soir; **good —** bonjour; **in the —**
le matin, dans la matinée; **the
next —** le lendemain; **this —**
ce matin

most la plupart (de *plus the def.
art.*)

mother la mère; **— -in-law** la
belle-mère

mouth la bouche; **to live from
hand to —** vivre au jour le jour

moved ému, –e

movie le cinéma; **—s** le cinéma;
(*fam.*) le ciné

Mrs. Mme (Madame) *f.*

much beaucoup

murderer un assassin (*through
premeditation or betrayal*); le
meurtrier (*in all senses*)

music la musique; **a — student**
un étudiant de musique

must falloir, devoir

my mon, ma, mes

N

name le nom; **What is her —?**
Comment s'appelle-t-elle? Quel
est son nom?

Napoleon Napoléon

near *adv.* près; *prep.* près de; **—
each other** l'un près de l'autre

necessary nécessaire; **it is —
that . . .** il faut que . . .

need avoir besoin de; falloir; **she
—s** elle a besoin de, il lui faut

neighbor le voisin, la voisine

neighborhood le voisinage, le
quartier; **in this —** dans le
voisinage, dans ce quartier

neither ni (*with* ne); **— . . . nor** ni
. . . ni; ni l'un ni l'autre

nervousness la nervosité

never jamais, ne jamais

new nouveau, nouvel, nouvelle;
neuf, neuve

New Orleans la Nouvelle-Orléans

New York New-York

news la nouvelle; **that's — to me**
c'est du nouveau pour moi

newspaper le journal

next prochain, –e; **— door to you**
à côté de chez vous; **— week** la
semaine prochaine; **— year** l'an
prochain, l'année prochaine; **the
— morning** le lendemain matin

nice gentil, –le

night la nuit; (*equivalent to evening*) le soir; **from morning till
—** du matin au soir; **last —** hier
soir; la nuit dernière, cette nuit

no non

noise le bruit

none (not one) aucun, –e

nonsense; to talk — dire des
bêtises

noon midi

not ne . . . pas; **— at all** (*equivalent to: don't mention it*) de rien

note *v.* remarquer, noter

nothing rien (de); (*with verb*) ne
. . . rien; rien ne; **she does —
but study** elle ne fait qu'étudier

notice s'apercevoir de; remarquer;
(catch sight of) apercevoir

novel *n.* le roman

novelist le romancier

novice le novice; (*unknown
author*) un (auteur) inconnu, un
débutant

now maintenant

nurse la bonne

O

oblige obliger

obstacle un obstacle

occasion une occasion; **such a
simple —** une occasion aussi ordinaire, une affaire aussi simple

ocean un océan; **to cross the —** faire la traversée

o'clock l'heure; **ten —** dix heures

offend offenser

offer offrir

office le bureau; (*teacher's, doctor's*) le cabinet

often souvent

old vieux, vieil, vieille; **— man** le vieillard; (*affectionate term*) mon vieux; **to be ten years —** avoir dix ans; **how — is he?** quel âge a-t-il? **to be a year —er than** avoir un an de plus que, être plus âgé d'un an que

on sur

once une fois; **at —** immédiatement, tout de suite

one un, une; *indef. pron.* on; **the —** celui, celle; **you're the — who** c'est vous qui . . .; **no —** ne . . . personne; personne . . . (ne); **not a —** aucun . . . (ne)

one's *adj.* son, sa, ses

only ne . . . que, seulement; **not — . . . but also** non seulement . . . mais encore (mais aussi)

open ouvrir; (*int., as of a door*) s'ouvrir

opera un opéra

operation une opération

opinion une opinion

oppose s'opposer (à)

opposite *prep.*, en face de; vis-à-vis de

opposition une opposition

optimistic optimiste

or ou

order: in — that pour que, afin que

order *v.* ordonner, commander

original original, –e

other autre

ought devoir

our notre, nos

out: — of (*after* prendre, chercher) dans

over sur; **— one ear** sur l'oreille

overcome vaincre

overnight du jour au lendemain

overture une ouverture

owe devoir

own propre

P

package le paquet

page la page

palatable être agréable au goût, avoir bon goût

paper le papier; le journal

parents les parents *m.*

Paris Paris

park le parc; **Monceau —** le parc Monceau

parlor le salon

party (*political*) le parti; **the radical socialist —** le parti radical-socialiste; (*entertainment*) la soirée

pass passer; **to — an examination** réussir à, être reçu à, un examen; **to — a law** voter une loi; **to — quickly** (of time) fuir, s'enfuir

patience la patience

patient le malade

pay: to — for payer; **to — attention to** faire attention à; **to — back** rendre

pen la plume; (*fountain*) le stylo

pencil le crayon

people les gens *m.* (*sometimes takes fem. adj.*); **young —** jeunes gens *m.*; **many —** beaucoup de (bien des) gens; **few —** peu de gens

pepper le poivre

performance la représentation; **to go to matinee —s** aller au théâtre en matinée

period: within a — of dans un délai de

perseverance la persévérance

persuade persuader (à) qqn de faire qqch

philology la philologie

pick (*flowers or fruit*) cueillir; **to — up** ramasser

picture le tableau; (*movies*) le film; la photo(graphie)

place le lieu, la place, un endroit; **in the first —** d'abord, en premier lieu, primo; **in the second — en** second lieu, secundo; (*and then*) et puis

plain clothes: — man un inspecteur (de police, de la Sûreté)

plan le plan

plan *v.* avoir l'intention de

plane un avion; **by —** en avion

play jouer; (*game or sport*) jouer à; **— cards** jouer aux cartes; **— tennis** jouer au tennis; **— the piano** jouer du piano

please plaire (à qqn); **to be hard to —** être difficile

pleasure le plaisir; **to give — to** faire plaisir à

pocket la poche

police la police

policeman un agent (de police)

politics la politique

poor pauvre

position la situation

possible possible

post: —card la carte postale

postpone ajourner; remettre (*the pleonasm* remettre à plus tard *is quite common in colloquial language*)

pound la livre

pour: to — rain pleuvoir à verse

poverty la misère, la pauvreté

precaution la précaution

prefer préférer, aimer mieux

prescribe ordonner

present *n.* le cadeau; **to make one a — of something** faire cadeau à qqn de qqch

present *v.* présenter

present *adj.* actuel, –le

president président, –e

pretend faire semblant, faire mine

pretty joli, –e

prevent empêcher

princess: the crown — la princesse royale

principal principal, –e

prison la prison

private particulier, –ière; privé, –e; **— lessons** des leçons particulières

probably probablement

problem le problème

professor le professeur; **some — or other** un professeur quelconque

progress le progrès

progressive progressif, –sive

project le projet

prolong prolonger

promise promettre

promotion l'avancement *m.*

proposition la proposition

protection la protection

provided that pourvu que

publish publier; **recently —ed** qui vient de paraître

publisher un éditeur

publishing house une maison d'édition

puff: cream — le chou à la crème

pupil l'élève *m. or f.*

purchase une emplette, un achat

purpose le but; **that doesn't serve any —** cela ne sert à rien

purse le porte-monnaie

put mettre; **to — aside** mettre de côté; **to — away** ranger; **to — into** il y mettre; **to — on** mettre

Q

quai le quai
quarter (*fraction*) le quart; a — of a century un quart de siècle; a — to ten dix heures moins le quart; a — after ten dix heures et quart; (*of a city*) le quartier
question la question; to be a — of s'agir de, être question de; to ask a — poser une question
quickly vite
quite (*entirely*) tout, tout à fait; (*very*) bien; — evident bien évident; (*rather*) assez
quiz une interrogation écrite; (*fam.*) la colle

R

racket la raquette
radical-socialist radical-socialiste
radio la T.S.F. (télégraphie sans fil); la radio; (*receiving*) set le poste (récepteur) de T.S.F. (la radio *is sometimes used in the sense of radio set*); to listen to the — écouter la T.S.F., la radio
raft le radeau
rain *n.* la pluie; to pour — pleuvoir à verse
rain *v.* pleuvoir
raise lever
rate: at any — en tout cas
rather plutôt; — than *plus inf.* (*with* préférer) plutôt que; (*with* aimer mieux) que
reach arriver à, parvenir à
read lire; to — aloud lire à haute voix; to — to faire la lecture à
ready prêt, -e; — to prêt à
realize se rendre compte (de)
really vraiment
recall se rappeler
receive recevoir

recently récemment
reception la réception
recognize reconnaître
recommend recommander
reconstruct reconstruire
record: to make a brilliant —, brilliant —s faire de brillantes études
red rouge
refugee réfugié, -e
refuse (to) refuser (de)
register se faire inscrire
regret regretter
rejoicing les réjouissances *f.*
relative un parent
remark le propos
remedy le remède
remember se rappeler, se souvenir de
rent louer; for (to) — à louer
reorganization la réorganisation
repeat répéter
request prier
research les travaux de recherche *m.*; to do — faire des travaux de recherche
resign: to — one's self to prendre son parti de
resist résister (à); to — all progress s'opposer à tout progrès; to — someone (*in his presence*) tenir tête à qqn
rest le repos
rest *v.* se reposer
retire: to — from business se retirer des affaires
return (*go back*) retourner; (*come back*) revenir; to — a call rendre une visite
review le compte-rendu; to write a — of a book rendre compte d'un livre, faire le compte-rendu d'un livre, faire l'analyse d'un livre
rich riche

ride aller, venir, en auto, à bicyclette etc.

ridiculous ridicule

right le droit; **to (on) the —** à droite; **— to vote** le droit de vote

right: — away tout de suite; **to be —** avoir raison

Rip van Winkle Rip van Winkle

road le chemin, la route; **to take the wrong —** se tromper de chemin

roll le petit pain

Romanticism le romantisme

room la pièce; (*bedroom*) la chambre; **living —** le salon

roommate le (la) camarade de chambre

rosy: —- cheeked rose; aux joues vermeilles, de rose

run courir; **to — up the stairs, come (go) running up the stairs** monter l'escalier en courant; **to — down the stairs, come (go) running down the stairs** descendre l'escalier en courant

S

sale la vente; **white goods —** journée de blanc

salt le sel

same même; **It's all the — to me** ça m'est égal

satisfied content, satisfait; **to be — with** être content de

save sauver; (*use sparingly*) ménager; **to — one's self the trouble of** s'épargner (*fam.*, s'éviter) la peine (l'ennui) de

say dire; **how do you — ...?** comment dit-on ...? **I should — I do know him!** Je crois bien que je le connais! **I should — so** je crois bien; **Say!** Dites

donc! **to — something about something** parler (dire qqch) de qqch; **they —** on dit

school une école; **to, in, at —** à l'école; **to attend summer —** suivre les (des) cours de vacances

scientific scientifique

scold gronder

sea la mer; **—shore** le bord de la mer

season la saison

section (*of a city*) le quartier

see voir; **to — again** revoir; (*to discern, distinguish*) distinguer

seem sembler, paraître

sell vendre

send envoyer; **to — for** envoyer chercher, faire venir

serve servir; **that doesn't — any purpose** cela ne sert à rien

set: to — the table mettre la table, le couvert

several plusieurs

sew coudre

shake: to — hands with serrer la main à; **he shook my hand** il m'a serré la main

she elle

shine briller; **the sun is shining** il fait du soleil

shoe le soulier (*low shoe*)

shopping les emplettes *f.*; **to do some —** faire des emplettes

short court, –e

should (*equivalent to* ought) devoir

show montrer, faire voir

shrill strident, –e

sick malade; **to be — and tired of** (en) avoir plein le dos de

side le côté; **on which —** de quel côté; **on the other —** de l'autre côté; **to take the — of** prendre le parti de

sideboard le buffet

sight la vue; (*of a city*) les curiosités *f.*
silhouette la silhouette
silk la soie; — **stockings** des bas *m.* de soie
simple simple; **such a** — **occasion** une occasion aussi ordinaire, une affaire aussi simple
simply simplement
since (*cause*) puisque; *prep. and adv.* depuis; — **then** depuis lors
sing chanter
single seul, –e
siren la sirène
sister la sœur
sit s'asseoir; **to** — **down** s'asseoir; **to** — **down at the table** (*to eat*) se mettre à table
situated situé, –e; **to be** — être, se trouver, être situé
sleep dormir; coucher; **to go to** — s'endormir; **to** — **late** faire la grasse matinée; **to** — **soundly** dormir bien, dormir profondément, (*fam.*) dormir sur les deux oreilles
slowly lentement
small petit, –e
smile sourire
so (*before adj. or adv.*) si, tellement, aussi; — **much,** — **many** tant (de); — **that** *conj.* (purpose) pour que, (*result*) de sorte que; — (*equivalent to* **therefore**) aussi (*at beginning of sentence and with inverted order*); par conséquent; — **be it!** Soit! ainsi soit-il! **Mrs.** — **and** — madame une telle
soldier le soldat
solution la solution
solve résoudre
some (*partitive*) du, de la, des, en; *adj.* quelque; *pron.* quelques-uns; —**one,** quelqu'un, on; — . . .

others les uns . . . d'autres (les autres); — **day** un jour
somebody quelqu'un
something quelque chose *m.*; — **to write with** (*writing materials*) de quoi écrire; **a certain** — **about them which is insulting** (un) je ne sais quoi d'insultant; **I need** — **to live on** il me faut de quoi vivre
sometimes quelquefois
son le fils; —**-in-law** le gendre; **her little** — son petit garçon
song la chanson
soon bientôt; **as** — **as** aussitôt que
sore: to have a — **throat** avoir mal à la gorge
sorry: to be — **that** regretter (que)
sound le son
Spain l'Espagne *f.*
speak parler; **to** — **about, of** parler de
speech le discours; **to make a** — faire un discours
spell le charme
spend (*time*) passer; (*money*) dépenser
spite: in — **of** malgré
spoil gâter
spoon la cuiller
spring le printemps
spy un espion
square carré, –e
staff: the general — l'état-major
stair un escalier; **to run up the** —**s** monter l'escalier en courant; **to run down the** —**s** descendre l'escalier en courant
stake: to be at — y aller de (*impersonal subject*)
stamp le timbre-(poste)
stand: to — **in line** faire la queue
start: to — (*the car*) démarrer; **the chauffeur suddenly**

started the car le chauffeur a démarré brusquement, vivement

starve: to — to death mourir de faim

starving affamé, –e

station la gare

statue la statue; the Statue of Liberty la statue de la Liberté (éclairant le monde)

stay rester; to — at home rester chez soi, à la maison

still encore, toujours

stingy chiche, avare, (*fam. and emphatic*) pingre

stocking le bas; silk —s des bas de soie

stop arrêter, s'arrêter; (*to leave off at*) en rester à; to — (in) at passer à

store le magasin; department —s les magasins de nouveautés, les grands magasins

storm un orage

story une histoire

straight droit, –e; to go — ahead aller tout droit

street la rue; to take, go to, the wrong — se tromper de rue

strike: to go on — se mettre en grève

strong fort, –e

student un étudiant, (*pupil*) un (une) élève; a music — un étudiant de musique

study une étude

study *v.* étudier, apprendre

studying (*equivalent to* studies) les études *f.*

stupid stupide, bête; to say — things dire des bêtises

style la mode; out of — démodé

suburb la banlieue

succeed (in) réussir (à); to — in an undertaking réussir dans une entreprise; mener une entre-

prise à bien; venir à bout d'une entreprise

success le succès

successful: to be — avoir du succès

successfully: to carry out — mener à bien; venir à bout de

such tel, telle; pareil, –le; — a un tel, une telle, un pareil, une pareille

suddenly soudain, vivement, brusquement; he turned around — il se retourna (s'est retourné) brusquement, vivement

suffer souffrir

sugar le sucre

suit le complet

suitcase la valise

summer un été; in — en été; last — l'été dernier; to attend — school suivre les (des) cours de vacances

sun le soleil; the — is shining il fait du soleil

Sunday (le) dimanche

sure sûr, –e

surmount franchir, surmonter

surprise étonner, surprendre

surprised: I am not — ça ne m'étonne pas

surrounded entouré, –e

suspect *v.* se douter de, soupçonner

swim nager

T

table la table; to set the — mettre la table, le couvert

take prendre; (*carry*) porter, conduire, emmener, mener; to — down descendre; to — out of sortir; to — the side of prendre le parti de; to — upstairs monter; falloir: How long does it —

(you) to ...? Combien de temps (vous) faut-il pour ... .?

tale le conte

talk about parler de

tall grand, –e

taste le goût

tea le thé

teach enseigner, (*also, if ind. and dir. obj. are present*) apprendre

teacher le professeur

tear déchirer

tell dire; **to — someone about something** parler à qqn de qqch; **to — someone something** dire qqch à qqn; **to —** (*a story*) raconter; **I am told** on me dit

ten dix; **about ten** une dizaine (de)

tennis le tennis; **to play —** jouer au tennis

terminate conclure

than que

thank: — you very much merci bien, beaucoup

thanks merci; **no —** (non) merci

that *rel. pron.* qui, que; *dem. pron.* cela, ça, ce; **— one** celui-là, celle-là; *dem. adj.* ce, cet, cette, ces; *conj.* que; **—'s what ...** voilà (c'est) ce qui, ce que ...

theater le théâtre

their leur

them les; leur; eux, elles

then puis, ensuite, alors; **and —** et puis

there là, y; **— is, are** il y a; voilà; **there she is** la voilà; **— he comes** le voilà qui vient

they ils, elles; eux, elles, on

thing la chose; **any old —** n'importe quoi

think croire; **to — of, about** penser à; **What do you think of** (*something*)? Que pensez-vous de (qqch)?

third *n.* le tiers; *adj.* troisième

thirsty: to be (very) — avoir (bien, très) soif

this *dem. adj.* ce, cet, cette, ces; *dem. pron.* celui-ci, celle-ci, ceci

thorough approfondi, –e

those *dem. adj.* ces; *dem. pron.* ceux, celles, ceux-là, celles-là

thousand: a — mille; **—s, des** milliers (de); (*in dates*) mil

three trois

throat la gorge; **to have a sore —** avoir mal à la gorge

through par

throw jeter; **to — violently to the ground** projeter violemment par terre

Thursday (le) jeudi

ticket le billet; **second-class —** billet de deuxième classe, de seconde (classe); une seconde, (*pop.*) une deuxième

time le temps; la fois; **ahead of — en avance; all the —** toujours; sans cesse; **to study all the —** ne faire qu'étudier; **a long —** longtemps; **a long, long —** longtemps; bien longtemps; **at the same —** en même temps, à la fois; **at the — of** au moment de; **at what time?** à quelle heure? **for a very short —** pendant un temps très court; **for hours at a —** pendant des heures; **from — to —** de temps en temps; **in — to** à temps pour; **it is — to** il est temps de; il (c'est) l'heure de; **(the) next —** la prochaine fois; **this is no — to** ce n'est pas le moment de; **three or four —s a year** trois ou quatre fois par an; **to be (arrive) on —** être (arriver) à l'heure; **to have — to** avoir le temps de;

what — is it? quelle heure est-il? to have a good — s'amuser

tiptoe: on — sur la pointe des pieds

tired fatigué, –e; to be (very) — être (très) fatigué; dormir debout; to be sick and — of (en) avoir plein le dos de

to à; in order — pour

today aujourd'hui

together ensemble

tomorrow demain

tone le ton; in a low — à voix basse

too, adv. trop; — much, — many trop (de); (equivalent to also) aussi

tooth la dent; to have the —ache avoir mal aux dents

top le haut; at the — of one's voice à tue-tête

touch: to — one for a few hundred francs taper qqn de quelques centaines de francs

tour la tournée; to make a tour of the United States faire une tournée aux États-Unis

tourist le (la) touriste

town la ville; down—, to — en ville; in — à la ville, en ville

train le train; to travel on the — voyager en chemin de fer

transmit transmettre

travel voyager; to — on the train voyager en chemin de fer

traveling: in our — abroad quand nous voyageons à l'étranger

treatise un traité

trick: to be up to one's old —s faire des siennes

trip le voyage

trolley le trolley; trackless — le trolleybus

troops les troupes f.

trouble (work, effort) la peine; (annoyance) l'ennui m.; to have one's work for nothing en être pour sa peine; to save one's self the — of s'épargner (fam. s'éviter) la peine (l'ennui) de

trousers le pantalon

truck le camion

true vrai, –e

trunk la malle

truth la vérité

try vouloir, essayer

Tuesday (le) mardi

turn tourner; to — on (off) the light allumer (éteindre) (l'électricité); to — one's back to tourner le dos à; to — around se retourner

tutor le précepteur, la préceptrice

twentieth vingtième

twenty vingt; I am twenty j'ai vingt ans

twenty-second vingt-deuxième; the — of December le vingt-deux décembre

twice deux fois; — a week deux fois par semaine

twin le jumeau, la jumelle; — brother le frère jumeau; — sister la sœur jumelle

two deux

typewriter une machine à écrire

U

ugly laid, –e; vilain, –e

umbrella le parapluie

unable: to be — ne pas pouvoir

under sous

undergo subir

understand comprendre

undertaking une entreprise; to succeed in an — cf. succeed

undoubtedly sans aucun doute

unfortunately malheureusement
uniform un uniforme
United States les États-Unis, *m.*
university une université
unless à moins que
until jusqu'à ce que; (*after* attendre) que; **not . . . until** ne . . . que
unusual insolit, –e *inedite (m+f)*
up: to be well — on être ferré (ferré à glace) sur
upstairs: to take — monter
us nous
use: what's the use? à quoi bon ?
use *v.* se servir de, employer
useless inutile; **it will be — for you to study more . . .** vous aurez beau étudier (davantage) . . ., il vous sera inutile d'étudier davantage . . .; **that will be —** cela ne servira à rien
usual habituel, –le; **as —** comme d'habitude

V

vacation les vacances *f.*; **about a ten-day —** une dizaine de jours de vacances
valise la valise
various (*several*) plusieurs; divers, différents
vegetable le légume
very très, bien
Vienna Vienne
village le village
violently violemment
visit: (*to — a place or to — a person in an official capacity, as a doctor, charity-worker, etc.*) visiter; (*to make a social —*) rendre visite à, faire visite à, aller voir
visitor le visiteur, la visite; **to have** (*receive*) **—s** avoir (recevoir) des visiteurs, des visites

voice la voix; **at the top of one's —** à tue-tête
volume le volume
vote le vote; **right to —** le droit de vote

W

wait (for) attendre
wake (up) réveiller
walk marcher; se promener; (*distinguished from* to ride) venir, aller, à pied; **to — along** passer; **I was walking along Vaugirard St. . . .** je passais rue de Vaugirard . . .; **to — down** descendre
walk *n.* la promenade
war la guerre; **Civil —** la guerre de Sécession
warm chaud; (*weather*) **it is —** il fait chaud
wash laver; **to — one's hands and face** se laver les mains et la figure
Washington Washington
waste gaspiller; **to — one's time** gaspiller (perdre) son temps à
wasteful gaspilleur, –euse
watch la montre
water l'eau *f.*
way la façon, la manière; **on the — chemin** faisant; **on the — back** en rentrant, en revenant; **to let one have his —** laisser faire qqn.
wear porter; **to — one's hair (cut) short** porter (avoir) les cheveux courts
weather le temps; **the — is good (fine) bad** il fait beau, mauvais (temps); le temps est beau, mauvais
wedding le mariage
Wednesday (le) mercredi
week la semaine, huit jours; **a —**

from **today** d'aujourd'hui en huit; **last** — la semaine dernière; **next** — la semaine prochaine

welcome: you're — il n'y a pas de quoi; de rien

well bien; **to be** — aller bien; —! eh bien! tiens! (tiens!) — **known** bien connu

were: as it — pour ainsi dire

what *inter. pron.* que, quoi; *inter. adj.* quel; *rel. pron.* ce qui, ce que; *exclam.* comment! — **a** quel, quelle; **What's that to me?** Qu'est-ce que cela me fait?

whatever quoi que *plus subj.*; quel que *plus subj.*

wheel la roue

when quand; lorsque (*not used interrogatively*)

where où; — **she comes from** d'où elle vient

whether si

which *pron.* qui, que; lequel; quoi; — **one** lequel, laquelle

while pendant que; tandis que

while: a little — **ago** tout à l'heure

white blanc, blanche

who qui, quel, quelle

whoever qui que

whole tout; entier, –ière; **the** — tout le; **the** — **day** toute la journée; **a** — **year** toute une année

whose dont; à qui

why pourquoi; (*exclamation*) mais

widower le veuf

wife la femme

willing: to be — **to** vouloir (bien)

win gagner

wind le vent; **the** — **blows** il fait du vent

windy: to be — faire du vent

wine le vin

wing une aile

winter l'hiver, *m.*; **in** — l'hiver, en hiver

wise: it is — **for one to . . .** on fera bien de

wish vouloir

with avec

without sans; **to do** — se passer de; **to do** — **meat** se passer de viande, faire maigre; (*conj.*) sans que

woman la femme

wooden de bois

word le mot, la parole; **to keep one's** — tenir (sa) parole

work *n.* le travail; (*literature*) une œuvre; **to do written** — **in French** faire un devoir de français; **to go to** — aller à son travail

work *v.* travailler; **to** — **hard** travailler dur, bien; **to** — **on something** travailler à qqch

workingman un ouvrier

world le monde; **to go around the** — faire le tour du monde; **in the** — (*after superlative*) du monde; **in this** — ici-bas

worse pire, plus mauvais; — **than ever** de plus belle

worth: to be — valoir; **it isn't worth the trouble** cela ne vaut pas la peine, ce n'est pas la peine

write écrire; **to** — **about something** dire qqch., parler de qqch; **something to** — **with** (*writing materials*) de quoi écrire

wrong: to be — (*mistaken*) se tromper; **to take the** — **road** (*street*) se tromper de chemin (rue); **to be in the** — avoir tort

Y

year un an, une année; **a whole** — toute une année; **from** — **to** —

d'année en année; **last —** l'an dernier, l'année dernière; **next —** l'an prochain, l'année prochaine

yell crier

yes oui; (*after a negative*) si

yesterday hier; **all day —** toute la journée d'hier

yet encore

you vous

young jeune; **— people** jeunes gens

your votre, vos

INDEX

Numbers refer to paragraphs.

23 - *qno.*
24
25

29,